Eleven Exercises in the
Art of Architectural Drawing

This book offers eleven servings of "slow food" for the architectural imagination as opposed to the tasteless "fast food" that dominates many drawing tables or digital tablets. The implementation of "fast drawing" has generated the present graphic obesity and indigestive architecture, thus the eleven slow exercises presented in the book aim to make the facture of architecture a much leaner and digestible process.

Organized around eleven exercises, this book does not emphasize speed, nor incorporate many timesaving tricks typical of drawing books, but rather proposes a slow, meditative process for construing drawings and for drawing constructing thoughts. Detailing the critical nature and crucial role of architectural drawings, this book is a manual which is essentially not a manual; it is an elucidation of an elegant manner for practising architecture. The book identifies the inauguration of architectural theory within the craftsmanship of architectural drawings and emphasises a non-division between the mind and the hand in the facture of drawings.

Highly illustrated throughout, with the author's own original drawings, this book is an indispensable reference text and an effective textbook for students seeking to advance their appreciation of the nature and exercise of architectural drawings.

Marco Frascari is Professor of Architecture at Carleton University, Canada. He studied and worked with Carlo Scarpa at IUAV and received his PhD in Architecture from the University of Pennsylvania. He taught for several years at the University of Pennsylvania, and as Visiting Professor at Columbia and Harvard. He then became a G. Truman Ward Professor of Architecture at Virginia Tech and is currently director of the David Azrieli School of Architecture and Urbanism in Ottawa, Canada.

Eleven Exercises in the Art of Architectural Drawing

Slow Food for the Architect's Imagination

Marco Frascari

Routledge
Taylor & Francis Group

LONDON AND NEW YORK

First published 2011
by Routledge
2 Park Square, Milton Park, Abingdon, Oxon, OX14 4RN

Simultaneously published in the USA and Canada
by Routledge
711 Third Avenue, New York, NY 10017

Routledge is an imprint of the Taylor & Francis Group, an informa business

© 2011 Marco Frascari

Typeset in Stone Sans and Univers by Alex Lazarou, London
Printed and bound in India by Replika Press Pvt. Ltd.

British Library Cataloguing in Publication Data
A catalogue record for this book is available from the British Library

Library of Congress Cataloging-in-Publication Data
Frascari, Marco.
Eleven exercises in the art of architectural drawing : slow-food for the
architect's imagination / Marco Frascari.
    p. cm.
Includes index.
1. Architectural drawing—Technique. I. Title.
NA2708.F73 2011
720.28'4—dc22

                                                              2010023422

ISBN13: 978-0-415-77925-8 (hbk)
ISBN13: 978-0-415-77926-5 (pbk)
ISBN13: 978-0-203-83585-2 (ebk)

This book is dedicated to my wife Paola

Contents

Acknowledgements

My deepest gratitude goes to Francesca Ford, the Architecture Commissioning Editor at Routledge, Taylor & Francis Books, for understanding the nature of this book; her enthusiastic support has made my unusual combination of images and text a reality in ink and paper.

I must also show my appreciation for Alex Lazarou, this book would not have existed in its present graphic form without his masterful capability to compose words and images on a page.

In addition I would like to acknowledge the support of the Canadian Center for Architecture for a wonderful interlude in Montreal where I had the opportunity to do research on scale figures during the day and to work on the manuscript of this book in the evening.

My wife Paola deserves my most felt thankfulness for being my first reader and my best critic. Her loving support and encouragement are in the end what made this book possible.

As always, I owe recognition to Rosa Vecchi Contessa Bolza, my grandmother and my first teacher of an unusual critical thinking.

Lastly, I offer my sincere thanks to all the people who have contributed to and worked on these Eleven Exercises and to all of those who supported me in any respect during the completion of the project.

Preface

"It is all too easy to confuse data with knowledge and information technology with information."

Peter F. Drucker[1]

"Perspicuous representation brings about the understanding, which consists precisely in the fact that we 'see the connections'. Hence the importance of finding connecting links."

Ludwig Wittgenstein[2]

Drafted as a wondrous dwelling within a dreamland of architectural drawings, this book should be assimilated in the same way architectural drawings are read. It is a reading that takes place by projecting otherness in the drawing and wandering from room to room, from detail to detail, from plan to section, from section to elevation in a meandering path of perceptions and memories. To the readers, I suggest to wait until after dinner to read the puzzles, the riddles and the enigmas that I am offering in a collection of exercises. They will have the delight of indulging on the exercises by using their post-prandium active imagination, hence taking advantage of the best mental images elaborated during lull moments of reverie and contemplation.

The text offered here is not about right or wrong simulations and dissimulations in architectural drawings, but rather about a discerning process that takes part in the interplay generated by our sensorial assimilation. Sensorial assimilation is an act of a proper cognitive musing, a procedure of incorporation by which we ingest the outside world into ourselves and transform it by an

0.1 (left)
Architectural World-Making

0.2 (right)
Cosmopoiesis and
World-Making

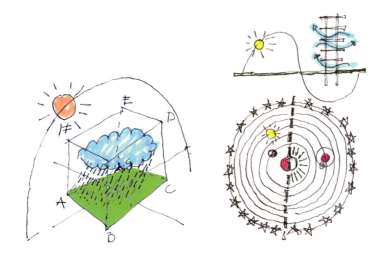

act of world-making. Architectural drawings are representations that facilitate the understanding of buildings, conditions, processes and events in human world-making, in other words they are the interactive and generative mapping of architectural cosmopoiesis. Cosmopoiesis can be described as "world-making". In *Ways of Worldmaking*, the philosopher Nelson Goodman observes that a "world" is not only a physical universe, but also the cultural artifacts, the systems of organization and meanings created by a group of people at any one time.[3] In this way, the formation of structure and spaces in architecture plays a significant role in the creation of and contribution to a world. Architectural cosmopoiesis encompasses the different ways architects have thought about the world in their architectural conceiving. In cosmopoiesis, we store the memories of our daily inhabiting and create systems through which we understand the existence of the phenomenal world and our own existence within it. Cosmopoiesis offers us a plan, a perception of our existence and where we are, tells us why we are here and, most often, where we are going.

Architects with their drawings participate in the praxis of a world-making that rises to the synesthetic landscapes of intimacy and participation. The drawings produce an interplay of signs that reveals the transfer of the cognitive dimensions into mundane and extramundane worlds of architecture. These worlds often might have remained unknown within a domain of architectural materials and substances.[4] Architectural nubs and their translations into the graphic media continue along the interplay of cultural, demographic, socio-economic, temporal and spatial variables, ultimately determining architectural conceptions with a trans-historical gauge combining factors of tradition and novelty.

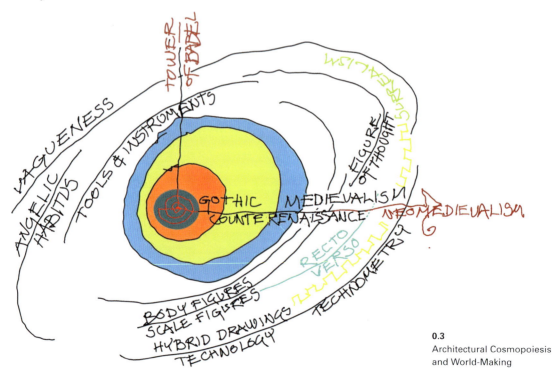

0.3
Architectural Cosmopoiesis
and World-Making

As both a communication contrivance and a conceptual implement, the act and making of drawings is essential to all facets of architectural process. Much of the practice of architecture is removed from the physicality of building and drawings act as mediators between conception and construction, between architect and builder and between architect and client. Inherently, both a process to a construction and an end in themselves, drawings are the means by which architects order, catalog and express their cosmopoietic intent. The techniques used in performing these drawings can vary from artwork and technical modeling and from poetic to prosaic drawings. Most of these drawings do not just reproduce merely physical realities, the solid stuff, but can also transmit metaphysical conditions, the dream stuff, ranging from forms of sacred places to mundane shapes embodied within the realms of fantasy and myth as explored by human imagination.

In non-trivial architectural drawings, imagination, fantasy, vision and memory, combined with sensual perceptions and projections, are all part of cognitive clusters. They are so entangled that, in comparison, the Gordian knot is a simple love knot. To solve this cognitively tangled knot by just cutting through it would only give an ambiguously defective characterization, even if it is purely intended to produce an operational definition of architectural drawings. I am proposing instead to analyze and describe this tangle, as it exists: an impenetrable unsolvable knotted-snarled phenomenon, entangled with causes, concomitant causes and causes of causes. It is essential to acquire a real operative condition to observe it and to question it, to inquire on its nature, without untangling the knot of the cognitive cluster, but through our finite perception

0.4
Architectural Representation
Knot as a Holy Icon

reaching an infinite number of relations. These are the reasons of the eleven exercises. First, the knot is given to you and then, through the exercises, the operative condition desired to attain an understanding of the nature of non-trivial architectural drawings may be reached.

The method for the comprehension of the nature and role of architectural drawing is a slow assimilation that takes place in the proposed exercises. The drawings exercises are not just instructions for accompanying illustrations of the arguments being made, but rather, they represent significant and signifying tactics that can be highly emblematic, critical and compelling, driving forward specific arguments or, sometimes, setting up counter-accounts.

Drawing is an elemental action. It belongs with counting and speaking to the field of the initial forms of cognition. However, to teach and to learn how to draw architecture is extremely difficult because our graphic imagery is often sabotaged during our early years of schooling. Drilling ingenuous children into prescribed routines to produce kitsch and cutesy images is the powerful wooden clog thrown into the mental machinery of children's graphic production by the many cultures that cannot distinguish between vision and visuality. In primary school children are forced to follow step by step instructions for trite results that have been predetermined by teachers. These procedures are effectively damaging the way children develop modes of drawing. A distinguished researcher of the origin and development of drafted representations and graphic expressions in early childhood, John Matthews, believes that most of the current teaching of drawing amounts to "child abuse".[5]

Despite the power and ubiquity of graphic images, educational curricula continue to pay little attention to graphics training and education. In response to pedagogical requirements, people with standard education produce more drawings during their first ten years of schooling than during the remainder of their lives. These drawings can be divided in two kinds:

1.   drawings subsidiary to other schoolwork: illustrations of texts, maps and diagrams, figures of geometry and so on; and
2.   drawings in art classes as an ancillary product of self-expression.

Both of these kinds of drawing are taught with instructions that will negatively effect the understanding and reading of drawings. The negative effect increases in secondary and post-secondary education. Elementary students are frequently asked to draw pictures as a way of expressing themselves, i.e. to communicate artistically. High school students, with very few exceptions, are seldom asked to do so; when asked, they usually produce something akin to a first or second grade school project. A parallel would be for a senior year student to write an essay consisting of a series of sentences at the level of "Tell dog run".

Probably no architect would challenge the importance that drawing has in practicing architecture. Furthermore, only a few architects would deny that to talk sensitively and sensibly about architectural drawings is an extraordinarily difficult undertaking. A fair amount of understanding of what is true and relevant about the nature and practice of drawing can be derived by providing facts about the materials, history and usage. Nevertheless most of the ideas and issues that are central and seminal to the essential make-up of architectural

drawings remain strangely elusive and inexpressible in terms other than those used in the facture of the drawings themselves.

"What are architectural drawings?" Can one really give an answer or even approach such a question today without any references to the human brain and the human body? I do not think so. When we speak of surprise, or pleasure, or surroundings, or unity, or abstraction, we can say quite a lot—even in our present state of imperfect knowledge—about brain activity connected to these cognitive experiences.

Architectural drawing is a way of acting. It is a particular way of exploring the built environment because drawings are the very condition of architectural experimentations; they exist before tectonic experiences could take place. Accurately speaking, they are not representations as photographic, artistic or commercial representations. They belong to a specific category of embodiment that makes architectural ideas possible since architecture itself is not disembodied, but arises from the coalescing of our brain and bodily experiences. This is not just a simplistic and obvious claim that we need a body to build and inhabit architecture, but it is the claim that the very structure of our thinking comes from the embodiment that takes place in architecture. It is important to remember, though, that embodiment refers generally to the entire physical context of cognition, including not just bodily states, but also modality-specific systems and environmental situations.

The idea of embodiment challenges the Cartesian dualism that has had such a long and pernicious influence on architecture and architectural drawings.

The same neural and cognitive processes that allow us to perceive and move around also create our conceptual system. Therefore, our conceptual system is generated by the architecture around us; we make buildings and they make us. Architecture is framed by embodied experience and embodied experience is framed by architecture, and this mirroring action is also embodied in the drawings. Consequently the ability to read and to make architectural drawings generally originates within an architect's perceptual and motor systems.

Nowadays, people working in the subject of Artificial Intelligence and "natural stupidity" are aware of the weird contradiction of the cloven Cartesian world. They know that it is uncomplicated to develop computer-processing systems that can straightforwardly substitute the work of engineers, lawyers, and physicians, but it is an impossible Sisyphean task to develop systems that can replace draftspersons, cooks, rôtisseurs, gardeners, and architects. Engineers, lawyers and physicians base their profession on a sequence of logical protocols worked out by deduction and induction, whereas draftspersons, gardeners and architects practice imagination and base their profession on analogies, homologies and demonstrative metaphors generated by conjectural imagination that transcends professional boundaries.

Conjectural imagination is configured as a double-sided coin: we know that there are images on both sides, but we can see only one side at the time. On the one side, imagination is the human faculty that keeps together what has been collected by different and discrete perceptions. This faculty has the gist of the Aristotelian koiné aesthesis, also known as "sensus communis" (amalgamated sense), an internal sense by which the complex configuration of objects such as architectural and culinary products make sense. The sensus communis is not our "common sense", but an amalgamation, a combinatory perception through an internal sense coordinating the data perceived by the external senses. An example of it is the clinical eye of pre-statistical medicine able to recognize the always-changing configurations of a syndrome.

On the other side of the coin, imagination is shown as the virtue by which the sensory images of a building we have seen and the flavors of food we have tasted can be transmuted in new buildings and novel dishes. Imagination can reconstruct something absent, but can also reelaborate the absent in a different composition of forms; we can imagine a man riding a horse as we can imagine a centaur. Imagination is the power by which I can remember my grandmother's roasted chicken but it is also the virtue by which Bonaparte's Swiss chef, Dunan the Younger, could figure out a new recipe and serve the Emperor a *poulet a la Marengo* to celebrate the strategic victory during the second Campaign in Italy, on June 14 1800.[6]

Imagination works within the alchemic modus operandi conceived by Paracelsus, a mercurial alchemist who located the origin of iatrochemistry in the processes of daily cooking. Paracelsus coined the German word "einbildungskraft" (the craft of image-building) to translate imagination. Imagination is the crafty power of the mind to reproduce the appearances that are prearranged by intuition, thereby making possible meaningful representations. That is, imagination is the indispensable hinge between intuition and understanding and therefore a necessary component of any cognitive knowledge. The synoptic character of knowledge could not be realized were it not for the reproduction of images, or representations, accomplished by the imagination.[7] In his alchemic dictionary, a Paracelsus' pupil, Martin Roland, defines imagination as "astrum in homine" (the star within man), a light that was more powerful than any star to achieve a prudent sapience.[8]

The issue is to discover how architects achieve sapience. Architectural sapience is grounded in prudence, i.e. phronesis. According to Aristotle, phronesis is the most important kind of knowledge because it deals with how you use the other kinds of knowledge, that is whether you use them "well" from an ethical point of view. Phronesis is knowledge that helps man to act wisely and make good determinations. Phronesis concerns values and goes beyond analytical, scientific knowledge (*episteme*) and technical sapience (*techne*). Phronesis is focused on particulars and is also context-dependent and has priority over universal rules. Phronesis is lucid, competent and ethical, and deals with things that are good or bad for humanity.

Non-trivial drawings are the place where architectural ethics occur because in the drawings architects considered the mode of action to deliver change, especially to enhance the quality of life. Not only does drawing involve the ability to decide how to achieve a certain end, but also the ability to reflect upon it and determine the achievement of a beatific life, a vita beata, a merging in a single embodiment of three complementary arts: the art of drawing well, living well and building well.

Prudent architects are able to extract "knowledge" from drawings that for the majority of non-architects look just like mere scribbled images or doodling that, in their opinion, have nothing to do with architecture. Architects may extract knowledge useful in a specific architectural project without ever giving to it any verbal descriptions. This is episodic knowledge, a "cognitive" form of memory based on personal experience. Willemien Visser presents the substance of episodic knowledge as not being abstract knowledge, but as a specific knowledge not especially linked to problem solving:

> "The knowledge used in problem solving, which has been studied most, is abstract knowledge … referring to types, or categories, of problems and solutions. Recently, researchers have started to discover the importance of problem-solving reuse: the use of "episodic", i.e. particular, experiences-linked sources which are at the same abstraction level as the target problem ("cases"), rather than general knowledge structures at a more abstract level."[9]

The actual cognitive activity implemented by architects during their work on professional projects is based on the re-use of previous successful episodes of architectural conceiving: Ludwig Mies van der Rohe's I-beams, Carlo Scarpa's interlocking circles, Frank Gehry's titanium sheathing. Architectural episodic intelligence is based on a triadic system of re-uses. One re-use is based on a faculty of knowing procedures generating the same formal result, the second re-use corresponds to a faculty that uses again materials and procedures in an ostensive and tangible manner, and a third re-use is based on the sensual capacity of knowing materials and procedures in an imaginative and bodily manner.

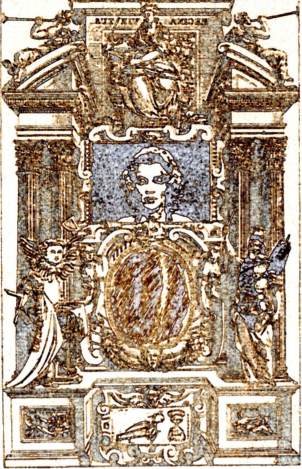

Non-Trivial Architectural Drawings

Labor intensive and slowly drafted non-trivial drawings belong to the forgotten aging-cellar of a refined multi-sensorial and emotional understanding of architecture. Our contemporary world is based on unnecessary hastiness: temporal speed and forced growth are the prevailing attitudes of our age meanwhile unhurried attitudes seem to imply stagnation and inertia. We live in a constant rush. Building and conceiving of building no longer goes on at a proper pace; everything has become increasingly fast. The conceiving and construction of a building exists within the overlapping of three spheres of influence: the push of finance, the urge of technology and the pull of fashion. Consequently buildings and drawings are prejudiced by hasty occasions and must respond to interest rates and rises in site prices that ascribe merely financial value to each instant. Architectural drawings are also pulled toward speediness just because it is possible. Digital technology speeds up tasks and, in theory at least, increases precision and photographic actuality, but produces buildings that lack grip and traction in time.

Non-trivial architectural drawings are the very condition of architectural experimentations; they exist before all the other kinds of architectural experiences. If properly done, these drawings are quite different from artistic or illustrative drawings. They belong to a specific category of representation that makes architectural thinking possible. They depart either from the Platonic view that sees visual reality as a function of ideal essences or from its Cartesian counter-view in which a drawing is assumed to be an internal mental construct of an external reality. Non-trivial architectural drawings offer idiosyncratic approaches, which controvert the presence of the entity presented in the drawing yet to elaborate it further. In that respect, the authority of this construction is a matter of apprehending a reference system between what is internal to the

0.7
Non-Trivial Architect

frame and what is external to it. In these drawing, the relation to a physical reality and what is involved in the drawing is provided by the techniques and methods of their factures.

Architectural drawings result from different forms of storytelling based on sapient factures. The word "facture" derives from the past participle of the Latin verb "facio", "facere", meaning both to make or to do; it thus has the same derivation as "fact", which might be defined as something evidently done. Understood in this way, "fact" and "facture" are closely related; to consider an artifact the same way as its facture is to consider it as a record of its having been made. Architectural drawings don't just represent something—they are something in their own right. Any architectural drawing is not just an aggregate of arbitrary signs that stands for something else—two lines make a wall, dash lines indicate something hidden, and so on—but they bring together signs that derive their meanings from the embodying of their tracing into the events that they represent.

In Italian, "facture" is *fattura* and the word carries mostly the same meanings as in English, however there is an additional meaning worthy of note: *fattura* is also the casting of the spell of the evil eye, a process based on the power of the invidious gaze. A *fattura* can progress from attempting to influence the behavior of the unknowing victim to the intentional making of special objects, "deliberately prepared with a distinct ceremonial, and with a power meaningfully incredible to achieve results, and in particularly frightening case, the *fattura* is done to kill".[10] The power is in the aura generated by ceremonial

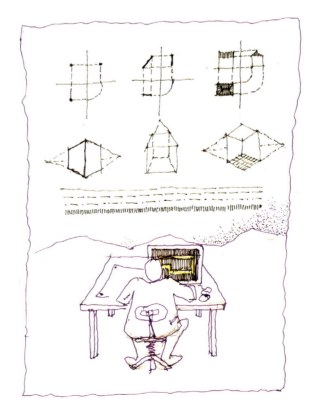

0.8
Trivial Architect

making of the *fattura* and how it can be interfered from the object itself by a simple casting glance from both the *fattura* maker and the victim. The "fattucchiere", the sorcerers that perform the *fatture*, have been applying neuropsychology anti litteram, they have always known that there is no Cartesian separation between mind and body.

Gianbattista Vico, a Neapolitan philosopher, who probably believed in the *fattucchiere*, adds a philosophical dimension to the understanding of human factures.[11] Vico overturns Descartes by developing a new philosophy of knowledge based on the verum-factum principle. The real is what humans make: the foundation of human knowledge is based on the homo faber. Geometry, mathematics, history and other areas of human constructs are sciences only because humans make them. Since humans can construct the elements of a system, a human apparatus, they therefore know how its different parts are arranged. The internal awareness of these human conceived mechanisms of material mediation, the factures, is the source of humanity's real knowledge. The positive power of the material mediation by signs ascribable to the designative character of architectural drawings is instituted by merging analytical and symbolic properties, amalgamating discreteness, finite numbers, combinatory power, pictograms, hieroglyphs and ideograms, all of which epitomize direct, prudent and temperate inscription of human thoughts.

Architecture is not a work of art, but the art that makes the work. Its embodiment formulates factures, because architecture makes things (architectura artefaciens) rather than accepting things that make architecture (architectura artefacta). To believe naively that just thinking of a building will bring a corresponding artifact into existence is a highly misleading notion. The idea of architecture is not a building, for architecture to exist in human consciousness someone has to draft a story. By analogy, it is possible to state that the idea of magic is not a magic event; in order for magic to exist, someone must tell a tale. To create a fairytale is to produce a facture. In order for a fairytale to exist, someone must write a plot. In this case, to write is not to know, but to produce something. In writing fairytales, authors do not know what is the crowning moment of magic in their story, but, saliently and sapiently, the authors fabricate the "magic in the story" by writing the story.

Chapter one

Architectural Iconoclasm

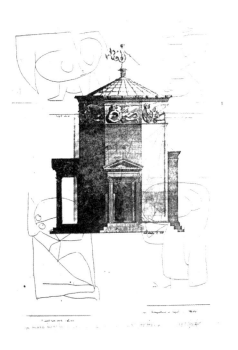

By using the language of the Second Council of Nicea II, where the most crucial discussion of the role of images took place, it is possible to say that the majority of architects and probably many chefs have shifted from "iconophilia" to "idolatry". Iconophilia is not a love for images for themselves but for the translations that takes place from one form of image to another. By contrast, idolatry can be characterized by a morose concentration on the image per se. Thus, the phenomenon of iconoclasm may be defined either as an aggression to idolatry or as an annihilation of iconophilia, two very different wars. Because it seems so difficult to resist the temptation to freeze-frame all images, the iconoclast dream is an unmediated access to truth, which operates within a complete absence of man-made images. If we follow the path of iconophilia, we should, on the contrary, pay even more attention to the series of transformations of which each image is only a provisional condition.

Architects should destroy the frozen images of the idols nibbled or gobbled down by architectural gluttons. A demonstration of the idolatrous misuse of images is in a report published in the Real Estate section of the *Washington*

Post. The article describes how model homes used for marketing have a unique clientele where individuals buy all the objects paraded: furniture, curtains, pictures on the wall, including the fake food displayed on the dining table.[1] In buying these houses in their commercial totality, people buy the image because these model homes have become numb fetishes to live in.

Even if digital technologies have increased unnecessarily the number of images that architects have to handle, the seductive "coolness" of digital representation fascinates architects, clients and architectural students—paradoxically even before they are enrolled in their first design studio. Many are won over by the striking otherworldliness of digital imaging, while others are swayed by the notion that using digital representations will expedite the conceiving of buildings, but above all there is the belief that digital imagery grants instant legitimacy to architectural proposals through a superficial appearance of completeness without considering that this pseudo-completeness hides a loss of rigor. Strangely, the result of this passion for digital representations has not been the creation of iconophile factions bursting with iconodules, but rather iconoclast ones. In a strange reversal phenomena, the digital iconodules have moved on the other side of the barricade and have become part of iconoclast groups that accept only images which have not been elaborated by human hands on drafting boards. Indeed, many offices have no drafting tables and many architectural schools are reaching the same iconoclastic standing.

In the production of digital drawings, realistic images have always been one of the major research aims. These constantly shifting and ameliorated technologies have sped up architectural presentations: photo-realistic representations of future buildings are considered the media of choice that allow architects and clients to make informed decisions. The computer screens that show visualizations of architecture in three dimensions have become powerful "crystal balls" or "magic mirrors" capable of showing "truthful views" of the future. Because the characteristics of the human facture does not show up in the presented images, they have become a modern version of the images accepted by the iconoclasts who are holding the doctrinal assumptions that the ideal, perspicacious and truthful representations would be the result of acheiropoietic (not-handmade) undertakings.

The iconoclasts thought that the only genuine and acceptable representations of Christ were those in which the divine figure was presented instantaneously, as in the Veronica Veil of the Holy Face and the Mandylion or Holy Face of Edessa. The Veronica is a vera-icona, "real icon" or "authentic image", a representation made without any human interference, an acheiropoietic icon. Holy Face images and other acheiropoietic icons are images that allow humans to approach the divine authority. Similarly, a merging of substantial-realism and photo-realism, digital renderings are considered better than photos because nothing in them is literally out of focus. They gain their cultural power because of the awareness that, being digital, these renderings follow true mathematical principles. The associations between digital images and the algorithms that generate them create the conviction that the digital rendering and the file inside the computer are interchangeable. This relationship posits an acheiropoietic likeness between the digital files and the drawings according to which the mathematical basis and the resulting images can both make similar claims to truth.

A common definition of architectural drawings—an architectural drawing is in essence a translator of a mental vision and that vision's physical manifestation—embodies the most common conceptual hindrance that has ever handicapped the education of architects and the understanding of architecture.[2]

There is no such thing as a mental vision of architecture to be translated or mediated in drawing, the architecture embodied in a non-trivial architectural drawing is the result of a formative facture, a process equivalent to the process of formativity (formatività) as delineated by the Turinese philosopher Luigi Pareyson.[3] Formativity is the central concept in his aesthetics which Pareyson defines as "a way of making such that, while one makes, one invents the way of making".[4] For Pareyson, a formative component is inherent in every human activity: human actions aim to produce form, so that even knowledge takes on constructive and intuitive procedures. Since the formative is present in every human activity, it will be a special activity based on specificity and concentration.

Pareyson describes an identity of form and content as the "way of forming" that not only expresses emotions and feelings, but also enhances the intellectual demands and techniques of execution. Inside the formative principle, there are no fixed rules, but each time we go in search of standards for the "making" it becomes an "attempt", a "construction" generating each time the necessary rules to take action. Pareyson's emphasis is on "making", and the absolute centrality of interest is aimed towards facture, viewed as vital to the physical development and history of the work. Architectural drawings rely on the physicality of their formative making as a construction of meanings, and, as factures, they encompass the entire sensorial life and makes possible the exercise of other specific operations, that not only expresses emotions and feelings, but also enhances the intellectual instances and technical demands.

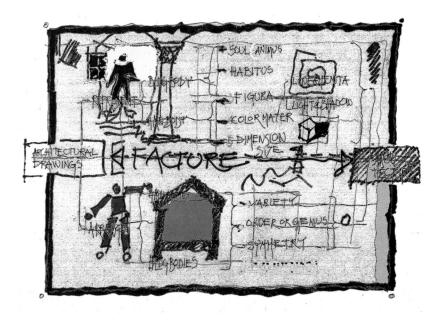

1.2
Diagram of a Facture

A drawing of architecture is a result and it is a process. On the one hand, its form does not exist before it is drawn, but, on the other hand, it is present in its drawn implementation. This is the enigmatic nature at the core of the process that uses drawing to conceive architecture. Architects, in their production of drawings, are guided by the act of drawing itself. They are aiming for a goal that they know will be revealed to them when they will reach it. It is an act of graphic divination able to discern the rules that have been followed only when drawing is near completion. To draw architecture is a sequence of felicitous glimpses that slowly and quickly leads to the construing of a building in absentia.

Slow Food for Architects' Imagination

In "Material Stone", a collection of essays dealing with the building technologies of contemporary architecture, Friz Neumayer remarks that there is "a deeply rooted cultural significance between the arts of cookery and building, one that still awaits adequate description". For Neumayer, these two arts are joined by a fundamental constant of the mutual beneficial production that is growing from "awareness of the characteristics and of materials and their correct methods of handling".[5] It is more than a cultural significance, it is a cognitive embodiment expressed in a metaphor, understood as a conceptual construction central to the development of thought.

The acquiring of the perceptions presented in the exercises in this book are based on metaphorical drinking and eating, and the resulting architectural drawings are presented as metaphorical food even if the first one of the exercises requires the use of edible foodstuffs. This metaphor is much more than just a matter of language: the concepts and influences shape how the architects conduct their graphic conceiving of architecture.

The essence of metaphor is understanding and experiencing one kind of object with other objects. It is not merely a literary turn of phrase, but an

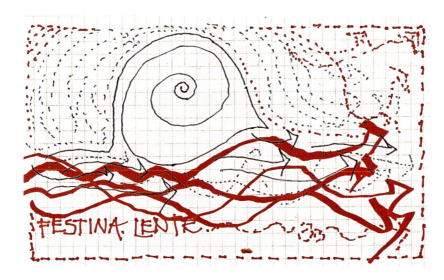

1.3
Festina Lente and Slow Food

Architectural Iconoclasm

essential part of how we define our everyday reality in an ontological condition. Metaphors through storytelling turn our experiences into artifacts. Food is an ideal poetic paragon that allows architects to uncover hidden levels of meaning in human and technological relationships and arrives at new understandings of the architectural experience. The notion of cooking is used to structure the conceiving of ideas. Food making and eating are something concrete that we experience directly, so we can use these physical notions to structure parallel concepts. This structuring is systematic, thus we can speak of "half baked drawings", "digesting the constrains of a design brief", or we can say, "the client can't swallow that elevation". Preparing drawings to represent ideas is food preparation and considering is chewing on them, an event that sometimes shows up metonymically as the chewing on the ends of pencils or pens.

The eleven exercises in this book are intended as a kind of architectural "grimoire", "a manual of construction magic" and "a book of graphic spells".[6] These exercises try to make architects aware of their tacit knowing by using stories concerning the practical knowledge of drawing and of architectural theory. In *Personal Knowledge*, Michael Polanyi argues for the epistemological significance of both these forms of knowledge.[7] Using the act of riding a bicycle, Polanyi proposes that the knowledge of the theoretical physics of balance cannot replace the practical knowledge of how to ride, and that knowing-how and knowing are established, grounded and interfaced.[8] In *The Tacit Dimension*, Polanyi points out that we can know more than we can tell. He termed this pre-logical phase of knowing as tacit knowledge.[9]

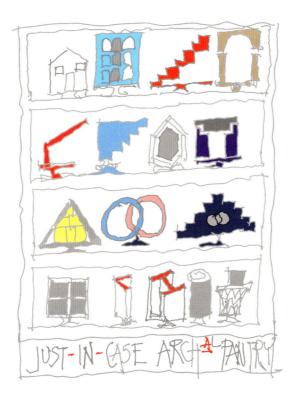

1.4
"Just-in-Case" Architectural Pantry

Tacit knowledge comprises a range of conceptual and sensory information and images that can be brought together to make sense of something. Many pieces of tacit knowledge may constitute a new model or theory, a combination of the architectural understanding and processes of discovery. By merging activities of the body and mind, the eleven exercises are planned as tactics to access this tacit knowledge by a construction of a habitus. The habitus, an operative condition is based on Pierre Bourdieu's notion of it as presented in his Postface to the French translation of Erwin Panofsky's *Gothic Architecture and Scholasticism.*[10] This habitus is a blend of experiences and functions within an array of perceptions, appreciations, and actions that makes possible an unlimited variety of architectural engagements, thanks to the discovery of homologous configurations.

Conjuring up again the food analogy, it is possible to compare tacit knowledge as "just-in-case" ingredients that are stocking a pantry. As two Australian management scholars, Ursula Mulder and Alma Whiteley, point out, "just-in-case" ingredients are things that might be necessary, but the cooks do not know when they will need them. There are also some standard ingredients that each pantry has, for example, pepper, salt, sugar, flour, coffee and tea, and they represent common explicit knowledge. Representing tacit knowledge is the judgment of cooks in selecting and combining "just-in-case" ingredients with a vision of their potentiality for finished products that are not yet in their mind. Tacit knowledge materialization begins by selecting the essential ingredients for a "non-recipe-planned savory pie" that will win a first prize in a culinary context.[11]

Eleven Exercises

The fruitful vagueness embodied in the eleven exercises comes from the polysemic nature of the Latin term "linea" (line). In architectural drawings, linea is then a heuristic device that it could be understood as a line of writing, as a line in a drawing or as the pulling of a line on a construction site, but not as a request of linearity. Architecture is an interfacing of writing, drawing and constructing of lines. These lines are investigational media, a point of departure for a symbiosis between physical materials and cultural ideas. Lines define everything from the tectonic character of rooflines to the anthropometric profile of a bathtub. Images are written and words are drafted and crossings of cultural events and material expressions take place within the lines of a drawing. By borrowing from geometry, geology, alchemy, philosophy, politics, biography, biology, mythology, and philology, architects should write and draw with hesitation, slowly discovering the multiple aspects of architectural inceptions and the consequent hybridization by which they are able to bring together disparate knowledge.

Architectural factures are operational process by which architects actualize architecture from without and it settles for mediated usefulness, arbitrated circumstances, and immediate sorting. In architectural drawing, the compilation of thoughts is not self-evident, but can be decoded and may be used to generate a crucial structure within which architecture can be understood and

read as culturally coded expressions of knowledge with their own epistemological assumptions and powerful ancestry.

The fundamental nature of the eleven exercises is perception and imagination in action. "Perception is not something that happens to us, or in us. It is something we do".[12] We only perceive that to which we attend. In architecture, as in many other fields, imagination depends on perception and perceptual consciousness, but also on the procedures used to record what has been attended. On their drawing and imaging procedures architects develop their talents for action and capability for thought. In tracing, marking and measuring lines, architects refine their abilities of architectural perception and by these ministering actions they evolve thoughtful processes of imagination. Architectural drawings are an assimilation of mental and environmental data and an elaboration of them in architectural artifacts. As Daniel Marcus Mendelowitz puts it:

> "Just as the written or spoken word, by fixing fragments of thought in logical sequences, makes possible the formulation of intellectual concepts of the greatest complexity, so drawing, by fixing visual impressions in static forms, makes it possible to build knowledge step by step and eventually come to know the nature of forms that are too complex to be comprehended at a single glance".[13]

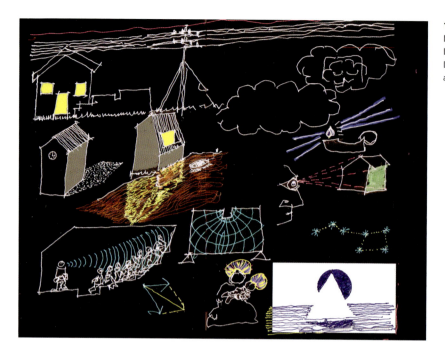

Drawings, the products of architects' work, are more intimately connected with an identification of what actions are performed than pictorial representations. These artifacts are called "drawings" because they were drawn—this is what architects attend. To pictorially represent, on the other hand, is to produce a picture, and there are many ways to produce pictures of things other than by drawing them. Pictorial representations may even look like drawings when they are not, simply because they were not drawn, but executed with other techniques that do not draw, such as a photo, watercolors, tempera, oil paint, woodblock prints, etchings, or lithographs. In addition, someone may produce a pictorial representation of something by drawing something other than what is pictorially represented. Architects' sketches are fragmentary and incomplete versions of architectural drawings and even if they are not made using the conventions of orthographic projection they cannot be regarded as pictures. Nevertheless, there are plenty of examples of architects illustrating details or spatial conditions as three-dimensional sketches, to investigate pictorially the effect of a certain massing of forms or spatial organization.

Chapter two

The Cosmopoiesis of Architectural Drawings

"[la] gastrosophie est une science de la plus haute sagesse qui doit réunir aux lumières de la médecine et del'agronomie celles de plusieurs autres sciences inconnues des civilizes …"

Charles Fourier[1]

In 1965, the architectural theoretician Peter Collins published a book titled *Changing Ideals in Modern Architecture* that is still commonly read as a major critical text on modernism. In the book, Collins listed four analogies used to explain architecture:

1. mechanical;
2. biological;
3. linguistic; and
4. gastronomic.

The mechanical, biological, and linguistic analogies were already well known, even if other or parallel naming were used for them. However, the gastronomical analogy introduced a novel approach. In his explorations of the many different launches of modern architecture, Collins located the modern beginnings of the gastronomical analogy in a lecture given by a nineteenth-century Scottish architectural writer, James Fergusson. Talking to a group of military engineers, Fergusson made a remarkable point regarding the true principle of architecture:

> "The process by which an image is refined into a temple, a hut to shelter, or a meeting house into a cathedral, is the same as that which refines a boiled neck of mutton into côtelettes à l'impériale or a grilled fowl into poulet à la Marengo. So essentially is this the case that if you wish to acquire a knowledge of the true principle of design in architecture, you will do better to study the works of Soyer or Mrs. Glasse than any or all of the writers on architecture, from Vitruvius to Pugin."[2]

Several architectural critics and theoreticians have appreciated Fergusson's consideration. However, whenever it is quoted it is always used as a way to reveal a significant intuition, it is only rarely analyzed for its critical content. Fergusson did not compare the alpha and omega of the architectural discipline of his time—that is, Marcus Vitruvius Pollio, author of the only surviving Roman treatise on architecture, and Augustus Welby Northmore Pugin, an English architect who contrasted medieval and neoclassical architecture to realize modernity—with possible corresponding characters in the history of food preparation, such as Marcus Gavius Aspicius, author of a renowned treatise on Roman cuisine art, and Marie-Antoine Carême, a sustainer of a modern method in cuisine who had contrasted ancien cuisinier with moderne cuisinier. Fergusson preferred to juxtapose the selected architects with two less-celebrated cooks who had shown pioneering approaches to the world-making of food, a novel gastrosophical modus operandi: Alexis Benoît Soyer (1810–1858), a flamboyant French chef who became a renowned cook in Victorian London, and Hannah Glasse (1708–1770), the mother of the modern dinner party and a successful cookery writer of the eighteenth century.

Biographies describe Soyer as a very conspicuous chef. However, Soyer took a leave at his own expense from his position as chef de cuisine at the Reform Club in London during the Crimean War to join the troops and advise the army on healthy cooking. Together with Florence Nightingale, Soyer reorganized the provisioning of the army hospitals. He invented his own field stove, the Soyer stove, and trained and installed a regimental cook in every regiment so that soldiers would receive adequate meals and not suffer from malnutrition or die of food poisoning. A few years before, during the Great Irish Potato Famine, he devised a soup kitchen and was asked by the government to travel to Ireland and implement his idea. While in Ireland, he published *Charitable Cookery*, a book that sold for sixpence a copy to raise money for charities helping the poor.[3]

Good ingredients, simple techniques, and quality dining available to all constituted the gastrosophy held by Hannah Glasse. She is best known for her cookbook, *The Art of Cookery*, first published in 1747. It was reprinted within its first year of publication and in twenty further editions during the eighteenth century. It continued to be published until the middle of the nineteenth century. Although Glasse rejected extravagance and wastefulness in cooking, she held that the careful presentation of dishes on the table was vital. Colors and shapes were meant to complement each other, and different dishes were always arranged symmetrically on the table. These gastrosophical manifestations were of the utmost importance, especially for the upwardly mobile middle-class audience for whom Hannah Glasse wrote.[4]

The dominant Western way of life aspires to supremacy and ascendancy. This pursuit also characterizes modern Western cooking, in which gastronomy seeks an imperious cultural presence and an overbearing visual significance as expressed in a domineering gastrosophy. Although representing two very different approaches to the cookery art, Glasse and Soyer are both concerned with a secularization of cooking and a prudent gastronomy. They are against a glorification of simulacra; in other words, they are for a weak gastrosophy. A strong gastronomical notion aims to impress through outstanding singular images and consistent articulation of dishes, whereas, a weak gastronomy is contextual and responsive and, as in the present-day Slow Food crusade, recognizes a precise, but gently prudent, material association between the conceiving and making of plates within a regional cosmopoiesis.[5] The hypothesis of a weak gastrosophy stems from the philosophy of weakness proposed by the Italian philosopher Gianni Vattimo. Introducing an approach of philosophizing that does not totalize the multitude of human discourses into a single scheme, Vattimo elaborated the idea of weak ontology and weak thought.[6]

Weak cosmopoietic gastronomy is concerned with real sensorial exchanges instead of idealized and conceptual manifestations. These later forms are manifested in the art of cuisine initially elaborated by Carême, carried on by the "haute cuisine", and brought to its extreme by the formal appearances of lightness carried on by the "nouvelle cuisine". A weak gastronomy grows and opens up from details of food elaboration, rather than the reverse process of closing down from concepts to the details. Within the cosmopoiesis of weak gastrosophy, the images arising from the foodstuffs project are deeper and more profoundly emotional experiences than images of food form. Foodstuffs evoke unconscious images and emotions, but modern gastronomy has been primarily concerned with visual biases; a demonstration of that is the flourishing of the difficult and even pornographic art of food photography.

Contemporary architecture also has been dominated by a photographic bias. Beatriz Colomina has argued that twentieth-century architecture was constituted within its own photographic representations.[7] However, as theorized by the Catalan architect Ignazi Sola-Morales, who interpreted Vattimo's philosophical work in architectural theory, weak architecture is without the visual bias. It allows the inhabitants to understand architecture by cross-modal sensorial experiences that are achieved when inhabitants cease to be mere spectators and begin to be participants in the art of living well through a corporeal interaction.[8] The main aim is for the inhabitant to understand architecture through slow prolonged periods of interaction in which a balance of the senses is achieved.

EXERCISE #1

Food Colors

According to a tradition, Master Valerio of Flanders, when working the windows of Milan Cathedral (those representing the history of St. Helena), was accompanied by an assistant called Zafferano, so named for his habit of mixing a bit saffron in any shade of yellow he used. Jokingly, the Master told him if he continued to do so he would eventually even put saffron in the risotto. At the wedding of Valerio's daughter, Zafferano plotted with the cook in charge of the banquet and added saffron to the risotto, usually seasoned only with butter and cheese. The recipe was a success, thanks not only to the savory flavor of saffron, but also to its joyful golden color.[9] Of course this is a myth, but the saffron earthly aura is left.

The term aura has a triadic origin. Aura (in Latin *aura* means "breeze, wind, air", and in Greek it means "breath, breeze") is a sensory stimulus detecting invisible smells and aromas used to indicate the distinctive but intangible

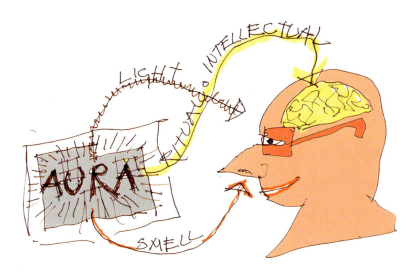

quality that seems to surround a person or thing. In overlapping realms of parapsychology and spirituality, an aura is a subtle multicolored luminous halo or nimbus surrounding a person or object. The association in the physical world is an optical phenomenon that appears near or around the Sun or Moon, and sometimes near other strong light sources such as streetlights.[10] The uses of aura in medical terminology reveal the perceptual connections between vision and smell. Aura can be a premonition before a migraine or a grand mal seizure. The aura may consist of flashing arcs of sparkling zig-zag lines or a blotting out of vision, or both, or strange odors, or the feeling of a breeze.[11]

In a far-reaching essay entitled, "The Work of Art in the Age of Mechanical Reproduction", Walter Benjamin applies the word "aura" to the sense of awe and reverence that an individual presumably experiences in the presence of unique works of art. Benjamin's aura is not in the object itself but rather in cultural attributes and values. Aura identifies art's traditional association with structures of power, magic and religious or secular rituals. With the inception of art's mechanical reproducibility, and the development of new forms of art (such as film) in which there is no actual original, the experience of art could be freed from the constrains of place and ritual and brought under the gaze and control of a mass audience, leading to a shattering of the aura:

> "For the first time in world history, mechanical reproduction emancipates the work of art from its parasitical dependence on ritual."[12]

A revealing note that points to architecture as having a unique relationship with aura is found in the footnotes of Benjamin's essay,

> "Distraction and concentration form polar opposites … this is most obvious with regard to buildings. Architecture has always represented the prototype of a work of art, the reception of which is consummated by a collectivity in a state of distraction. The laws of its reception are most instructive."[13]

All senses should be involved in the act of architectural drawing to make it a facture that deals with human distraction. This should be done through a rediscovery of the media used during drawing and how they relate to other senses beside the usual sight.

"It is obligation of man to eat and to build" is an amazing remark put forward by Filarete, a Renaissance architect and theoretician, at the beginning of his treatise, an architectural storytelling that appropriately initiates with a discussion around a dinner table.[14] The problem with the denigration of the corporeal dimension in architecture is not simply that the fundamental relationships bonding food production and eating with architectural production and inhabitation fails to get the bona fide attention that it deserves. Rather, the present interest in it demonstrates that architects, as most nouvelle cuisine chefs, are off-track. On the contrary, the belly-affirming chefs and architects— not the heavy eaters, but the corporeal ones—do not waste time with a search for the universal power of image prestige by imposition. They begin within an inherited local sapience that they, with their belly-quickening dishes or drawings, seek to further. The body and its desires for both food and architecture immerse us in the world, engage us in all sorts of interactions, and blur rigid boundaries between our surroundings and ourselves.

Draw a sequence of building details using a pen holder completed with a good selection of different kind of nibs, and a good set of watercolor brushes on watercolor paper. Instead of dipping your nibs or your brushes in store-bought inks and paints, use exclusively liquids, pastes, juices or powders that you normally eat, drink or use to spice and flavor your food.

The foodstuffs to be used in liquid form for drawing could be saffron, mustard, paprika, cocoa, blackberries, blueberries, curry, beets, red currants, different kinds of wine, tea, coffee, lemon, orange juice (ideal for tracing occult lines which can be revealed later on by heat), nocino, egg yolk and any other suitable foodstuffs.

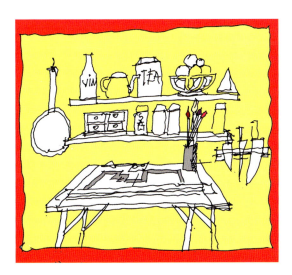

2.2
Drawing with Foodstuff

Some of the dry foodstuffs can be dissolved in water, white wine, and milk. For instance, saffron, usually found in desiccated form, can be first pounded into powder and then dissolved in a little hot water and it gives you an alluring gold-yellow and a long lasting earthily smell. Many of the mentioned foodstuffs have pleasant or unpleasant odors, nevertheless these odoriferous media increase the sentient nature of the readers of the drawings. As fixative, sprayed whole milk can be used to stabilize the powdered foodstuffs that cannot be dissolved or absorbed by the paper; it can also be fixed with beaten egg-white painted over—the use of the albumen will also enrich the tonality of colors.

In this exercise, experimenting first with the different coloring materials and the proportions between the selected materials and the diluting agents is very important, although direct attempts with whatever is at hand can often give surprising results.

Synesthetic Processes

Known to medical science for almost three hundred years synesthesia, a technical expression meaning crossing of the senses (in Greek "syn" means together, and "aisthesis" means sensation or perception) has been recently confirmed as a legitimate and positive human condition. Synesthesia is not a neurologic disorder, but a different way of experiencing the environment. It is a sequence of idiosyncratic, automatic, involuntary and consistent experiences across an individual's lifespan. Synesthesia occurs through the associations of two or more physical senses and other sense modalities. In other words, it denotes that sensory stimulation of one sensory modality (the inducer) will elicit an involuntary or automatic sensation in another sensory modality (the concurrent). Called synesthetes, the individuals with synesthesia may "smell" colors, "see" sounds and "feel" tastes. During the early part of the twentieth century the Russian neurologist, Aleksandr Romanovich Luria, observed that "S", one of his patients, was a synesthete and "S" experienced words as having a "taste and weight ... something oily slipping through the hand". Upon hearing a specific sound pitch, "S" saw "a brown strip against a dark background that had red tongue-like edges" and tasted it as "sweet and sour borscht".[15] Richard E. Cytowic, a physician trained in neurology, neuropsychology and known for rediscovering synesthesia and returning it to the scientific mainstream, points out,

> "After decades of neglect, a revival of inquiry is under way. As in earlier times, today's interest is multidisciplinary. Neuroscience is particularly curious this time—or at least it should be—because of what synesthesia might tell us about consciousness, the nature of reality, and the relationship between reason and emotion."[16]

The critical concerns in material substances or material artifacts developed by architects and cooks, and how they achieve transformations and transubstantiations of what they have at hand, can be understood by approaching the phenomena as result of synesthetic processes. In synesthetes, the stimulation of one sensory modality causes a reliable perception in one or more different senses.

During the cooking or drawing processes, one of the human senses is considered dominant, but the result as well as the making—a dish or a building—ought to be conceived and appreciated with the totality of senses. By looking to the color of the food during the cooking process a chef will evoke if is ready or not, and in the case of architecture by a color pencil delineation of a room, an architect can evoke its thermal or acoustical delights. This phenomenology makes clear that synesthesia is not an idea, but an experience, it is not reasoning but emotional. This experience takes place in the brain, a neuro-phenomenon, and although it is the root of poetic devices, it differs substantially from shaded metaphors, literary tropes, sounds, symbolism. Commonplace expressions such as "loud colors", "dark sounds", "sweet smells", "soft voices" and "sound structures" are employed to describe complex experiences. These expressions probably antedate intentionally formal manipulation of language and are derived from real synesthetic experiences.[17]

In architectural drawings the roles of reason and emotion are reversed. Creativity is an experience, not an abstract idea that a mind and body incessantly analyze. In drafting, the elicited sensations perceived by synesthetes are emotional and noëtic and the conclusion is reached when lines rest in an emotional balance. As long as the searched result is not achieved, the drawing cannot rest; the battle lines and colors are changed until the intended nuances of synesthetic perception are achieved. Its reality and vividness are what makes architectural synesthesia so motivating in its violation of conventional perceptions of what drawings look like.

To the fin de siècle artists, synesthetes appeared to be at humanity's psychic forefront, rising above the sensually segregated masses. At the beginning of the artistic and scientific fascination with synesthesia, son et lumiere multimodal concerts, sometimes including aromas and scents, were popular and often featured color-organs with keyboards that controlled colored lights as well as musical notes. Russian composer Alexander Scriabin, a known synesthete, featured an organ that produced multihued light beams in his symphony Prometheus, the Poem of Fire.

After a peak of fascination between 1860 and 1930, synesthesia was forgotten and disregarded mostly because its subjective character was considered unsuitable for proper scientific study. The lack of obvious agreement among synesthetes on the crossmodalities was taken as evidence that synesthesia was not actual. The possibility of scientific comparison was not evident because researchers were looking at the terminal stage of a conscious perception, instead of taking into account the previous processes that led to that perception. The scientific world was baffled by synesthesia's impenetrable nature. Scientists could not understand or share synesthetes' unique perceptions. Two individuals with the same sensory cross-modality do not report identical, or even similar, synesthetic responses; Scriabin and Nikolai Rimsky-Korsakov, for example, disagreed on the color of given notes and keys.

Lately, a comeback of scientific interest in synesthesia is taking place following cognitive and multimedia studies that are contemplating the condition not as an anomaly of the mind, but as a norm of human perception, imagination, and creativity. As Bulat Galeyev points out, synesthesia is not merely a psychic abnormality, but a powerful variety of tacit knowledge.[18] The additional

2.3
A Synesthetic Alphabet

perception is real, often outside the body, instead of being projected by the mind's eye. Synesthesia is perceived externally in peri-personal space, the limb-axis space immediately surrounding the body, never at a long distance as in the spatial tele-reception of vision or audition.

Synesthetes perceive by merging primary and secondary qualities in the cloven world of the res extensa (subjective corporeal substances) and cogitans (objective thinking essences). They associate the delight of res extensa with the judgment of the res cogitans in a new perception reconciling the subjective with the objective. The most common type of synesthesia is grapheme–color (i.e. number–color or letter–color) synaesthesia. The perceptual richness of synesthetes' texts and computation is not just pedantry. Each is unique, and saliently so, and gives to the synesthetes an advantage in figuring out texts, formulas and calculations. Synesthetic cross wiring of sensory associations are emotional states of affairs appreciating that there are ineffable things you hear, invisible things that you see, and impalpable things that you touch, that are describable but beyond words. Nevertheless, these experiences are accompanied by a sense of certitude—the "this is it" feeling—and a conviction that what is perceived is actual and valid. They are noëtic illuminations based on facts that are experienced indirectly but at the same time coupled with a feeling of assurance of the perception. As Richard Cytowic points out, synesthetic experiences are a third-person verbal description of a first-person sensory experience.[19] It is a way for handling the "primitive" functions of emotion, memory, and attention. The role that emotion plays in our thinking and actions is often misunderstood and even minimized, but synesthesia implies emotional evaluations, not the reasoned evaluations that ultimately inform our behavior. Scientific studies of synesthetic individuals have demonstrated that the color of a number is a much more precise perception than the graphic form of the digit in verifying the accuracy of a computation, and the feeling of shapes evoked by tasting food is better than aromas for judging if a victual is properly made.[20]

The Cosmopoiesis of Architectural Drawings

Chapter three

Festina Lente

"Our century, which began and has developed under the insignia of industrial civilization, first invented the machine and then took it as its life model. We are enslaved by speed and have all succumbed to the same insidious virus: Fast Life, which disrupts our habits, pervades the privacy of our homes and forces us to eat Fast Foods. To be worthy of the name, Homo Sapiens should rid himself of speed before it reduces him to a species in danger of extinction. A firm defense of quiet material pleasure is the only way to oppose the universal folly of Fast Life."

Folco Portinari[1]

Slowness is often related to negative values of clumsiness, disinterest, sloth and tedium, conditions that do not include the positive effects resulting from paused, well-thought and safe attitudes. Architectural drawings are islands of slowness within the stormy sea of the pseudo-fastness of the building industry. Bad architectural drawings are fast food and good architectural drawings are slow food for architects' thinking. However, it does not mean that slow food drawing is based on slow tempo and the fast food drawing on fast tempo. Slow and fast in architectural drawings are not physical expressions of chronological conditions, but cognitive perceptions. Speed is a concept resulting in a continuum of individual and socio-cultural perceptions. Without the fast we can't appreciate the slow, and vice-versa.

In *Slowness* (La Lenteur), a philosophical-tragic-comedy novel, Milan Kundera connects slowness to remembering, and speed to forgetting. When one wants to savor, remember, or prolong a moment, one moves and acts slowly. On the other hand, one travels fast to forget an experience.

"The man hunched over his motorcycle can focus only on the present instant of his flight; he is caught in a fragment of time cut off from both the past and the future; he is wrenched from the continuity of time … in other words, he is in a state of ecstasy; in that state he is unaware of his age, his wife, his children, his worries, and so he has no fear, because the source of fear is in the future, and a person freed of the future has nothing to fear."[2]

3.1
Sensorium or Common Sense

Under the powerful emblem of "festina lente" (hasten slowly), architecture refers to the process of building architectural artifacts gradually by taking the immediate functions, structure and materiality, together with other mediated factors into account.[3] The resulting buildings are not just aimed at economic and functional efficiency, but at cultural value and historical characteristics by using unique and natural materials minimizing artificial feeling and assimilating the local culture.

"Slow" is both a condition of world-making and an approach to everyday life. The notion of "slow" is not only pointing out a magnificent procedure but it is an inflection of senses, emotions, spaces and sustainability. Because of their speed, technological advances of the past one hundred years have meant that the work we do more often than not creates a sense of disconnection from time and place.

Slow architecture does not imply idleness, but rather taking the necessary time to consider and envisage positive and negative consequences and possible positive alternatives. Festina lente aims at a highly efficient and effective method for practicing long-term thinking within architecture.[4] The notion of festina lente has major implications for the pace of drawing because it prevents individuals from acting in the heat of the moment and avoids swift and arbitrary decisions by fulfilling a slow building up of careful work.

Why has the pleasure of slowness disappeared from the making of drawings? Architecture is meant to transcend its epoch and so are architectural drawings. Buildings should accommodate the requests of their own epoch, but at the same time they should be able to adapt to requests that cannot be easily anticipated or even imagined. Drawing should not be done only to fulfill the request of a specific building construction, but to respond at the same time to unanticipated requirements, because architects draw situations, not just buildings; and situations are the most powerful determinants of behavior: more powerful than personality, habit, education, character, genetic make-up, more powerful than anything.

3.2
Festina Lente,
Aldo Manuzio's emblem
from the Hypnerotomahia

The Facture of Drawings

This work is not intended as a reactionary proposition trying to start a counter-revolution against the exploitations caused by the present conditions of architectural representations, but rather its aim is to gain a critical understanding of the processes at the base of architectural conceiving to obtain a better handling of computer technology. Non-trivial architectural representations are not merely algorithmically generated depictions, but recognize the need for processes to address the materiality and sensuality to be embedded in the drawings. Non-trivial architectural representations can allow architectural students and professionals to really take advantage of the incredible potential of digital drawings. The epistemology of architectural drawings must be synthesized at the chaotic and cunning junction of humanistic and scientific concepts of knowledge. In drawing, the lines become just as much a part of the meaning as the conditions in which the lines had been traced.[5]

The drawing surface and its materiality is the location where the essential synesthetic experience of the architectural preparation to the act of building takes place. Investigating the mapping of a structure, originally composed in one medium, onto another structure in another medium is the fundamental undertaking of architectural drawings. The acts of making, reading, or interpreting architectural drawings are not usually acknowledged to involve expressions associated with other senses; paradoxically, vision is deemed the exclusive sense necessary and sufficient to accomplish such tasks, even if architects use drawings to figure out dwellings that are bundles of intertwined sensory perceptions.

Architects work on their drawings by using graphic processes that allow the exploration of specific physical events of construction and inhabitation. Architects' drawings are a never-ending alternation between what is representable and what is not representable. Consequently, the drawn surface becomes a glimmering receptacle of architectural desires, a rich vessel simmering with architectural factures rather than a transparent vessel within which, in a futile stillness, the lines precipitate into "graphic dregs" that describe future buildings, a numb drawing that reject any reflection and perception of architectural factures.

A proper cosmopoiesis feeds on intuition, on caring, and nurturing, and drawing factures feed with the creative energy of architectural imagination. It reveals and manifests emotional and mental activities by connecting the act of drawing to a delighted construction of satisfied dwelling conducive to happy thinking and happy living. Many of the conventionally elaborated views of drawings deal with buildings from without and it settles for mediated usefulness, arbitrated circumstances, and immediate sorting. The same condition is within the realm of cooking; it is clearly expressed in the opposition between the emotional inconsequentiality of processed food imposed for convenience and other conditions and the meaningfulness of slow food that gives a sense of emotional well-being.

If architectural cosmopoiesis is not to be made of "outlines alone", what else goes in its making; what do architects work with? Drawing factures connect the construction and use of buildings with the sensorial cosmology of its inhabitants and makers. The facture of signs that is used to generate traces during construction also forms the basis for sorting the facture of the marks used in architectural drawing. These factures fall into these three categories:

1. Marks made directly by the human body: scratches, grooves, furrows in clay or soft materials, smears or smudges contrasting materials with hands and fingers on surfaces and by spitting paint from the mouth. In drawing there is no transformation; the only difference is that the support is different from the construction site.
2. Marks made by wood, bone, stone, and metal tools, an enhancement of the previous class of signs; these tools adapt themselves to different surfaces and they become complex instruments that in addition to marking can guide the drawing; tools of this kind range from brushes, pencils, pens, scribers and chalks to templates, elipsographs, proportional dividers and pantographs.
3. Signs made by light and shadows: the historical range of these kinds of signs extends from contemporary laser tracers to shadow casting and tracing as described by Vitruvius in the discipline of dialing. In drawing factures the range goes from blueprints to digital screens.

In the factures to which these productions of signs belong, surfaces play an essential role because tools do not translate ideas but produce ideas with their interaction with the surface. There are four classes of drawing tools in relationship to their acting on the support:

1. Scoring tools: they are sharp or dull tools that cut, incise, notch, etch, slice, gash, scratch and nick the surface. They are chisels, gouges and the like. In this case, the support contains the vestiges.
2. Tracing tools: they are charred, chalky or waxy tools but always friable; these tools leave part of their matter on the surface by scouring. They include pencils, chalks, and pastels. In this case, the supports hold the marks.
3. Depositing tools: the tools do not act unless they are loaded. They set down a pigment by spraying or by dragging liquid, viscous or powdered materials. They are pens, brushes, and markers. In this case, the supports retain the traces by absorption.
4. Luminous tools: they do not touch the support and they act by light and shadows; the drawings disappear as soon as the energy feeding the instrument or the light sources casting the shadow are interrupted. They are mostly digital tools. A proper selection of supports or output can preserve the drawings, but they are byproducts and, most of the time, they are fashioned to emulate any of the three previous classes of tools.

The supports can be opaque or transparent and luminous; the materiality of their surfaces reacts differently to the acting and the materiality of the tools.

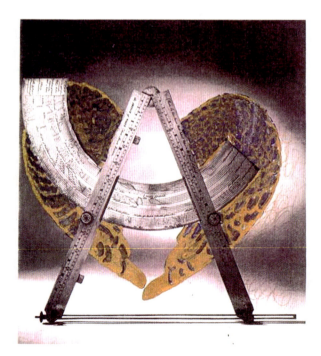

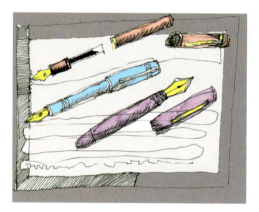

3.3
Tools: Fountain Pens

3.4
Angelic Tool

A great variety of supports have been used for architectural drawings: stone, paper, fabric, clay, plaster, bone, metal, glass. The dimensions have varied from the extraordinarily small to the exceedingly large. The tension of the suitability between the materiality and dimension of supports and drawing tools is what rules the facture of architectural drawings and it also has a major impact on the resulting architecture. As the nature of grounds and soils plays a major role in the erection of buildings, the drafting or drawing supports are the material condition for making future buildings visible and tangible. With the support, architectural drawing finds its own place and time; the materiality of the surfaces and the dimensions of the supports determine these aspects.

EXERCISE #2

Tools

3.5
Tools ad hoc

Buildings and architectural drawings are the result of affordances given by tools. The affordances of a tool become obvious in its use. An American psychologist of perception, James Jerome Gibson, defines affordances as the opportunities for action provided to the observers by the environment within which they operate. Furthermore, Gibson proposes that observers perceive the reality of these affordances rather than abstract physical properties of objects and environments. Affordances are real and have a relational ontology since they do not exist as a function of either the environment or the observer alone, but exist in the interaction between the physical capabilities and properties of the observer and the physical properties of the environment.[6]

Tools have a dual function. On the one hand, instruments as objects contribute to the affordances of the environment: before being used, a tool has its own affordances, inviting certain actions; drawing tools are theoretical products of the continuous modeling effort that aims at rationalizing perception and production of shapes. On the other hand, during their use instruments extend human effectiveness; drawing instruments are physical objects of the world to be modeled. To understand their architectural function means to be able to make instruments that realize a desired action. The relationship between the body, mind and instruments is a dialectic one, and the "reflexivity" inherent in this relationship constitutes the very nature of our interaction with cognitive instruments.

Drawing instruments have been indirectly described since early Greek treatises on geometry, straight edges to draw even lines, and compasses to describe circles or section of circles. This long tradition demonstrates that tools are replicatable and reusable and that tools encapsulate information as well as behavior. Furthermore, tools can combine or interact with one another for achieving different effects.

Vincenzo Scamozzi gives a rare but clear explanation of the role and nature of the tools he used (see appendix). He used folded paper to create temporary squares where he could mark the fundamental measures and proportion of the building in that moment on the drawing board. He also used the magnetic compass combined with a rose of winds to analyze sites and he was the first that represented the rose of wind in drawings of architectural plans.

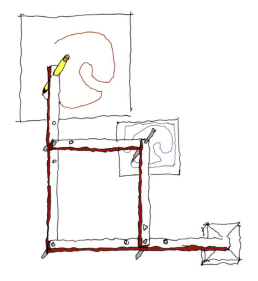

A cosmogony and a cosmopoiesis of architectural instruments:

Before undertaking a project make you own drafting tools using paper, paperboard, light wood, metal, plastic or any other suitable material. Fashion these tools in a way that will make them specific to the project you are undertaking. Only planar drawing instruments will be considered in this exercise, even if spatial drawing instruments such as perspectographs have played a major role in specific practices.

The metaphor of tool-use for describing the interaction between a human and a computer is pervasive in the user interface with the program. However, it is surprisingly difficult to define the affordance of tool-use precisely, especially in cognitive terms; the making of your own tools will raise a different body, mind and drawing facture connection.

Make your own marking tools (pencils and pens that have been produced industrially are not allowed), for instance it is possible to use drinking-straws or stirrers cut into quill pens.

Make your edges for drawing lines: they do not need to be straight but rather they should be related to your design intention, the same condition should be followed in the facture of the necessary squares.

Make your own compasses or dividers; disposable chopsticks provide excellent legs for a compass, you need only to fasten points or markers, and then figure out a variable joint or a tie-up one—this solution requires a divider for each different curve.

Also make a pantograph. The original use of the pantograph is for copying and scaling drawings and to enlarge the small sketches you drew at the beginning of this exercise. To make a pantograph cut four strips out of stiff cardboard or rigid plastic, about 25 millimeter wide, and 300 millimeter long. Put them together according to the picture above. Make a hole for the drawing tool. The pushpins go in upside down; you must put a piece of cork over the sharp end that sticks out, for protection. Use a nail to make a pointer. Make the fix point very heavy so it does not move.

3.6
A view of the tools on a tilted drafting table

3.7
Pantograph

Chapter four

Drawings as Loci for Thought

"My line wants to remind constantly that it's made of ink, I appeal to the complicity of my reader who will transform this line into meaning by using our common background of culture, history, poetry."

Saul Steinberg[1]

"It is impossible to explain clearly this business of building if it is not seen in a drawing. It is even difficult to understand it in a drawing. Anyone who does not understand drawing cannot understand it well, for it is more difficult to understand a drawing than to draw it."

Antonio Averlino Filarete[2]

The facture of architectural drawings is not obvious, as the marketing for digital architectural instruments is trying to convince architects, builders, and clients. The facture does not presume what traces, lines, and scores in the drawings are worldly or unworldly, existing or non-existing, physical or mental, subjective or objective. The facture of architectural drawing must avoid such descriptions. The only thing that in the facture must be assumed is that that which is marked, inked, penciled, brushed, chalked, and printed comes into being. Architectural drawing is wholly based on a sapience of a process of materialization, in which the materiality of the lines becomes the carrier of fluid, and generates invisible lines that become lines of thought.

In their drawing, architects select inscribing processes that allow the exploration of specific physical events of construction and inhabitation. In their drawings, architects create and explore synesthetically all the sensory necessities of building and dwelling. Infusing their drawings with "invisible tinctures" architects link and elaborate thoughtful architectural morsels. On the surface and in the thickness of paper, architects inscribe rooms for thoughts by planning sensory transitions from disorder to order. Space on paper can be made contiguous with three-dimensional space. The two-dimensional quality of inscriptions allows them to merge with a three-dimensional geometry. The result is that architects can work on paper with rulers and numbers, but still manipulate three-dimensional facture "out there", by having learned how to manipulate drawings and then to array them in "cooking" sequences. Through drawing, delineating and tracing, architects cook their raw thoughts in edifying

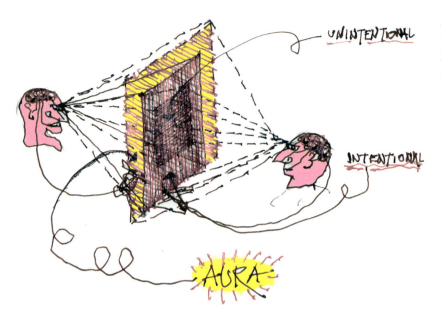

4.1
Architectural Drawing Related
Communication Divided into
Three Areas: 1) Intentional,
2) Unintentional, 3) Aura

considerations.[3] They construct or deconstruct through a variety of formal, conceptual, and physical actions on paper anticipating the yet to come conceptual and physical events in the buildings. They do so in a manner analogous to the one by which cooks are able to relate the process taking place in a pot or in the oven with the upcoming experience in the mouth.

Architectural drawings are instrumental as well as demonstrative and representational; they serve several functions; they are subject to the laws of physics and it is also a craft form. Architectural interpretation through drawings involves a wide of variety of media and genres. Simply to represent architectural drawings as documents tout court misconstrues the multiplicity of possibilities involved in a drawing.

Is a non-trivial discipline of architectural drawings possible? How can a systematic, endlessly growing stratified structure of architectural representations maintain its original meaningful condition through mediate abilities? Is architectural cognitive thinking able to produce something novel without reactivating previous levels of knowledge? The problem is that non-trivial architectural drawings are a particular sort of text: one that bears very little similarity to verbal, linguistic, or even artistic text. As such, the idea that they can be read in the same way that one reads a novel, a portrait, or even a city map simply does not stand up to analysis.

Why raise the issue of architectural drawing? With the present proliferation and maturation of digital technologies, what is the use of the hand and the traces that the hand can make on clay, stone, wood or paper? Why waste time to examine the nature of drawings, their marks, lines, scratches, furrows, incisions, touches, dots and dashes, inscriptions, string lines, stains and blotches; penciled, inked, chalked, brushed, illuminated or erased on diverse grounds? Where is the gain in it for improving architectural thinking? When considering the character of thinking, most people associate it primarily with words, with language. When visual is taken into account inevitably it becomes visual thinking. Unfortunately, in the locution the concentration is on the "visual" and the "thinking" component is almost forgotten and fades into the background. Visual thinking in architecture is an even more complicated issue because it is part of the larger structure based on sensorial thinking.

What does a non-trivial drawing really represent? Traditionally, architects express their thinking about a construction externally by drawing manually or digitally on different kinds of supports, and then they examine, interpret, and perhaps reinterpret them. The interpretative process continues even after the pen has been put down with the work of the reader of the drawing picking up where the drawing stopped. Drawing promotes a positive and objective detachment because decisions are made based on the story of conception and development present in the drawing itself in addition to the necessary architectural issues at play. The drawing operates in a manner seeking to resolve the multiple and contradictory forces at work within architecture and encompasses a larger set of criteria. After interpretative readings and re-readings, these formulations by drawings may inspire changes in the proposed architecture and a transformation of the architectural thinking is put down again perhaps in a different media to be re-examined again, re-conceived, redrawn, re-examined, and so on.

Architectural drawings are a class of peripheral and internal representations, one of many cognitive tools that facilitate the relationships between imagination, memory and thinking. Architects' thinking ability is limited simultaneously by the amount of information and data that they must keep in mind, by the number of mental operations they ought to apply to data and the detailed information that they are handling in conceiving a buildable artifact. By offloading memory to drawings that can be inspected and re-inspected, architects may lighten their burden, and the memory limitations can be reduced.

An architect should attempt to understand the evolution of conceiving a building in a drawing facture as a series of transpositions. The meaning of each transposition is shaped by the logic of the medium and the support used in making the drawing. These multiple transpositions—these manifold drawings—together set in motion the work of architecture. The architects' role

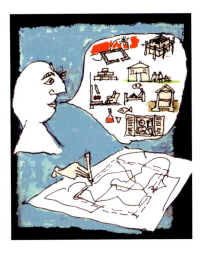

4.2
Verbalization of Architecture

is to perform these transpositions, and in them uncover the various theoretical meanings embodied in architecture. The question then is: is it possible to analyze the architectural theories that have never been verbalized as a result of the study of architectural drawings? It is obvious that such a study can be composed only from that which is intrinsically present in the drawings. Drawings have an order of their own because they construe and refine motives and configurations that already exist in facts. In the facture of each drawing, there is an order in the genesis, multiplication, combination, dissolution and re-synthesis of delineations. This order can change from drawing to drawing and this condition makes the sorting of the order not so obvious. Furthermore, the architectural business by selling itself as a problem-solving profession has put forward a sequential order for the production of architectural drawings that does not exist in the reality of an architectural facture. To bill clients, the regulators of the profession have set a sequence of steps and a bipolar order of "design" and "production" drawings that do not correspond to the real conceiving of building. For instance, a construction detail can be conceived and worked out before a preliminary sketch of the plan of the building is put on paper. Regardless of all these difficulties, by carefully reading the drawings it is possible to work out the real procedure followed by an individual in conceiving architecture.

Is the world of architectural drawings chaos or cosmos?

In spite of its mystifying appearance of arty and non-arty drawings, the world of architectural drawings is cosmographic. The tension between cosmos and chaos, order and disorder, can be reflected in the word chaosmos—a Joycean coinage.[4] The drafting cosmographies take place within a Scholastic-like world subjugated by drawing habitus, a social making based on a set of bodily operations related to mental schemas.

The inception of bodily operations and mental schemas is one of the primary foundations of the habitus. This is a procedure of lasting, transposable dispositions which, by integrating experiences, functions at every moment as a matrix of perceptions, appreciations, and actions, and makes possible the achievement of infinitely diversified tasks, thanks to analogical transfers of schemes permitting the solution of similarly shaped challenges. Habitus, as "modus operandi", is the solution to the making of architectural drawing and its origins can be found in the medieval architectural drawings and in the tradition of tracing floors. Medieval architects and masons used to draw out their details well in advance. Because of the cost and size limitations of parchment sheets, they would draw by incising directly onto conveniently placed sections of floors or on floors prepared with a layer of plaster, which would show the drawing more clearly.

Although the notion of the habitus may have ancient roots, its substantive content is extremely modern. I am borrowing the notion of habitus from the revaluation of it done by Pierre Bourdieu, a French sociologist. Bourdieu acknowledges his appropriation of the habitus idea from the work of art historian Erwin Panofsky, who himself was influenced by the proto-cognitive theory

4.3
Cosmography Diagram

4.4
Cosmography as Drawing

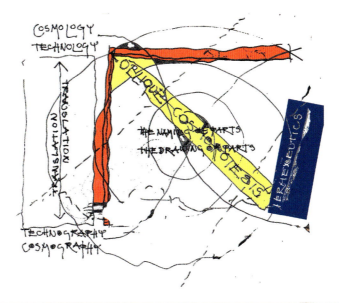

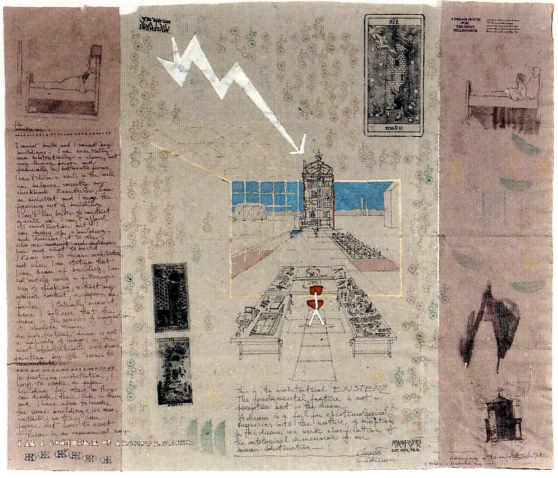

of "symbolic forms" formulated by Cassirer.[5] Bourdieu gives his earliest definition of habitus in the Postface, written for the French translation of Panofsky's Gothic Architecture and Scholasticism.[6]

Non-trivial architectural drawings are the result of habitus and fall within the framework for habitus clearly indicted by Bourdieu. Drawings are:

> "Systems of durable, transposable dispositions, structured structures predisposed to function as structuring structures, that is, as principles which generate and organize practices and representations that can be objectively adapted to their outcomes without presupposing a conscious aiming at ends or an express mastery of the operations necessary in order to attain them. Objectively 'regulated' and 'regular' without being in any way the product of obedience to rules, they can be collectively orchestrated without being the product of the organizing action of a conductor."[7]

In architectural drawings the habitus leads to a coordination of graphic procedures that persistently orient drawing selections, which, although not premeditated, are nonetheless systematic. These drawing selections without being arranged and organized deliberately according to an ultimate end are nevertheless permeated with a sort of determination to be revealed only at the end of the drawing.

Drawing forms are nothing but descriptions to which one tries to attribute the consistency of concepts, with the sole result of demonstrating that even concepts are drawings and that the intellect is still another sector or segment of the act of drawing. The understanding of architectural drawings must include a personal awareness, because the drawings are the resuit of a facture that involves a lively, productive and advancing formation of meanings. Architectural drawings are not a handed down ready made form of documented presences. To be meaningful, architectural drawings must have room for perspicuous interpretation. Architectural drawings exist only if we are conscious of them, and for one to be alertly conscious of architectural drawings, architectural drawings must touch on more levels of our lives than just a mere logic of visualization of depiction and delineation. How do architectural drawings mean more than the marking out of buildings parts and illustrative renderings?

Aesthetic Habitus

Drawing architecture is a skill and as for any other skill there are those who have the skill of drawing as an innate talent, but it can also be learned through practice. It is like playing chess; if you move the pieces without knowing the rules and never having anybody explain to you the possible strategies, you may be able to figure out how to play by watching others, but you are at a great disadvantage; yet this is how most people approach architectural drawings. They expect to win in their first try; but there are challenges they must learn to face and there are methods to do it.

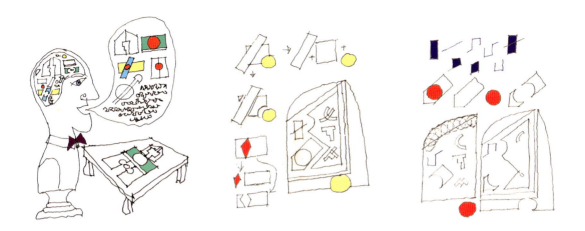

When individuals begin to set themselves up to draw, they must realize that they are only practicing and that what they are doing is a training exercise and the outcome is about getting better, not producing masterpieces. Eventually they may be ready to go into the game, but if they take the pressure off themselves they will be freer to relax and do their best without unrealistic expectations, especially as Ludwig Wittgenstein has explained:

"The aspects of things that are most important for us are hidden because of their simplicity and familiarity. (One is unable to notice something—because it is always before one's eyes.) [...] we fail to be struck by what, once seen, is most striking and most powerful."[8]

Architectural drawings are not about realistic representations of buildings. The most important thing to learn about drawing is more about seeing what the hand does with the chosen drafting tools on the selected support than about a vision of the absent building. If someone can write his or her name in a non-trivial way—and believe me this is not so easy—he or she has learned enough control of a tool to make a drawing facture.

What most often stops the majority of people from drawing an architectural artifact that is not abstract, for example an alphabet letter, is not being able to break up the artifact they are drawing into lines, curves and angles. Once these individuals learn to break up intangible, tangible, visible and invisible lines composing the artifacts they are drawing, they will be well on the way. When someone learns to do this, any building can be drawn.

The key for learning to draw is an understanding primarily concerned with the sensorial knowledge of the world. This seems to be a given, except that, more often than not, the reason that individuals say they can't draw a building is because they believe they must draw from a vision. On average, this vision is the result of nothing but a muddling memory of many forms. Unfortunately, this is the most prevalent myth that discourages the majority of architects from drawing in a non-trivial manner. A non-trivial method of mimesis is to draw the ways through which we perceive the world, a bodily logic, as it were, as we can find it.[9]

The nature of the human faculty of aesthesis is entirely without distinction between the sensorial, the extramundane and the structural, and it can be revealed by telling a short fable, an apologue. The fable revealing the ineffable nature of aesthesis is embodied in the following conversation that took place between Guillermo Jullian de la Fuente (J) and Amedeo Petrilli (A). They are recalling a moment of the life of Le Corbusier that can be a perfect apologue to demonstrate an aesthetic assessment of the reality of architectural drawings as slow food for architectural thinking. Jullian is telling the story of a repast between Le Corbusier and Pier Luigi Nervi, a dazzling Italian engineer, that Julian had witnessed in a famous restaurant in Rome in the spring of 1960:

> "J. ... Then, they had to decide what to eat and they selected the chicken after a long debate. When the plates arrived, Corbu said to Nervi that he would teach him how to eat a chicken … a poulet. He took it with both hands and tore it in many pieces, adding that this was the right way, because all the senses begin to work all together. A. Sight, touch, smells … J. Definitely … and then, Nervi said: 'Excuse me, old friend, it is not done in that way.' He took up knife and fork and, in a moment, he divided his chicken in four perfect pieces, working on delicate structural points … You know, I do not want to make complicated architectural theories, but for me that was a fantastic lesson, because I was in front of different points of view, both equally deep: two knowledgeable approaches … At the same time, to see these two characters make this thing … And if memory does not fail me, when Nervi had finished cutting his chicken, with high regard Corbu said to him: '... chapeau!' A. ... And ... how did it end? J. As always these stories end up ... we ate our chicken ..."[10]

Aesthesis is in both the approaches and in the final eating of the chicken, and it confirms the sensorial nature of the event. Aesthesis can be in any element of a drawing that is perceived by the senses. Aesthesis refers to those characteristics that, by being perceived by the senses, can influence the inner world of an architect either in a positive way, by causing pleasant feelings, or in a negative way, by causing unpleasant feelings. In simple words, what architects might like or dislike about a drawing that they are drafting plays a fundamental role in the conceiving of buildings. This is not as simple as it sounds. The variety of interfering influences, their interactions and the complexity of these interactive outcomes render the way individuals perceive and process drawings as a set of idiosyncratic stimuli.

The sensorial condition turns architectural drawings into showers of "gifts", and this complex and felicitous showering of gifts is the basic nature of architecture itself. Architectural drawings are, in other words, wholly based on a sapience of the givenness and the appearing of a cosmopoiesis. Givenness is not understood as a fact, but as a facture. Through drawing factures, architects study how architecture is performed and translated in building factures; it is a giving-act in which the given is given.

When architects practice drawing, they must be looking at what they are drawing and how the selected media interact with the paper and constantly be comparing what factual and non-factual lines they have drawn. The request for factual and non-factual lines and a defining mood is that architects, in tracing lines on paper, are not giving evident notations but synesthetic presentations. Ranging from study drawings prepared for "dining-in" to construction drawings for "carrying-out", this synesthetic cooking of drawings then becomes a real act of architectural digestion followed by a proper assimilation. These drawings demand our intellectual, emotional, and extramundane engagement. The study and making of these drawings is an examination and an execution of that which is not obvious. The key postulation is not that what architects trace on paper is worldly or unworldly, existing or non-existing, physical or mental, subjective or objective. Architectural drawing must stay away from such labels. The only thing that the facture of architectural drawing assumes is that which appears on paper comes into the totality of our discernment of a world-making.

To read and understand "between the lines" is not to read and understand elsewhere; it is not to look behind some sort of curtain, to remove some sort of shroud, to raise some sort of wrapper. Architects do not sneak a look behind built or drafted occurrences of architecture to see what is "really there". For what is really there between the lines stands right before them, not in some other place, not behind the lines, not hidden out of view. The sensual and emotional presences of an artifact are not miserly advertised; yet they are manifested and presented between the lines. Architecture is thus, as architects point out, an underlying presence that moves back and forth between the lines and the walls.

Instead of looking at occurrences, drawing and reading the drawings line-by-line, architects draw and read "between the lines". For architects, that which is "between the lines" is more actual than the lines in themselves; for that which is shown "between the lines" is that which appears most powerfully and directly. What is not shown directly—but only "between the lines"—is that which appears most candidly in a distracted use of architecture, manifesting and developing itself in the everyday use of it. Architects are not passers-by. They linger, have patience and hasten slowly and abide in places where architecture abides. In the everyday world, individuals that are passing-by can briefly catch a glimpse of buildings and edifices, but if they study them carefully, for instance, they can see the architecture of a boutique hotel in downtown, but they do not see what makes that specific building architecture "as such". In their drawings, architects seek to elaborate on this "as such".

Chapter five

The Pregnancy of Drawings

"The Door to the invisible must be visible."

René Daumal[1]

In a sketch traced on the margin of one of the drawings for the restoration of an unusual Gothic building, Palazzo Steri in Palermo, Carlo Scarpa drew the figure of a pregnant woman encompassing a colored rendering of the screen-grate detail for a window within her belly. It was not very difficult to imagine how this strange and cross-bred portrayal of theory and practice of architecture came about. Scarpa, an extraordinarily gifted Venetian architect of the late twentieth century, had sketched several possible solutions to the interweaving of the horizontal and vertical elements composing the grid-iron of the screen. Suddenly, one of sketches revealed to his eyes the desired solution and, with a fast hand, Scarpa traced a quick circle to single it out and casting in a graphic mode the expletive: "that's it". The circle combined with other minor pencil marks and dots, probably pre-existing around the area of the colored sketch, worked as a Rorschach Inkblot and Scarpa's saw in it a pregnant woman and such delineation was completed with a few other minor traits of pencil. This is an ideal reflective instance of inference from the facture. In a drawing, most of the times, facture goes unnoticed, and it is nearly invisible to the viewer. Nevertheless, facture embodies the idea that the object itself carries some record of its having been made. It's the over-arching theoretical construct from which all architectural traits stem.

Facture is a way for pursuing a non trivial geometry, i.e. a geomaternal formativity in architecture. The term geomater was coined by James Joyce, who combined matrix, mater (mother) and meter with geo-(earth) in a pregnant metaphor making geometry a discipline of measurement, prediction and conceiving.[2] To conceive comes from the Latin concipere which means "to lay hold of entirely", "to absorb" (as liquid), "to catch" (as a fire), hence "to conceive" (as a child). In the embodiment of the metaphor, imagination is a matrix or womb. In conceiving a building, architects are geo-mothers who construct and construe material-maternal-artifacts in and on the world.[3]

Factures are expressed by the materialistic nature of the "graphplots" and "poetographies", powerful terms coined by Joyce, that when transferred into the full-bodied sapience of architectural drawings that question they stimulate emotional associations in their readers.[4] An architectural graphplot is structured in three concurrent geomaternal articulations according to the nature of the architectural imagination.

1. Geomantic Geometry: it induces emotional correlations through prophetic tokens and it is based on a vivid tracing of lines.
2. Body Geometry: it throws specific architectural emotions onto the corporeal imagination and it is based on measuring procedures, preparing the ground for the next articulation.
3. Longing Geometry: a molding of intellectual and emotional associations capable to turn into material the immaterial.

These geometries have been used to unfold the meaning-making potentiality of architecture, historically and didactically. They are different aspects of the imaginative metaphysics that is geomater. These geomaternal articulations overlap in their procedures and share the acumen of a maternal touch.

In Book II of his Treatise, Filarete (Antonio Averlino) likens the architectural patron to the father and the architect to the mother of a building, after the fertilization the result of the architect's gestation is a preliminary wooden model, a facture that the mother-architect must grow in a complete building.[5] Many architects have never acquired a maternal touch and the ability to deliver factures through expecting graphic similes. Many theoreticians and professional architects have drunk the waters of the Lethe River and forgotten the possibility of any auspicious maternal thinking; meanwhile architecture has become a commodity to be kept under control by critics whose fashionable and factional admonishments weight down any possible redeeming opportunity. This ominous view of the constructed world precludes the development of conjunctions between wombs and buildings, even in the marginalia of a drawing.

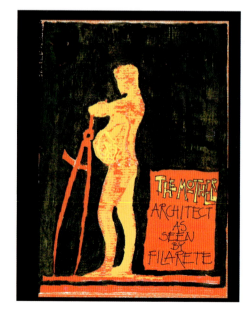

5.1
Geomatrician

5.2
Architect as a Mother

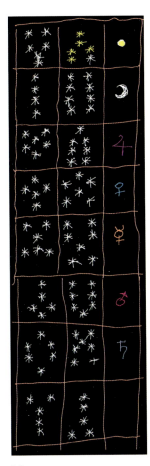

5.3
Marks Used in Geomancy

Combinations of shallow censoring and narrow-minded professional concerns mostly related to question of market have undermined the extraordinary architects' capability of being arbiters able to prognosticate and predict future constructions using a proper geomaternal play of vestiges to make their buildings places for thinking. I am using the word geomaternal with a specific sense similar to that of geomancy because geomaternal tracing has to do with our space-temporal presence as humans, a play of line on the soil or on the sand as seen in many forms of geomancy. "Geomancy" is derived from the Latin "*geomantia*", which in turn is derived from the Greek for "divination by earth". The Arabic name for geomancy, "*ilm al-raml*", means "the science of the sand". In their original forms, the geomantic figures were generated by making lines of random numbers of dots in the sand.

An Arab myth on the origin of geomancy tells of Idris (the Arabic name for Hermes Trismegistus), who one day, without work and out of boredom, began to trace doodles in the sand. A stranger appeared before him and asked what he was doing. Idris replied that he was simply entertaining himself, but the stranger replied that he was doing a very serious act. Idris denied that his doodles had any meaning, but the stranger explained the significance of the figures Idris had drawn. He then commanded Idris to draw another figure, and upon doing so the stranger explained the meaning and significance of that figure. The pair continued doing so until Idris had discovered and understood the sixteen figures. The stranger then taught Idris how to form the figures in a regular manner and what the results meant, teaching him how to know things that could not be known with just the physical senses. After testing Idris' newly found knowledge and skill of geomancy, and after revealing himself to be Jibril (the Arabic name for archangel Gabriel), the stranger disappeared.[6]

There are sixteen possible figures in the geomantic tableau. Each one of the figures bears a name and a specific set of significant attributes or qualities, e.g. good health, imprisonment. Their traditional names in Latin are: Acquisitio, Amissio, Laetitia, Tristitia, Caput Draconis, Cauda Draconis, Albus,

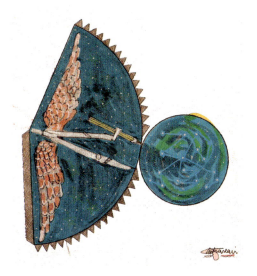

5.4
Unfolding of Synthetic
Geometry

Rubeus, Puer, Puella, Fortuna Major, Fortuma Minor, Populus, Via, Conjunctio, Carcer. Associated with geomancy there is an interesting metal tablet made by Muhammad ibn Khutlukh al Mawsuli, now in the British Museum, designed for geomantic divination. The tablet seems to be unique and is dated 639 AH (1241–2 AD). When turning the dials on the front of the tablet, random designs of dots would appear, which then can be interpreted. The tablet predates nearly all the extant treatises on geomancy, a condition that heightens the importance of this mechanical computer for the understanding of geomantic practices.

Leibniz, who despised geomancy, nevertheless points out in his *Discourse on Metaphysics*:

> "For let us suppose, e.g., that someone makes a number of marks on paper quite at random, as do those who practice the ridiculous art of geomancy. I say that it is possible to find a geometrical line, the notion of which is constant & uniform according to a certain rule, such that this line passes through all these points, and in the same order as the hand had marked them."[7]

The geomantic figures can be considered a precursor of a parametric shape grammar as calculation from heuristic or metaphorical conditions to a rigorous relationship in which design and calculation each inform and enhance the other. As in a shape grammar, spatial relations and shapes are defined. A spatial relation is specified by a finite number of shapes arranged in a certain way. A shape grammar provides for the recursive generation of arrangements of shapes in given spatial relations. A shape grammar elucidates the composition of actual objects and at the same time provides the basis for the description of these objects in other terms. In *Shape*,[8] a shape grammar compilation, George Stiny argues that seeing shapes—with all their changeability and ambiguity—is an inexhaustible source of creative ideas. Understanding shapes, he says, is a useful way to understand what is possible in design.

Making Sense of Geomater

What kind of maternal and material mimesis is required for succeeding the play of lines that is currently mostly lacking from contemporary architectural drawings? The answer is simple: the feminine nature of geometry. Greek mythology holds that our human capacity for geometric vision is a gift of the divine feminine—energetic sources of wisdom thought of as a lineage of goddesses.[9] Born from primal chaos is Gaia, from whose name comes "geometry", this mythological account explains also Joyce's "geomater". Plato regarded geometry as the ultimate mnemonic device that organized primeval chaos. In *Timaeus*,[10] he describes how the Demiurge "remembered" itself within Chora (Greek for "place") the site in which *Forms* developed and initiated order in the human world.

Mathematical abstract thinking evolved the discipline of geometry from being a sensual play of compasses, rulers and other drafting tools on drawing surfaces to a mere algebraic and digital understanding. The teaching of

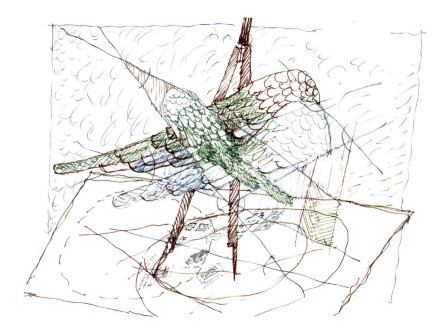

geometry moved from the level of sensual perception—the real area of geo-mater—to the level of cerebral discernment. At the level of sensual perception, there are no major differences between a Chiliagon and Myriagon, but, at the analytical level, the difference between 1,000 and 10,000 sides is critical. Consequently, descriptive geometry has refocused its aim and shifted from being based on a synesthesia, a combination of sense modalities of sharp lines, weight and sound configurations, to anesthetic expressions, a negation of sense modalities through algorithmic descriptions of lines and configurations.

This move from sensual, but sensible, approximations to analytically intelligible precision endangers the human ability to produce delightful architecture. Architecture must be measured with both a degree of mathematical precision and with an appreciation of the innate dimensional inaccuracy of the materials selected for construction. In building, every part and every detail is exactly approximate.[11] Stone, metal and brick all possess different capacities to retain finished dimensions; every constructive part of a building has its order and measure: masonry, in decimeters; wood carpentry, in centimeters; metal works, in millimeters; nowadays everything is increasingly expressed in millimeters.

The transfer from hand drawing to computer drawings has caused an important change in the appearance: the "softness" of handmade drawings or models is replaced by harshness. The computer light illuminating the model shapes makes the buildings look impossibly exact and "hard", even if they are rendered with an atmospheric perspective. The streets look brand new, the colors artificial; everything seems too perfect. Real building edges are less precise than their equivalent in the computer model, their surfaces are less uniform; windows sit differently in a facade plane. However, there is no easy way to add imperfections to the model because the lines that give shape to volumes are created by strings of numbers. The appearance of the renderings reflects the faultless geometry of the vector files. The scale models made by hand did not suffer from this artificiality: the hand-cut edges, the surfaces of the material selected for the model (paper, cardboard, wood, plastic) reveal flaw lines and surfaces appear nearer to veracity when viewed in photographic close-up.

The imprecision is true when using descriptive geometry in a hand drafting of architecture, as Ernest Irving Freese points out in "The Geometry of Architectural Drafting", a remarkable work on the art of architectural drawings published in installments, in *Pencil Points*, from 1929 to 1931:

> "On the drafting board, points and lines are material things: marks made with sharpened instruments. In the art of geometry, then points and lines not only possess a magnitude, but magnitude in three directions. Just try to erase some of the 'ornery' ones and you will discover the third dimension—perpendicular to the plane of paper."[12]

The reality of the geomater is related to the materiality of chora, i.e. the surface upon which the footprint or the traces of pens and pencils are cast. Vitruvius tells a number of stories, and one of them concerns the philosopher Aristippus (435–366 BC), who was shipwrecked on the coast of Rhodes. The philosopher saw a few geometrical figures drawn in the sand, and cried out to his companions: "Let us be of good cheer, for I see vestigia of man!"[13] Vestigia means footprints, but Aristippus used it metaphorically to indicate the geometric tracings he saw in the sand. When meeting with real or metaphorical vestigia, we have an uncanny sense that somebody was here before us. The indentation in the

ground made by a person leaves powerfully evocative signs because footprints make present an absence. Vitruvius tells us that footprints are clues for the configuration of the Ichnographia (ichnos = foot impression, graphia = drawing), the plan of a building.[14] The materiality of geometrical drawing impressed on paper is not purely a set of arbitrary symbols, but it is directly connected indexically (physically or causally) to what those symbols represent and to whom had impressed them. Three powers, the vis geometrica, the vis imaginativa and the vis designativa become evident in the depth of the strong vestigia generated by the geomater's dancing of the lines. These strong lines unfold within the chora of drawings through a corporeality subordinated to fluid and manipulable systems of multi-sensory perceptions.

5.8
Synthetic Geometry

5.9
Descriptive Geometry

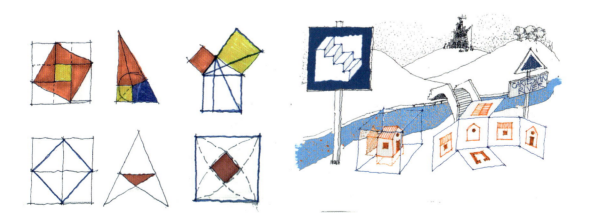

Fathered by Gaspard Monge, under the influence of Descartes, descriptive geometry was born as a crossbreed, a merger of drafting procedures amalgamating synthetic geometry and analytical geometry.[15] During the evolution and fruition of descriptive geometry, the advocates of analytical geometry slowly phagocytized the synthetic side of geometry present in it. Since then, descriptive geometry has become purely a bodiless geometry by having coupled with projective geometry. The result of this sad affair was that mathematicians lost their interest in teaching descriptive geometry for architectural students who easily get bored by the abstractness of calculus. As a consequence these students could not bridge the gap between ministrations of numeric anesthesia and the material inscribing of a graphic synesthesia.

Confronted with this situation, the architectural faculty who remained convinced that the understanding of descriptive geometry is intuitive, began to teach a few fundamentals of descriptive geometry and rely on the geomaternal instinct of many of the future architects. The possibility of undertaking such an approach had already been suggested at the official origin of descriptive geometry, in a statement by Joseph-Louis Lagrange,[16] who, after having listened to a Monge's lecture on descriptive geometry, had uttered, "*Je ne savais pas que je savais le geometrie descriptive*" (I had not realized that I knew descriptive geometry).[17] The teaching of the basic principles of descriptive geometry directly in the studio environment was a quite acceptable solution. "Playing" with the required tools on a drafting table was a rich enough experience to develop a self-learning of descriptive geometry as the students were constructing plans, cross-sections and elevations on paper. By holding drafting tools in their hands, the students of architecture could bridge the gap and understand the geomaternal nature of the union of descriptive and synthetic geometries. This playing with tools, i.e. squares, parallel bars, compasses, dividers, pantographs, strings, rulers, assorted kinds of paper, diverse pens and pencils, and different techniques of reproduction, would have made explicit what was the implicit constructive nature of a sensual geometry.

Diagram showing the Progress from Orality to Typography in Architectural Representations

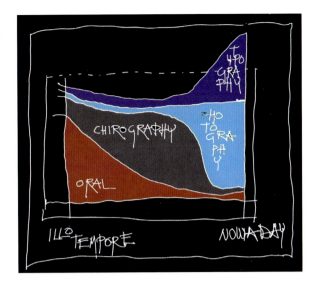

Drafting tools originated as copies of the hand tools used on construction sites, consequently drafting tools embody in themselves the norms and the kinesthesia of architectural making. By musing themselves with the tools, the students could feed their natural inclination to geomaternal procedures and develop analogical understandings. However, architecture has moved from being rooted in a chirographic culture to a typographic performance and screens, mice and keyboards have substituted the traditional drafting tools.

In proposing a "science of depiction", James Gibson proposed a primary distinction between human-generated markings on surfaces: between photographic and chirographic pictures, that is, literally, pictures formed by the workings of luminosity on a surface, and pictures made directly by hand. Nowadays, at these two sets of depictions must be added a third set: typographic pictures. They are pictures produced through the "black boxes" of the computer stations. When projected or printed, these typographic pictures will resemble photographic or chirographic pictures, but instead have been produced by digital transformation generated by clicking and typing.[18]

If the traces are made by a possible number of hand tools: stylus, scribe, brush, pen, pencil, crayon, marker, with the help of other drafting tools, then the resulting product is *chirographic*. If a camera, including its accessory equipment, has produced the traces, we will have a *photographic* result. In both, the interaction of the trace maker with the support for the images plays a fundamental role. However, if the traces are generated by digital input without any direct physical interaction during the making of the image with the final presentation media, the result is *typographic*. This third kind has been the most harmful for architectural imagination; the lack of material play with drafting tools and shadows has further reduced the imaginal abduction ruling architects' conceiving.

The story *Thales at the foot of the Pyramids*, drawing lines in the sand to the light of the sun as told by Michel Serres reveals the nature of the abductive process.[19] Serres considers Thales's descriptive finding that the height of a pyramid could be determined by measuring its shadow. Thales is standing in the Egyptian desert before one pyramid; two others loom in the distance, they look the same and yet they are somehow different. The geometrical notion of similarity is already present in the fringe. Thales stands "in the domain of implicit knowledge"; all he needs to do is to make it explicit. Nevertheless, the pivotal conversion from implicit to explicit knowledge requires that the shadow be negated, its distinctive nature of constantly changing to become a "constant" and rendered as the mark of an idealized form. Thus at the birth of geometry, the "shadow of opinion, of empiricism, of objects" is sacrificed through synthesis not analysis to "the sun of knowledge and of sameness".[20] Thales' suggestive process is the process of inference that the pragmatic semiotician Charles Sanders Peirce, has called abduction. For Peirce, abductive suggestions are based on argumentation. In his "Lectures on Pragmatism", Peirce defines abduction as "the process of forming explanatory hypotheses",[21] and as the "only kind of reasoning which supplies new ideas, the only kind which is, in this sense, synthetic".[22]

Before further arguing for a geomaternal approach, I must make clear the difference between synthetic and analytic geometry and their presence on the drafting table or inside the black boxes of the digital programs. The best way to explain the difference is to pose a geometrical problem and solving it first synthetically and then analytically and see the effects it can have on drawings and constructions. The exercise selected to explain the difference between the two geometrical approaches is very simple, but it has many implications in the realm of architecture. It is merely the tracing of a tangent t to a circle, given the circle C with the center O and a point P on it. On the drafting table, a synthetic approach, the solution is to trace the radius OP and then to trace line t orthogonal to OP. In the analytical approach, inside the black box of CAD, the solution is: the equation of the curve $[x^2 + y^2 = r^2]$ and the point P is individuated by the coordinates [a, b] and the solution is to find the general equation for a line passing for the point P: $[y - b = m(x - a)]$ and the gradient m of the tangent t, the final result is $[ax + by = r]$.[23]

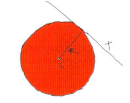

5.12
Synthetic Tangent

In the synthetic solution, t is perpendicular to r, but if a different curve is proposed, i.e. an ellipsis, the geometric affordances would be different, but in the case of analytical geometry if the curve is changed the procedure to reach the tracing of the ellipsis is the same circle.[24] The analytical method is general and generic, whereas the geomaternal approach is case specific and requires skills, cognitions and experiences that are not only epistemologically framed. Geometric affordances through analogical reasoning open the gate of understanding to other affordances. This procedure of analogical reasoning may be better understood by a simpler example of analogy between medicine and geometry that has its roots in Aristotle. In the *Posterior Analytics* I, 13,[25] Aristotle observes, "it belongs to the physician to know that circular wounds heal more slowly [than other kinds], but it belongs to the geometer to know the reasoned fact" (79a15–16). The reason is that healing occurs along the perimeter of a wound, and a geomaternal consideration tells us that the circle has the smallest perimeter for any given area; thus the wound will heal more slowly than a wound that has rhomboid shape.[26]

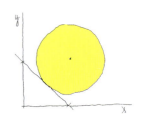

5.13
Analytic Tangent

The geometric affordances can be analogically translated in drafting and building affordances. For instance, in the case of drafting affordances, after a few frustrating experiences of having to remake almost completed drawings, the learning on the drafting table is that the first step in inking a drawing is to trace all the curves and then to trace the other lines. To explain the move from drafting affordances to tectonic affordances I cannot be generic and general but I will use a specific case from physical records of constructions. During the restoration of the crypt floor in Leon Battista Alberti's San Sebastiano in Mantua, the foundations were exposed and carefully surveyed. The resulting discovery was that the square columns placed on the foundation plinths of the north side of this central plan building proceeding from the center to the perimeter were placed slightly off-center of every plinth every time to the point that the bottom bricks of the columns at the edge were cantilevering off their plinths a couple of centimeters. The story beyond this tectonic mistake is a predicament in the measured layout solved through a geometric layout. The plinths were laid down using the analytical procedure of orthogonal coordinates, and a minor mistake was repeated over and over. However, being a central plan edifice, the geomaternal affordances embodied in tracing a few circles detected the measuring trouble and allowed the builders to correct the mistake by relocating the columns in their proper positions—traces of the exercise of these measuring circles are recorded by markings left on the mortar covering the top of the columns plinths.[27]

Geomaternal design sets the relationship between measure and proportion. In a basic but non-trivial proposition of Euclidian geometry: the interior angles of a triangle total to 180 degrees. As long as we just look at the triangle, making no changes in our diagram, we also make no progress in our proof. However, when we move to the construction—let me stress "a drawing construction"—of a line parallel to a base through the opposite vertex, we see that propositions involving parallel lines solve the problem. The construction is by no means implied by the problem or by the postulates of geometry, but the constructed line gives us the affordances to act on them.

A geomaternal point of view helps to grasp the convoluted tectonic relationship between measures and proportion. From this point of view, for instance, it is possible to explain the constantly changing distance between the columns and the pilasters in Palladio's Serliana motive on the ground floor of the marble screen built by Palladio to encase pre-existing buildings. Palladio believed in an old Italian saying: *tra il dire e il fare c'e' di mezzo il mare* [between the saying (the woodcut in the treatise) and the making (the erection of the marble loggia around the Basilica) there is a sea (the preexisting constructions on site)]. This particular sea did not contain water but consisted of a pre-existing fifteenth-century building, known as the Palazzo della Ragione (a public structure), which was the result of the restoration of two older buildings after a fire. Such restoration had joined the two buildings connecting them with the addition on top of a vast gothic hall with a roof, a carena rovesciata (inverted hull), supported by a structure of crossed ogival arches. At the end of the fifteenth century, the city-fathers decided to give the building a new appearance and create covered spaces for the markets that were held around it. The model selected entailed full Roman arches in a double loggia forming a stone screen to

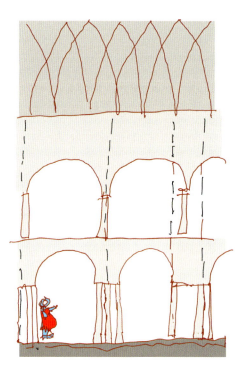

5.14
Diagram Showing the
Relationships between
Ogival Arches, Full Arches
and Serlianas in the
Basilica of Vicenza

be erected, around the brick gothic building, in the style of the loggias around the Palazzo della Ragione in Padua.

The chosen architect, Tommaso Formenton, planned the loggias as requested to surround the building. These were duly built. However, Formenton's addition collapsed only two years after completion, presenting the problem of rebuilding. Though many great architects were consulted, from Sebastiano Serlio to Michele Sanmicheli and Giulio Romano, a solution was not quickly found. Fifty years were to pass before the solution, conceived by Palladio, was chosen. He solved the problem with loggias composed of a series of Serlianas.

The general understanding at this point is that Formenton did faulty construction and Palladio did not. The reality is that Palladio knew how to play between measures and proportions using ruler and compass whereas Formenton did not. Formenton did not realize that ogival arches can keep the rise of the arch constant even if the clear span changes. Roman arches require that the rise and clear span should both be constant. After just a few arches, the structure built by Formenton no longer related structurally to the rhythm of the pre-existing structure of the inside body based on the ogival arches that had irregular clear spans. By using the Serliana (after that better know as Palladian window), a composition of an arch with two short horizontal beams on the sides, Palladio was able, without altering the dimensions of the arches, to respond to the variations in length between the structural elements, simply by changing the span of the side beams.

Chapter six

Nullo die sine linea

Architecture is a constructed virtue—or better, it is the Queen of Virtues, as Palladio labeled it on the frontispiece of his treatise—by which humans interact bodily, tectonically and culturally with a region that they modify to their advantage. Not too long ago, architectural drawings were made in limited quantities. A few lines sufficed to depict past or future buildings. Today, we need an inconceivable number of lines even to depict the tiniest building. As a result, the favorite motto used by Scarpa should be updated. Scarpa's "… nullo die sine linea" (no day [goes by] without line), should be unfortunately changed to "… no day goes by without *a thousand* lines". The huge number of lines needed

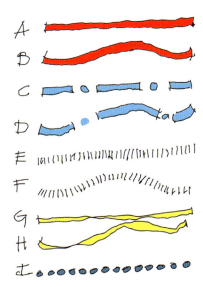

for a small house or an edifice no longer permits any drawing hesitation, any pause allowing the architects to discover and to generate the power of thinking that has always been embedded in proper architecture.

The tracing and pulling of lines facilitate a spatial understanding of things, concepts, conditions, processes or events in a cosmopoiesis. The techniques to trace the required lines can vary from graphic arts and spatial models to poetic, descriptive and technical drawings. Lines do not just reproduce physical realities, but can also transmit metaphysical realities, the shape of sacred space and the realms of fantasy and myth as explored by imagination.

My speculative account dealing with the virtue of architecture is founded on the principle of a non-trivial architecture, a forgotten canonical stance, that can be used as a basis for new thoughtful realizations. This principle rules the interface between mind, body and architectural constructs, because harmoniously intertwined mind and body connected with architectural activities make life not only possible, but also happy. Proper architecture results from the merging, in the constructed environment, of four complementary arts: the art of thinking well, the art of living well, the art of building well, the art of drawing well. These four arts can be organized as a rotating wheel to be adopted as a heuristic tool, a multi-modal representation for investigating the facture of architecture.

6.2
Lines in the Brain

Architectural drawings are not created as an end in themselves. They are produced to demonstrate architectural concepts, to determine tectonic procedures and to regulate functional uses, for the benefit of architects, clients, or someone else. Most importantly, they are the essential scaffold to form a transformative imagination since architecture begins not in thought (as other disciplines have often implied) but in the perceptual relationship between our bodies and the world. The specific methodology for the facture of these drawings is also based on the recognition that a drafting conjuring is not just a manual skill, but manifestation of a faculty acquired through appropriate techniques of visualization and storytelling exercises comparable to what Manfredo Massironi, a perception phenomenologist, calls hypothetigraphies.[1] As wonderful projections of buildings, these architectural hypothetigraphies provide tempered and prudent analogical places. The use of drawings as hypothetical scenarios help to understand the way things actually will be. There are many different kinds of thought experiments. All thought experiments, however, employ a method that does not derive from observation or physical experiment, but from planning and experimentation in subjunctive reasoning. An architectural drawing then moves from being a transactional and formalized ambiguity to be something that will raise the thought to a highest level. The subjunctive mood of drawings becomes a virtual experiment in architecture. In putting their musings on paper, architects perform thought-experiments (Ernst Mach's Gedankenexperiment) using anagogies which raise the architectural thoughts above the specificity of the drawing.

Anagogical Drawings

A term originated in textual biblical exegesis, anagogy becomes well known and consequential during the medieval age with a memorable distich attributed to

Nullo die sine linea

Augustine of Dacia describing the four senses of a text:

> "The literal sense teaches what happened. The allegorical what you
> believe. The moral what you should do. The anagogic where you
> are going."[2]

The word anagogia is a transliteration from the Greek and it is the union of the
word "ana" (above, high) and the verb "agein" (to lead).[3] Hugh of St. Victor,
in De scripturis et scriptoribus sacris, distinguished anagogy from allegory. The
latter takes place when a visible fact is signified by another visible fact. Anagogy
takes place when a visible fact or event "leads above" to something not visible,
that is, when what is visible opens the door to higher invisible events.[4]

Anagogy belongs to the layer of a deeper sense that summarizes and
encapsulates in a final reality the other three senses. In the list and description
of the four senses of the writings (literal, allegoric, moral and anagogy), anagogy always occupies the last place. Structural and qualitative reasons determine such a location: anagogy being the last of the four senses of writings
and also their purposes. Similarly the four senses can be detected in architectural drawings. On paper, concealed within the architectural lines, the literal
and the allegorical senses of a drawing strictly represent different analogical
constructs that articulate the tectonic and formal imagination. The literal and
metaphorical senses have obvious didascalic functions by describing the building envelope, its materiality, the correspondences and the aspects necessary
to represent the multiple functional nature of every building. The tropological
or moral sense of drawings addresses the intellectual constructions and it is
the argument by which technological, religious and social codes are defined
and transformed. Resulting from the interlacing of the logical constrains of the
other three interpretative senses, the anagogical sense substantiates the proper
purpose embodied in the architectural project by demonstrating an immaterial
reality beyond the material conditions.

Anagogy occurs when the connection between materiality and immate-
riality, and perceptible and imperceptible, are in a suspension of time. Closely
related to anagogy is the idea of transitus, which refers to the viewer's mental
journey across an image. In the mode of entrance there is depicted a three-
dimensional world and the viewer is drawn directly into the heart of the universe of the image, and perhaps even into the unappreciable world beyond the
scene itself.

An architectural transitus can be done with a sequence of transitions. The
first condition is the one generated by the transfer of analogical and allegorical
senses from the drawing performances taking place at the construction sites to
the paper on drafting tables and vice versa, then from the recto of the sheet of
paper to the verso of it. A way to understand the transitus from recto to verso
and vice versa that takes place by using paper in drawing architecture is a passage of Edwin Abbott's *Flatland: A Romance of Many Dimensions* (1884).[5] The
Abbot's Romance takes place during a cosmological transitus on the Eve of the
last Millennium. Flatland is the story of an individual living in a two-dimensional
world. The storyteller, A. Square, is a humble square that, through dreams, has
visited Lineland and Pointland and he tells us how Flatland is annually visited

by a three-dimensional sphere transiting through it: a pulsing phenomenon that he could not comprehend until he developed an impression of the third dimension in passing from a system of knowing to a different system of knowing consciousness.

Architects do not build, but merely draw

The tracing that architects do on the flatlands of drawing paper, what has it to do with the act of building? What makes these flat sheets relate with what we finally will call architecture? Nothing: different matter, different dimensions, other substances and materials. Do we label architecture the stones, the bricks or the inks on the paper? Conceivably, neither the stones nor the inks are architecture. Rather something that escapes us: beautifully vague traces of factures that we can only grab through drawing daily tracings of lines.

The recent changes in the conditions of production and reproduction of architectural documents have been so traumatic to put into question the boundaries of the discipline. As all legitimate disciplines, architecture has her own history and it has undergone a sequence of alterations of its technical and phenomenological foundations with consequent redefinitions of its theories and areas of action. It is essential to recognize—even more in our age of digital imaging—that the majority of architects do not build buildings but merely draw them, as Robin Evans had several times and powerfully pointed out.[6]

Presently architecture is laying bare, melted in a senseless commercial presence by, on the one hand, a visual exploitation of photo-renderings and, on the other hand, by the transformation and unifying colonization of the modes of production caused by Building Information Modeling (BIM). The significance of the impact of BIM software on the practice of architecture over the next decade cannot be underestimated. Hence the urgent need to rethink the boundaries, within an interdisciplinary context, of the drawing practice in order to give back to architecture a solid and graspable proper sense. Drawing practices need to regain proper disciplinary virtues by which powerful tools such as BIM can really help to bring their graphic productions into being as poetic, expressive, conceptually dense, and multivalent expressions of architecture.

EXERCISE #3

Improper Drawing

The widespread a-critical use of CAD, BIM, and any other varieties of digital modeling, and photo renderings, reduces drawings to "dream stuff" totally devoid of any connection with built "solid stuff"; the resulting buildings are "stuff" that is completely lacking the complementary "dream stuff". These results of digital application and modeling programs can be described as a quasi-abuse of architectural thinking. They are farcical representations that merely give information and show pointless adherence to programs, codes, and prescriptions, or they are pseudo-representations that show faddish renderings.

They are inauspicious graphic occurrences to be translated into buildings. This allegation may seem excessive, given that digital media offer a set of extraordinarily easy instruments for producing and delivering images. In reality, their superficial visually completeness vilifies architectural representations by hiding the cognitive problems and realities embodied in the built world behind the pleasing appearance of a pseudo-efficient neatness.

The most pragmatic sides of construction procedures endure consequences generated by the negative standard of completeness and neatness because these might hide costly consequences. Digital modeling allows architects to continually repeat their mistakes by presenting drawings that always look neat—which inspires security and conveys an air of authority—even when full of constructive inanity. These drawings can be considered comparable to a word processed text run through a spellchecker. The result is that mistypings and misspellings are completely absent, but, for instance, the mistyping of the sentence "architecture is a cience" has been automatically corrected to "architecture is a cense", which is no doubt a puzzling and curious idea, but misleading and meaningless if read in context. Another sample is the following sentence: "as spellcheckers progrades wilt not fined words witch are miss used butt spelled rite so digitalis muddling withy out tricycle revival will lead to knight garish designs!"

CAD and BIM have an effect akin to unskilled photography, which grasps everything, but holds nothing but unfiltered information, sometimes out of focus. These drawings and renderings are what an acute art theoretician, Federico Zuccaro (1542–1609), called "disegno esterno" (external drawing), a sheer graphic configuration without any substantial substratum.[7] These representations are nothing but shapes circumscribed by lines, devoid of mental and corporeal substances, filled with patterns and tiling. They produce not architecture but what has been called "buildings in drag".[8] The architectural details designed by using these three-dimensional software programs look two-dimensional and flattened when built, as if the building was still on a computer screen. A shallow architecture of pure exteriority is the dominant presence in strip malls, builder tract housing, office parks, and high rises. These buildings look much better on the flat and glossy pages of real estate brochures than in the reality of a world-making.

Let us consider the sets of images brought into being by BIM, a new approach of "Virtual Building Constuction" based on parametric CAD technology. Plans and cross sections, axonometric projections, and perspectives, appear similar to the drawings generated by several of the two and three dimensional modeling software products in widespread use both in practice and academia, and one might erroneously conclude that BIM is simply a more refined, and more robust, version of those other programs. However, the ground breaking characteristic of BIM software is that it organizes the information describing a building in a series of databases that may be used in a variety of ways: information in the databases includes properties related to materials, construction assemblies, structural and thermal performance, energy use, day-lighting, and a multitude of other attributes. Thus, BIM becomes a powerful means for coordination and collaboration, for testing and analysis, for materials selection, cost estimates, scheduling, structural and environmental analysis, energy

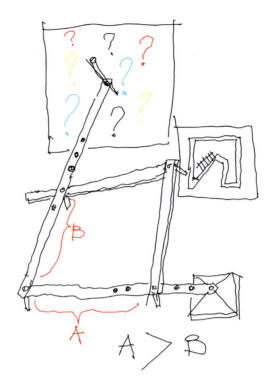

performance monitoring, the development and management of furniture and equipment schedules and deliveries, prototype design, digital fabrication, and post-occupancy facility management and maintenance. With the use of BIM, architects can create 3D, 4D and 5D models that show every little detail of buildings, but not of architecture. The relevance and importance of BIM is not only for 3D modeling, but also for 4D and 5D modeling which include scheduling and cost projection.[9]

In the traditional processes, architecture is translated from a material condition (drawing) to another material condition (building). Drawings are translated in buildings. With BIM, as in the other similar programs, a conversion takes place. Conversion is an event that results in a transformation of a building information (an algorithm) from the status in which it has been created (presentation, production drawings, and so on) to the status of building management (fabrication, cost estimates, maintenance, repairs, etc.). Conversion is justified as the elimination of unnecessary barriers in sharing and exchanging building data between computer applications. The aim is a continuous information flow though the processes of product development eliminating the need of human translation. BIM is a set of systems that enables users to integrate and re-use building information and domain knowledge through the lifecycle of a building.

To deal with such a powerful program or similar ones, the solution is to use them in an inappropriate way. Typically the programs use three-dimensional, real-time, dynamic building modeling software to increase productivity

6.4
BIM: the Wheel of Fortune,
Lady Architecture is Turning
the Wheel of Building
Management, Engineering,
Detailing, Fabrication and
Controlling Institution

in building design and construction. They encompass the characteristics of building geometry, spatial relationships, illumination analysis, geographic information, quantities, qualities and properties of building components. Of these characteristics, building geometry and the quality of building components are the ones to be tackled in an improper way.

James Vandezande, Associate CAD Manager at Skidmore, Owings & Merrill, says that the senior members of the design teams with less computer experience, but greater knowledge of design and constructability, seem to fare better with these tools than some of the younger designers because with BIM it is no longer necessary to know how to plot styles and layers, null blocks and empty text. Instead it is necessary to speak of walls and stairs, foundations and framing.[10]

The solution to BIM predetermined imposition is to use it improperly. To use it improperly, it is necessary to add a few other objects, i.e. scale figures. In Virtual Building, a door is not only a collection of points, lines, and curves arranged to look like a door—it is an object, with an object-oriented infrastructure, that displays many of the qualities and behaviors of a real door within the context of the building information model and it can be used only as door. In improper drawings, scale figures are not profiles but objects that model the animation of human movement. They are embodied agents, virtual humans, and their applications involve behavior-based animation of human movement especially for gesture, gait, and body expression, constructing a parameterized action representation for real-time simulation and animation. Then in this improper use—contaminated by human behavior—a door, as every architectural student knows, can be used as an inexpensive drafting table.

There are many applications for computer animation and simulation to model virtual crowds of autonomous agents. Most of them deal with simulations of entertainment, training, and human factors in the analysis for building evacuation. Others deal with scenarios where masses of people gather, flow, and disperse, such as transportation centers, sporting events, and concerts. However, crowd simulations include only basic locomotive behaviors possibly coupled with a few stochastic actions, but to solve the conceiving phase of BIM these simulations should present virtual humans going about their individual and personal agendas of work, play, leisure, travel, or entertainment.[11]

Take the pantograph you have built in a previous exercise and alter the ratio of connection of its arms and enlarge a drawing of a plan and a section that you are studying. The result of this improper use of the pantograph will be amazing. Then draw within this enlarged section scale figures performing mundane activities.

Chapter seven

Architectural Consciousness

7.1
Architect's Phrenology

Architecture consists of three fundamental entities—space, time and matter—played within human consciousness. Space, time and matter have their own degrees of freedom controlled by architect's consciousness that sway users' consciousness. Architecture is fundamentally the creation of controlled places and spaces, through the use of walls, columns, arches, beams, ceilings, surfaces, textures, lights, shadows, shades, music, noises, perfumes, and odors. Nowhere is this more evident than in the architecture of public-use spaces. The casinos, the malls, the stadiums, the commercial malls, the courthouses, the schools, the hotels, the theaters and the museums are all environments carefully orchestrated to orient, to disorient or to reorient the visitors and inhabitants, or to make a specific pitch effective. In these environments, the total exclusion of the sensory stimuli generated by the external reality of the world means that patrons are dependent on manufactured cues for their behavior. Eliminating all external stimuli prevents random reactions. As virtual modes become more sophisticated in providing an approximation of tactile environments into which we can lose ourselves, so does atmospheric architecture.

While the science of how architecture around us affects human neurological activity is still relatively new, its principles are not. For instance, the buildings of commercial businesses have been known to use their architecture to lure people into their stores since commercial trading began within cities. Lyman Frank Baum, better known as the author of the *Wizard of Oz*, was among the first professional retail art directors.[1] During the 1890s, Baum began by testing combinations of color surfaces and materiality played with light, glass and mirrors to find how to stimulate positive responses to certain products. Baum perfected an architectural spirit of affluence and opulence within the building's spaces and embodied sumptuousness and luxury in the architectural finishing and decorations deliberately studied to elicit feelings of class and provoke inferiority in the patrons. Baum's postulation was that for the patrons the only way to rectify their perceived inadequacy was to spend money on the products sold therein and prove their worth accordingly. During the medieval age, many church fathers suggested similar procedures for the architecture of cathedrals and holy places to elicit religious feelings and to persuade the faithful to accept religious coercions. Fascist government played the same game, Fascist architecture made people eager to accept political oppression.

There are genuine neurological connections between behavior and the physical space within which it takes place. Humans in different phases of development learn how to think their way through the world almost entirely through sensual stimuli, which are intimately connected to the surrounding environment. Contemporary architecture has generated an incredible number of places for living, eating, sleeping, playing, working, practicing sports, and so on. However, only a few of these places have "thinking" as the dominant dedication. Only the existence of places that allow thinking besides a merely structural functionality makes the neurological union of body and mind within the built environment the real project of architecture. Although I must recognize that too many professionals belonging to the present praxis deem this projection as ill fated. To hide the gratuitousness of their artifacts, these architects resist the projections of neurological life in the built environment and generate distressful architecture, which coerces the inhabitants into unnecessary mental or emotional conflicts.

The built environment in which we live sets an important backdrop to what we are and what we do, because we build architecture, but in return architecture builds us. The thinking and living within architecture reflects and casts light on the values existing in any society. In many constructions, the devising and nurturing of architectural happiness has been prevented by the fusion of fashionable elations with financial gratification. This fusion has changed the thought process of many architects: they no longer think within architectural consciousness, but merely think about architecture.

Consciousness, perhaps the most complicated brain-function involving, presumably, most of the other functions of the brain, remains one of the most daunting areas of human knowledge. In architecture the question is double sided. On one side there is a search for what constitutes the consciousness dynamics of an architect marshaling the large number of variables involved in a conceiving of a building. How will knowing the consciousness dynamics associated with the production of architectural drawings and representation enhance the art of building well? On the other side the quest is for understanding how consciousness, memory, and our sense of the "self" come about within a built environment.

How can the power of one's "thinking well" be enhanced by architecture? "Thinking well" is based on cognitive processes combined with the feeling of emotions, intuitions and sensations. What causes the "art of thinking well" to be tied to architecture and how is this approach to thinking mapped on architecture and how does it differ from other modes of thought? Architectural thinking aims to develop the human capacities of embodiment and embedment by fostering efficient body-mind activities and contemplations within the ecology of the built environment. This process will offer a liberating life-enhancing condition in opposition to an analytical thinking based on an ideal disembodied knowledge.

In architectural conceiving, the images of knowing are based on word-less storytelling framed within a natural cosmopoiesis, as Antonio Damasio, an internationally recognized neuroscientist has pointed out:

> "Wordless storytelling is natural. The imagetic representation of sequences of brain events, which occurs in brains simpler than ours, is the stuff of which stories are made. A natural preverbal occurrence of storytelling may well be the reason why we ended up creating drama and eventually books, and why a good part of humanity is currently hooked on movie theaters and television screens. Movies are the closest external representation of the prevailing storytelling that goes on in our minds. What goes on within each shot, the different framing of a subject that the movement of the camera can accomplish, what goes on in the transition of shots achieved by editing, and what goes on in the narrative constructed by a particular juxtaposition of shots is comparable in some respects to what is going on in the mind, thanks to the machinery in charge of making visual and auditory images, and to devices such as the many levels of attention and working memory."[2]

An architect's brain is primarily an organ for homeostasis—a center that collects and collates responses on body states, and acts to maintain constancy of the internal milieu. This notion vastly clarifies the role and nature of emotions, provides a feeling of knowing and an enhancement of architectural understanding, and allows the images of the human and built bodies, assisted by memory and reasoning, to become the fundamental core of architectural consciousness.

Emotions are vital to the higher reaches of distinctively architectural intelligence. According to Damasio and other scientists, in opposition to the common notion of unemotional rationality, emotions do not impede rational thinking but rather they are essential components of rationality. These emotions and the motion of human bodies shape non-verbal architectural inferences, architects' drawing factures that strengthen the processes of core consciousness at the base of architectural conceiving.

Thinking about architectural events makes active the sympathetic nervous system; just as real life built events can cause its activation. The bodies, as scale figures, used in drawing become inferences that reveal, for instance, the close linkage between the regulation of life and the processing of images that is implicit in the sense of individual perspective. Their presence makes clear when the following assumption can be made: if these scale figures have the perspective of this body I now feel, then these images are in my body—they are mine. As for the sense of action, it is contained in the fact that certain images are tightly associated with certain options for motor response. Therein is our sense of agency—these images are an architectural presence and I can act on the architecture that caused them.

Storytelling

> "The body believes in what it plays at: it weeps if it mimes grief. It does not represent what it performs, it does not memorize the past, it enacts the past, bringing it to life."
>
> Pierre Bourdieu[3]

Architecture is embedded storytelling based on sapient factures. These factures are formative works because they result from a making that, meanwhile, is in the process which invents its way of its own making.[4] Furthermore, architectural factures as formative works do not carry out their processes of formation in a sphere of pure intellectual and extramundane order, instead they are tangled in the concrete of experience. They are engaged in a body tackle with the materiality of drawings first and subsequently with the one of buildings.

To believe naively that just by thinking of a building a corresponding artifact will exist is a misleading idea since the thought of a building is not a building. For a building to exist, someone has to tell its facture in a "formative storytelling". The story is told by a hesitant delineation of many lines. A hesitant set of lines is a sensible and sensitive form of drawing, dwelling constantly on pensive borders, where the drafting and writing of lines are buzzing backward through history and igniting genetic and anagogic drawings. These lines are a way of reaching what it is beyond the functional quotidian. Hesitate comes from Latin *haesitare*, meaning to stick fast, to stammer. It is a momentary holding back in doubt, a difficulty in doing or making something. In our age of aggressive digital imaging and atrociously hasty construction, hesitation must be brought back into architects' drawings to make them truly heuristic devices.

For the ancient Greeks there were two different kinds of time: Chronos, straightforward chronological, historical time, measured with time-pieces and calendars; and Kairos, the less tangible, mercurial, unpredictable time of chance, of opportunity, synchronicity. Chronos, the god of linear time, is traditionally depicted as an old man, slow-moving and with a long beard. The god of opportunity, Kairos, called by the Romans Occasio (opportunity), is young and agile, he possesses winged feet to hover and dance, he seizes the opportunity at the right place and the right time and he can randomly cross the solidly planned trail of Chronos. These two aspects of time are interwoven as the warp and weft in a textile. Astounding drawings materialize when these two aspects of time cross or merge since drawing is based on the right timing. We often think of the duration of time as a chronological resource, as in the sentence: "we have three months to complete the project". We need to be equally aware that there is another manner for looking at time that it is also an essential resource: "now is our window of opportunity". Both types of time are resources for the architect. Patience in drawing, often overlooked as a resource, is more than the willingness to wait: it is also the willingness to facilitate rather than to dominate and to know when it is that the opportune moment presents itself.

Within the realm of cooking, the difference between culinary sapience and "filling food" is clearly expressed in the opposition between slow food and fast food and a parallel comparison can be made of the opposition between slow and fast drawing. The overpowering request for lines to erect an edifice or a small house no longer allows one to take time for slow drawing. Without a lingering drafting sapience, there is no architecture. Sapience stems from thoughtfully sensible considerations on how material transforms into matter and this is the foundation of thinking in architecture. Sapience comes from the Latin sapere, a tactile appreciation, which is a savoring and operates in the same manner by which the sense of taste discerns different essences or flavors.[5] During the process of drawing, architects determine and savor architectural objects and their causes.

The protracted translation of lines of drawings into building lines and vice versa is the most essential phase of the architectural process of imagination by which buildings are conceived and erected because the ontogenesis of architectural lines assimilate within itself the primary processes of designation that takes place on construction sites. Lines weave enigmas that are slowly translated on paper and their solution determines architects' ability to consider and savor the facture of the building.

Architecture is built to transcend its epoch so are architectural drawings; buildings outlive their builders and so too drawings should outlive their drafters. The implication of this parallelism is that both buildings and drawings carry in their facture the constructed virtue of architecture. Buildings should respond to the requests of their own epoch, but at the same time they should be able to adapt to requests that cannot be anticipated or even imagined. By the same token, architectural drawing done to accomplish the exclusive requests of a specific building construction should be able to be read for searching answers to constructive requirement of other buildings. These possibilities are achieved in the inauguration of both buildings and drawings.

The innermost intention of a facture is in its revealing the inauguration of a drawing, a building or a dish. At this point, a cosmopoiesis absorbs within the configuration of the artifact. The results are poetic artifacts. Poetic architects and poetic chefs are those who have mastered the often-complex techniques and comprehended the history and diversity of their cuisine or architecture. For instance, poetic chefs elaborate and cook "dishes full of feeling" that after being eaten are declared "pure poetry". Gastropoiesis underscores how the food of a certain cultural milieu makes itself first historical and then a-historical. For instance, this move from historical to a-historical can be seen in the sequence of appetizers, called "carpaccio" of salmon, beef, tuna and so on. The sequence was inaugurated with a plate devised by the great Venetian chef, Giuseppe Cipriani. The original carpaccio was made of thin slices of raw beef sirloin, arugula (rocket salad) and shavings of parmesan cheese all drizzled with extra virgin olive oil, it was a poetic artifact conceived to celebrate the reds, the greens and the whites typical of the paintings of Carpaccio at the opening of a great exhibition of Carpaccio's paintings held in Venice in 1963.

Within poetic artifacts, the intent lays in the edifying understanding of materials, in how the ingredients are ranked in the culture, the distillation of the objects' essence in the acts of making; consequently the fundamental role of the maker becomes a process based on nurturing, discovering, and revealing. Cosmopoietic artifacts always give a feeling that something strange concerning their nature is not completely revealed but it is still contained in them. Such a sensation results from the factual making of it since in making cosmopoietic artifacts architects and cooks bend the material stuff to their intent, to their insights of the ways of the world.

Cosmopoietic cooking and building defamiliarize the known world and make it strange; to that extent, the resulting artifacts inspire a consciousness that makes us realize how arbitrary and conventional relations actually are. The putting out of place of food components or building details or metaphorical hangings as one would hang a salami in a cellar allows one to defamiliarize the day-to-day experience, enables the "other" to peek behind the screen, to reach down into the deep bottom of an old coffer hidden in the attic of the brain, and reinvest the world with meaning. The first roots of cognitive neuroscience lie in *phrenology*, a pseudoscientific approach that claimed that behavior could be determined by the shape and bumps of the head. This hypothesis was initially proposed and championed in 1796 by Austrian physician Franz Joseph Gall, a marginalized curiosity that will allow us to say that architects have a phrenologic bump for architecture.

Having already recognized that most architects do not erect buildings, but merely formulate them in drawings, the tracings of real and non-trivial architectural drawings are not obvious and objective, as the descriptions of the accomplishments obtained with the use of building information modeling is trying to affirm them as a solution to architectural uncertainty. In making their drawings, architects do not presume that architectural traces are worldly or unworldly, existing or non-existing, physical or mental, subjective or objective. Architectural drawing must avoid such labels. The only thing that the act of drawing assumes is that which is marked, inked, penciled, brushed or chalked comes into being through a facture and not through an iconoclastic algorithm.

7.3

Diagram a la Giordano Bruno of the Arts of Living Well, Building Well and Drawing Well

Architectural drawings must not be understood as mere visualizations but as architectural factures. They are factures because they are made and done. Consequently, the reading of a drawing is based on the construing of the marks or touches, a productive procedure that David Summers calls "inferences from facture".[6]

Architectural drawings are factures captivating their makers and readers. They don't just represent something—they are something in their own right since the signifying power is in the ceremonial facture and how this aura can be interfered from the drawing itself. Architectural drawings have the same signifying power for architects, clients and builders — the aura of the drawings themselves will inspire awe and reverence that will lead to a better facture of edifices and buildings.

If a set of architectural markings and inscriptions stands for architects, builders or clients in some respect or capacity, then every pen stroke, brush stroke, pencil line, charcoal mark, wash run, smudge, erasure, pentimento and blur must have a signaling function and a meaning. For the most part, architectural criticism and history have concentrated on the large-scale question instead of on the process of assembly and interaction among different kinds of signs and productions, and on the interface between media and supports. There is no meaningless mark in a genetic architectural representation, they encode mundane, physical and extramundane qualities in the conceiving of an architectural artifact. Even accidental marks play a major role in a genetic representation.

The making of genetic architectural representations is a theoretical framework focused on the cognitive configurations of architectural factures. These configurations map out the expressions and patterns recording the physical or mental actions corresponding to specific acts of intelligence ruling the development of the multiple and interfacing stages of architectural projects. The practice of genetic representations always produces a speculative edifice—a mirror of the architectural cosmos—that will help to recognize the foundational nature of architectural imagination and how these acts of imagination can be transmuted within the triad of the arts of building well, thinking well and living well.

A critically constructed genetic analysis of architects' drawings is the most effective and efficient way to learn architecture. The critical investigation of genetic architectural representation examines the sedimentation of architectural materiality in weathered papers and models inscribed with pentimenti, additions, replacements, and erasures. Although it is a collection of tangible documents such as architects' sketches, notes, drafts, models and blueprints, the real objective is much more intangible: a movement of emotions that are not optically but imaginatively real. The world-making of genetic representations remains concrete, for it never posits an ideal architecture beyond those documents, but rather strives to reconstruct, from all available evidence, the chain of events in the conceiving processes. A critically constructed genetic analysis is a continuation of the architectural imaginative act itself. The study of beginnings, of alternative and concurrent architectural representation, makes possible to rethink and refine complex theoretical questions about the efficacy in the architectural production of buildings.

In one of his Socratic teachings, Scarpa points out that "drawing" is the only way for an architect to understand the built reality.[7]

> "Photographs are of no use: a drawing that is useful. Take a photograph and a drawing. I understand the drawing better. A bad photograph is a public act of falsification. The human eye is better than the camera, because is mobile, and a camera though you cannot reproach it for anything regard to … it does not state anything true, everything is false; or else, it is a great photographer who is taking the picture and then he seizes the particularly illuminating angle of view, and it is the artistic instinct of the photographer which is involved instead of colors, pencil or pastel strokes."[8]

Photographs, however, are extremely powerful in carrying human ideas. Chew on this simple example of non-architectural use of photo-renderings. Try to imagine how a future set of housing blocks could be represented in a photo-rendering to convey contrasting ideas. On the one hand, we could use a color-saturated image of the housing blocks shown during a mid-spring sunny day with the glass of the windows reflecting the sky, staging open, green space, children playing and group of people staging communal activities. On the other hand, we could use an aerial view, a grainy black and white image presenting a view of the surrounding environment of concrete housing blocks during a murky winter's afternoon. Furthermore, the view could use a telephoto effect that emphasizes their proliferation, crowding and gives a sense of dilapidated dereliction inhabited by scale figures of disaffected looking youths, urban anomie. Although both the representations look real, they are not accurate representations of the "reality" of the proposed architecture and what will be the genuine architectural effect of the housing. This is considered irrelevant because the representational strategies adopted have been selected to fulfill specifically the rhetorical and normative aims of their advocates very well.

Once built, those buildings will seem less real than the glamorous "photorealistic" renderings used to promote them. In part this is due to the gap between the growing sophistication of our means of representation and a corresponding visual impoverishment that results directly from the means of everyday construction. Crudely built rather than carefully executed, and generally devoid of the close range enjoyment of refined materiality that can compensate for the disappearance of craftsmanship, such buildings rarely offer multi-scaled architectural delights.

To persevere in my telling of edifying stories regarding the tellurian and cosmic twins that are architecture and cuisine, I must sit at a historical table at the Trattoria del Gaffaro. This was a small restaurant not far away from the IUAV (Istituto Universitario Architettura Venezia) main seat at the Tolentini in Venice, where, during the days devoted to the review of student work for Scarpa's studio courses, the Professore and his assistants enjoyed their lunch.[9] The event I am recalling happened during one of these communal lunches when the special dish ordered by him for his cohort and prepared by the patient chef of the Gaffaro was the risotto col tastasal (to taste the salt). Offered traditionally in the Venetian mainland at a specific time in winter when salamis are made, this seasonal risotto is prepared using some of the fresh blend of ground pork meat, salt and spices destined to be stuffed into the salami casings and subsequently properly aged. The fresh salami stuffing is not cooked in the risotto just to give it flavor, but because it is an excellent way to assess the balance of its ingredients, especially the proportion between ground meat and salt, therefore assuring the quality of the future salami. Indeed, as an alchemic procedure of analogies, the cooking process with the rice achieves the same result of the evaporation that will take place in the dry cellar where the salami are going to be aged and stored. Although the final flavor is totally different, the balance of spices and salt in the risotto will reflect accurately the balance in the salami made with that stuffing.

Making a few considerations on the strange nature and role of the food to be eaten—a fictitious victual (res ficta), to unveil something hidden, the salt, in something (res facta) that in the end will be completely different from the preparation tasted—Scarpa digressed by setting a parallel between the function of the risotto col tastasal and the function of drawings. A set of architectural drawings is completely different from a building, but its purpose is to taste in advance the architecture of a future building.

Spolia

The advocating of collage in architectural drawing is not meant in the pictorial sense, but rather related to the tradition of architectural spoils. The collage should be the drawing for a "pasticcio". Meaning an artistic work consisting of a medley of pieces taken from various sources, the Italian word "pasticcio" appeared in the English language during the early eighteenth century and means a work or style produced by borrowing fragments, ingredients or motifs from various sources, making a potpourri, a strangely disguised form of cosmopoiesis. The most famous English architectural Pasticcio is a 30-foot-high architectural folly acting as the central visual pivot in the Monument Court located at the center of Sir John Soane's House at Numbers 12–14 Lincoln's Inn Fields in London. Soane erected this structure composed of spolia, a collection of architectural elements coming from many different construction or archeological sites, to symbolize architecture, and he put his preferred Tivoli capital, used at the Bank of England, on the top of it. By the end of the nineteenth century Soane's Pasticcio was leaning dangerously to one side, and, as a result, it was dismantled in 1896, but it has been rebuilt recently. Soane's Pasticcio is a demonstration of the work of architecture produced by borrowing pieces, fragments, ingredients or motifs from various sources, a potpourri of spolia to coalesce unsightly building elements and attractive architectural spoils in a unique statement of the making of cosmopoiesis.

The fundamental condition of the spolia is that, on the one hand, the use of left-over building elements could either be intentional conservation or conscious subversion of the past, and on the other hand something that "just happened" as a result of the limited availability of materials in the locality. The use of spolia becomes common during the late period of Roman architecture, and for centuries it had been seen as a purely negative development. For instance, Vasari saw the use of spolia as disintegration of artistic capability, confirmation of pathetic efforts due to not having anything better.[10] Vasari's evaluation of the use of spolia in fourth-century church basilicas was less negative; he understood the re-use of exotic non-Italian marble and granite column shafts as an indication of good taste.[11] Only during the twentieth century, architectural historians and critics defined spolia as a purposefully tectonic development.

Following a constructive idea of spolia, a collection of blueprints of disparate buildings belonging to different time periods (scanned and reduced to the same drawing scale) should be used for this exercise: select sections or portions of plan, sections, and construction details from well detailed construction or production drawings and then with these pieces compose plans, sections and elevations of a new edifice. The chosen pieces should be cut physically with scissors and glued on a plywood board, composing a decoupage. The decoupage should be completed with grids of reference and measures. Gold paint should be used to highlight the sectioned walls, making it an effective spolia drawing. The striking example of this kind of drawing is Tiberio Alfarano's 1571 plan of St. Peter's Basilica in the Vatican Archives. The drawing was prepared by Alfarano, a scholar of the Basilica history, as source—a brutta copia or copia di lavoro—for the engraving—bella copia—that he made to illustrate his De Basilicae Vaticanae Antiquissima et Nova Structura.

Alfarano, combining pieces of traditional architectural prints and new drawings in a decoupage and completing the work by using representation techniques typical of icon paintings, has made his a perfect spolia drawing. He made the plan using several sheets of paper of different dimensions, quality, and consistency, glued together on a wooden board. On them, Alfarano drew in graphite the actual ichnography of the Constantinian Basilica on which he glued Michelangelo's ichnography of the New Temple using a fragment of the 1569 print by Duperac aligning Michelangelo's central plan to the base drawing portraying the

old basilicas. Then he redrew on the print the covered portions of the Constantinian Basilica, highlighting the presence of the ancient walls with a gold paint.

The spolia technique—collage plus drawing—goes well beyond representing a one-time likeness, providing an extramundane gate into the cognitive dimensions drawings.[12] The spoila of construction drawings used in this exercise seems to resonate with prominent themes of postmodern cultural criticism, such as appropriation, bricolage, historicism, the fragment, and ruin. However, these portions of drawings are spoils of construction drawings and consequently in putting them together it should be figured out a proper tectonic solution that should be drawn carefully in the point of commissure. Having done the decoupage (brutta copia) it should be generated into a new image (bella copia) using a scanner, then converting the raster image into a vector-based drawing and keep working on the building completing the missing parts.

The Drawing Body

"Buildings are as useful to our minds as they are to our bodies."
John Onians[13]

The fashionable practices of many architects today produce architectural bodies without qualities. The works they produce are unhappy figures without proper body-images or body schemas. These patched-together monstrosities are to contemporary architectural practice what Mary Shelley's monster was to the popular culture of nineteenth-century Britain. The prevailing stance among these architects is that building-bodies do not require the presence of building bodies. Indeed, many writings by architectural critics and theoreticians are curiously without references to human beings or human activity; rather, they tend to reflect on architects' obsessions with building form and aesthetics.

As inbred neurologists, architects carry on investigations and assessments of architectural consciousness through their drawings. Without becoming acquainted with neurology, they lead us to think about architecture with our bodies, but also to think about our bodies through architecture. Mary Douglas, in *Purity and Danger*, points out how complex the structure of the body becomes if it is used to understand the neurological chiasmus of bodies and their environment:

> "The body is a model, which can stand for any bounded system. It's boundaries can represent any boundaries, which are threatened or precarious. The body is a complex structure. The function of its different parts and their relation afford a source of symbols for other complex structures. We cannot possibly interpret rituals concerning excreta, breast milk, saliva, and the rest unless we are prepared to see in the body a symbol of society, and to see the powers and dangers credited to social structure reproduced in small on the human body."[14]

Architectural consciousness generally originates within individuals' perceptual and motor systems. Architecture is framed by embodied experiences that in turn are framed by architecture. In using and drawing architecture, the body knows things about which the mind is ignorant, as Vico has pointed out in his New Science:

"Rational metaphysics teaches that man becomes all things by understanding them (homo intelligendo fit omnia), this imaginative metaphysics shows that man becomes all things by not understanding them (homo non intelligendo fit omnia); and perhaps the latter proposition is truer than the former, for when man understands he extends his mind and takes in the things, but when he does not understand he makes the things out of himself and becomes them by transforming himself into them."[15]

In architectural drawings, human figures are much more than anthropometric references because, from Vico's point of view, they can be seen as the creation of base configurations that perform, form, reform and transform architecture by tracing metaphorical, metonymical and demonstrative patterns of life in plans, elevations and cross sections. They elicit human emotion with the use of mirror neurons.

During the last decade of the twentieth century, the purpose of mirror neurons was the radical discovery of Giacomo Rizzolatti and his team, a group of neuroscientists at the university of Parma, Italy. They have shown that part of the motor cortex in monkeys and humans not only controls movement but also perceive these movements in others. When a monkey or human sees an experimenter making a hand movement, the corresponding part of their brain becomes active: as if it had made the same movement itself. Indeed, when individuals see a hand movement in others, their own hand muscles get slightly more active, though not enough to move their hands.

The implications of the discovery of mirroring neurons and embodied simulation for empathetic responses to drawings of buildings, and to scale figures in particular, have not yet been assessed. The basic idea is that a crucial element of architectural response consists of the activation of embodied mechanisms encompassing the simulation of actions, emotions and corporeal sensation, and that these events are universal. This basic level of reaction to scale figures and architectural drawing is essential to understand the effectiveness both of everyday use of building and of their spatial and tectonic existence. Historical, cultural and other contextual components of the architectural discourse do not preclude the importance of taking account of the neural considerations that arise in the empathetic understanding of architectural factures.

Mirroring thought and emotions to architectural drawings redefines our relationship with them and enlarges our ideas about the relationships among drawings, body, mind and buildings. This closely interdependent relationship marks a turning point in the understanding of the connections between humans and its uses in architecture and in architectural conceiving. As Gerald M. Edelman, a 1972 Nobel Prize winner in Medicine, has pointed out: "The brain is embodied and the body is embedded."[16] Embedding is an essential architectural circumstance, since the "body is embedded and situated in a particular environment influencing it and being influenced by it", and this occurrence takes us in architecturally determined econiches.

During the last two decades of the nineteenth century a methodical examination of the empathetic and elicitation possibilities generated by movements of bodies began in France with the work of Francois Delsarte. A French acting, singing, and aesthetics teacher, Delsarte analyzed how people gesticulated in real life and elaborated a lexicon of gestures, each of which had a direct correlation with emotional states.[17] Delsarte observed that for every emotion, of whatever kind, there is a corresponding body movement. He also believed that a perfect reproduction of the outer manifestation of passions would induce, by reflex, identical emotions in the audience. He was a precursor to mastering the essential role played by the mirror neurons system in echoing and understanding not just the actions of who is performing in front of us, but also their intentions, the social meaning of their behavior and their emotions. Mirror neurons let us grasp the minds of others not through conceptual reasoning, but through direct simulation: by feeling, not by thinking.

Distorted body-images

The anorexics' distorted body-image inhibits them from seeing their starving bodies. When they look in the mirror, what they see is not what other people see. Recognition is altered. A morbid fear of fatness and obsessive determination to get thinner gives their mind control over their whole body, setting them on a course that leads to isolation and deep inner turmoil. Starving, excessive exercise and vomiting are methods used to keep the body miserably thin.

Distorted building body-images dominate in the production of many architectural professionals. When professionals look in the mirror of their drawings or computer screens they do not see the flatness of their architecture that others see. The morbid fear of not being up to fashion or the absolute determination to have their architecture green and sustainable gives to these architects a pseudo-commonsensical attitude, an obsessive control on the all-building body. Photo-renderings, excessive PowerPoint presentations and overworked CAD construction documents are strategies that keep the body of their buildings drearily dull and flat.

Evidenced in the graphic and photographic representations pervading contemporary architectural journals and magazines, these flat and dejected architectural bodies without qualities are the result of a process whereby prosthetic gadgets, mechanical carcasses, and perfunctory human remains supplant the time-honored portrayal of edifices as embodied constructs. These devices used in this body-less imaging intended to replace the habitus of corporeal figures that were used as inaugural mechanisms in the conceiving of architecture. The drawings and the resulting body-less building dissimulate the human bodies, suspiciously avoiding the more critical and nettlesome issue of how to assimilate a corporeal dimension within the context of architectural practice.

The coupling of human bodies and building bodies affirms that knowledge of architecture is supplied by the communal embodied experience of individuals. In *Philosophy In The Flesh*, George Lakoff, a cognitive linguist, and Mark Johnson, a philosopher, explain that "our conceptual system" is in the human beings' "perceptual and motor systems".[18] From this perspective, it is easy to recognize that the human conceptual grasping of architecture is inherently part of embodied experiences embedded in built econiches. Buildings can have a powerful effect, they can externalize things otherwise proscribed;

buildings are not repressed and they can express things that are otherwise taboo. Buildings have the capability to alleviate suffering in people who are ill, feel distressed or have a sense of dislocation, but if the buildings are conceived within a bodiless experience they can dislocate, distress and make ill their inhabitants.

The human body has long inspired architects who have in the majority acknowledged the role played by the body in the perception and understanding of architectural artifacts. However, too many architects today seem to suffer from an agnosia by which—to paraphrase a title used by Oliver Sacks in one of his stories—the nuptial's relationship with Lady Architecture, they constantly mistake their allegorical consort for their hats, as a well-known picture of a New York ball in 1931 demonstrates.[19] At the annual Beaux-Arts Ball, at least two-dozen architects came dressed as buildings and their hats were revealing which skyscraper or tall building they had designed. They included A. Stewart Walker as the Fuller Building, Leonard Schultze as the Waldorf-Astoria, Ely Jacques Kahn as the Squibb Building, William Van Alen as the Chrysler Building, Ralph Walker as the Wall Street Building and Joseph Freedlander as the Museum of the City of New York. Like many other architects, in their architectural imagination and in the produced images, they had merely reflected body-looks, not body-images.

A body-image is a system of perception, attitudes and beliefs, whereas a body schema is a system of sensory-motor capacities that functions without awareness or perceptual monitoring. Architecturally speaking the most important of these two systems is the body-image. The somatosensory system and the sensory nerves carry the body-image, a representation of one's physical appearance. Constructed by the brain from experiences and sensations, the body-image is a fundamental aspect of both self-awareness and self-identity, and can be disrupted by several external and internal circumstances. The body-image is not merely a representation of the body but also an anticipatory arrangement for the detailed movements of the body, and rather than being a fixed structure, it is dynamic and plastic, capable of reorganizing itself radically with the contingencies of experience. The body-image can also be supplemented by incorporating objects, implements, and instruments, such as a pencil, a roll of paper or compass in the hand of an architect's portrait. The body-image can be referred to as the "imaginable body", as theorized by Paul Schilder, that can be converted into the realm of architectural imaging.[20] The imaginable body, for Schilder, is a vivid and animated presence and is not merely the product of

sensation, representation, or perception, but results from a coalescing of the three.[21] The imaginable body is so real that, for example, when body-image distortions lead to phenomena such as phantom limb and body dysmorphic disorder, it can lead some people to request amputation of what they perceive to be a supernumerary limb.

Bodies as Imaginative Universals

> "I think it's one of the things that is part of the criticism about the way that architects are trained—they don't have a complex body in mind when they're designing."
>
> Anonymous architect[22]

By merging visible and invisible body-images and interweaving anatomy and posture with cultural and social conventions, it is possible to imagine a set of manifold tactics for architectural conceiving. These images offer the possibility of reuniting architectural production and human well-being: a union that has been substantially diminished by the majority of contemporary architectural practice.

The use of body-images and body schemas to conceive architecture ensures that the imaginable force of human bodies is impressed, received, and vividly transmitted into the built environment. This approach brings into play the lessons learned from the body, particularly the elaboration of the corporeal images evoked by mimes and dancers, especially when "counterpoised" to culturally bounded images of everyday people.[23] Lately, only a few architects, in their conceiving of buildings, apply in their drawings the presence of human bodies and the corresponding forms of multiple embodiment. The majority prefer to have no body presences in their drawings and in their photos of architecture, thinking that the absence of bodies in architectural representations helps to retain the clarity and purity of their designs. When the body is present as a scale figure, it is typically a "normal body", a body corresponding to precise anthropometric standards. This understanding of the body has its origin in Julien Offray de La Mettrie's view, he saw human bodies as physical machines and subjected to mechanical laws.[24] The scale figures, from this point of view, are little more than good-looking machines with fixed measurable parts; they have no gender, race, or physical differences.

Architectural drawing is not limited to envisioning the future construction of a building, but is also an implicit way of thinking about bodies interacting with other bodies (built and human). This manner of architectural imaging follows from corporal experiences constructed and construed in a corpus of body images. Dealing with the visceral character of building as fostering high spirits, these thoughtful embodiments bring forth the virtuous nature of architecture—an indispensable condition for implementing a proper life.

Body-images establish a potential architecture by delineating the relation of the visible and material icons of construction to the immaterial and invisible signs of architecture. These sketched scale figures reveal the noëtic geometry, an intelligible geometry of tangible matter, underpinning architectural detailing—establishing the material qualities necessary for a serene inhabitation. These drawings tell a story of an empathetic correlation between body and building, demonstrating how foreseeing corporeal reasons, architectural images can anticipate the interrelation of inhabitation, construction, and imagination. The mystery of the incarnate building is never entirely conjured by using the skin and the bones of only one specific body image. They are not Frankensteinian hodgepodges of heads, torsos and limbs, but Stoic assemblages of anatomical parts playing analogical empathies informed by the quotidian world, enhancing the "wunderkämmer" of architecture.

As scale figures, useful body-images can be ordered in three classes: (1) the nude mimes, (2) the dancers in leotards, and (3) the shadow people. These classes correspond to three realms of inscriptions of potential activators

7.9
Scale Figures

for the mirror neurons to understand the conditions of embodiment and the bodies' presence in the econiches generated by architectural artifacts.

Naked mimes are the essential expressions of the architectural mimesis, creating the counterpoint for the designed elements around them, meanwhile they portray a tectonic tale. Jean Dorcy, a voice for the silent theatre, describes the power of the mime:

> "[It] is neither a natural impulse nor a physiological reflex; censored and elaborated by the intellect, as by an architect, it therefore offers us sharp images."[25]

The mime is not a mimic. He is not a dancer. He does not perform pantomime. He uses his body as a tool in the language of expression dealing with something that is not present. The mime-scale-figures portray the ineffable tectonic and structural essences of the building surrounding them. The mimes, as metonymic figures, carefully evoke the constructive nature of the spatial containers and as dynamic and metaphoric figures; the dancers outline the spatial representation with crossing paths reflecting the disposition of the building. These two types of scale figures transubstantiate the corporeality of time, tempo and weather within an a-temporality of design. The mimes' dynamic actions condense events in evoking constructional principles.

Dancers describe spaces evoked in drawings by conjuring spatial configurations that delineate the tension of the surrounding structures:

> "The stage is a place where space changes nature, size and architecture according to the body occupying it; ... scenic spaces become a sky, a meadow, or a garden, thanks to the magic of a dancing body."[26]

Dancing scale-figures delineate space and time. The dancers' symbolic movements add perceptual details to future spaces. As dynamic and metaphoric figures, the dancers outline the spatial representation with crossing paths reflecting the disposition of the building.

In the drawings, the shadows detached from bodies set a dialogue between the possible use of spaces and programmatic requirements. The presence of these projections of ordinary individuals in the drawings enables one to comprehend the role of the two other classes of body-images. In contraposition, the shadows of the ordinary people in the drawings suggest the protean potential of architecture, regionally expressed. In "Les techniques du corps", Marcel Mauss discusses the wide range of activities that shape the mutable human body, from styles of caring, to gender formation, styles of work, exercises, sexual postures and ritual events, etc., that may seem innate but in reality they are acquired expressions of culture's values.[27] Particular expressions such as work positions or other aspects of the body differ, sometimes radically, from culture to culture. Individuals, raised in a climate of surgery, drugs, orthopedic devices, and constraining social fashion, image their body differently from those who have been raised to use meditation, movement postures, herbs, sensitive manipulation, and acupuncture to maintain their health.

The naked bodies are corporeal mimes as theorized by Jean Louis Barrault. The originating idea of Barrault's art of mime is the "counterpoids (counterweight) that is the use the use of a representation of the effort of the muscularity in performing the act to show the mirroring effort on the muscularity to show physically what is not present".[28] The counterpoid is the corporeal basis for assisting the imagination to disclose the intangible. Through their body, the corporeal mimes evoke that which is not present. The imaginary existence for an object becomes real when corporeal mimes express, through the tension and perturbation of their musculature, the intended effect that the use of a given object will impose on our bodies, revealing a presence, in absentia, through a projection.

The naked mime as scale figure is ultimately the direct expression of the tectonic being of architecture through the medium of the body. It is the connecting link between the traditional knowledge of columns as bodies, capitals as heads and so on, and a vital understanding of architecture, but at the same time the use of the naked mime avoids the use of the body as a perfect microcosm, or as a figurative condition to solve with compositional, proportional, and harmonic authority a Cartesian ordered geometry. It is the clue to the connection between mental and physical development and the power of architecture in tectonic expression.

The shadows are not organic, non-fleshy entities, but they are the best way to fight ergonomic standards by reaching through a projection the diverse sensory, emotional, and physical dispositions of the human body and at the same time avoiding the risk of using presentations enhancing bodies seemingly taut, normal, vigorous, and healthy. The body, when it is present as a shadow, is not a "nice" scale figure and consequently is not a menace or an endorsement to the aesthetic process, or "equivalent to a dangerous prohibition"; shadows are not dubious presences that with their impurities can perturb "the purity of architectural order".[29]

7.10
Section with Scale Figures

Scale Figures

A pre-Socratic philosopher, Protagoras, is famous for the statement: "The man is the measure of all things." This affirmation indicates the cogency of embodiment as a way for setting a proper cosmopoiesis. Since before Vitruvius wrote his treatise in the first century BC, the human body as a metaphorical and symbolic referent has provided what is perhaps the most prolific trope for architectural theory. The interrelationships between the body and geometric form, through circles and squares, and relating design parameters to the proportions of the human body have been at the core of Western architectural ideas and practices. The body was envisioned as a perfect microcosm, the figural basis of a cosmopoiesis, which located humankind at the centre of a regular or ordered macrocosm.

After Descartes, the human subject became divided into mind and body, with the body cast as an ancillary and detrimental counterpart of the mind. Cartesian conceptions conjure up the sterile spaces of screens or panels for geometrical projections, and the like. Presently, in architectural education, the critical discussion of the body is erratic and nearly extinct in professional practices. The intricacy of the human body's connections with architecture is rarely presented in any depth in architectural drawings. The human body is reduced to physical presence, subsumed by the rationality of geometry and mathematics, or to an anthropometric tool for the control of measures and dimensional operations.

The gift which we possess of seeing similarities between human bodies and building bodies is nothing but a weak rudiment of the formerly powerful compulsion to become similar and to behave mimetically. The forgotten faculty of becoming similar extended far beyond the narrow confines of the perceived world in which we are still capable of seeing similarities.

Everything mimetic in non-trivial drawings is an intention with an established basis that can only appear at all in connection with something alien,

7.11
Bloody Vitruvian Figure

the semiotic or communicative element of drawing. Scale figures as signatures occupy a "middle world", combining the virtual and the real into an environment of visualization that blurs the distinctions between subject and object—, part of a continuum of experiences generated by creative choices by the drafter. During the performance of a drawing, scale figures act as catalytic agents in helping architects to define the nature of building.

In classical buildings the "human scale" was built within them. Alberti's Palazzo Rucellai (1452–1470) in Florence, for example, meets the ground with a stone bench built to define the low margin of the facade. Even if it is not present, the human figure sitting on that bench determines the scale of this architectonic element. This does not happen in most of contemporary architecture. The human body, as a reference point for the scale of architecture showing human existential durability, is now absent. The stairs are the only presence of the embodiment left in many of the contemporary buildings. Scale comes from Latin by the way of Italian. The Latin word scala (from scandere: to climb) meaning stairs, in Italian, evolved also to mean: proportion of a representation to the actual object. If the scale of building is unknown, a look at the treads or raisers of stairs reveals immediately the proportional relationship of the drawing.

To do this exercise keep in mind that architecture is never autonomous from multiple embodiments and that the human body is the starting point and point of arrival of architecture. Begin a drawing of a section on a Bristol board by drawing several scale figures.[30] The aim is to use human bodies as instruments for the production of form while at the same time the experience and the communication of the experience of the body is expressed by different kinds of movement. Some of the patterns of movement are potentially implied by empty space, because architecture restricts potential movement through the imposition of boundaries and the creation of spatial structure.

Draw grosso modo the line of a section then start placing scale figures and use their bodies and their shortcomings to further define the functions, the tectonic and the spaces of the building. Begin by drawing shadowy silhouettes representing quotidian events that will take place within the building, i.e. sitting on the toilet, climbing stairs, resting against a wall or looking out of the window.[31] The use of shadows will avoid the risk of using the bodies as objects. Shadowy scale figures are concerned less with the symbolic nature of architecture, and more with the everyday practices "that shape the conduct of human beings towards each other".[32] In a projective way, shadows regard people as fleshy, corporeal matter as embodied in the making of the building.

Draw a second set of scale figures, a choreography of bodies that are dancing through the building. Dance is the art of movement and, through transfiguration, its figures introduce the element of time in the a-temporal conditions of drawing. The translational movement of dance amplifies times. Dance originates in common patterns of movement, as a conscious elaboration of correspondences and potentialities substantiated in such quotidian patterns. A dance script addresses the principles that generate dance movements as they connect bodies with the space around them.[33] The script involves a vocabulary of individual moves, a transformational grammar governing the sequence of such moves in time, and a generative syntax of different dance actions occurring simultaneously or in parallel.

The principles that generate dance include a reflective awareness of the interplay between a locally applied rule that becomes visible as a movement, and an overall form that unfolds over time as a collective effect of such a rule. The representation of the individual moment must be considered as part of an overall flow, and as part of a complex coordination of other movements. Make sure that you draw the scale figures of the dancers immersed in the very flow they are creating. Dance is not constituted as a series of images but as a unified and continuous image summarized in one scale figure, a synchronic capture of a diachronic phenomenon.[34]

The art of mime is a rhythmic art just as dance, but the rhythm is internal to mime. In drawings, the space-occupancy of naked mimes oscillates between the two poles of movement and rest. The idea of representing space as a relational structure among bodies (mimes and building) is fundamental for conceiving the tectonic nature of the building.

Being a multi-sensory morphology, intersecting the morphology of movement, the dancers and mimes do not need to be represented in the section as whole bodies, sometimes only fragments of bodies are enough, meanwhile the shadows should always be in their totality.

The bodies of the scale figures should challenge bodily stereotypes. They are not paradigmatically acquiescent and static bodies. They do not always need to be fit, slender and healthy personas, being about 1.8 meters tall, delineated by using ergonomic data and information contained in a number of design manuals. The bodies of scale figures are not devoid of sex, gender, or sensory capacities.

Chapter eight

Architectural Brouillons: work intended to be recopied

"Nothing is more beautiful than a beautiful manuscript draft …
A complete poem would be the poem of a Poem starting from its
fertilized embryo—and its successive states, unexpected interpola-
tions, and approximations. That's real Genesis."

Paul Valéry[1]

The forecasting of past constructions and back-casting future buildings demands
a coherent approach for establishing and constituting which representations
can be the real "arche" of "archi-tecture". This means to examine the operations and the outcomes by which representations are generated, grown and
delivered into the heterogeneous compilation of delineations and depictions
that makes a project of architecture. This genetic analysis is a continuation of

8.1
Venatic Drawing

the architectural imaginative act itself. The examination of beginnings, of alternative and concurrent architectural representation, makes possible to rethink and refine complex theoretical questions on the efficacy of architectural representation in producing architecture. The study of genetic representation is advantageous to the process of conceiving the development of a building in absentia because of the ability of architects to interpret the representation's backtalk and use it as an input in devising future conceiving. Borrowing a French idiom, particular sets of architectural representations can be labeled as architectural "brouillons", a term meaning "rough works or collections of notes intended to be neatly recopied later".[2]

The study of genetic architectural representations aims to restore a lost temporal aspect to the study of architecture that it cannot be identified with or derived from architectural history or architectural criticism. It includes features of visual and constructive hermeneutics, reception criticism, and historical research. The examination of genetic architectural representations is mainly concerned with how architectural drawings and models are produced and reproduced. Although based essentially on what Carlo Ginzburg has identified as a procedure based on clues, an evidentiary paradigm, the reading of genetic representations also grows out of a phenomenological understanding based on a venatic serendipity based on little traces.[3] This understanding sees drawings as mirroring plays of signs to be interpreted by confronting questions of authorship and author-guided imagination.

Sottolucidi

Within the Italian tradition of pre-digital practices, architects used to draw "under-drawings". Predominantly carried out on paperboards, called "sottolucidi", they are a blend of drafting, drawing and sketching combined with written instructions and thumbnail sketches arranged as marginalia. Then, interpreting this medley of graphic expressions and descriptions, the draftspersons or architectural interns had to trace the drawing in ink on heavy tracing paper called "carta da lucido" and this action was labeled "lucidare" (to trace). Then the resulting traced drawings were called lucidi and were mostly used to generate blueprints. The carta da lucido came into architecture from the practice of using oiled paper for preparatory drawings in painting. In the attempt to envisage a future building, the role played by the sottolucidi is genetic: they are brouillons to be interpreted through the filter of the carta da lucido.

The sottolucidi do not result from a mind vision of architectural artifacts, but instead they provoke one out during their factures, as in Pareyson's formativity.[4] A sottolucido summons the sensus communis, a sensorial amalgamation, by allowing the tiny traces to saturate the visible, but without any attempt or claim of reducing the invisible to visible drawing. The sottolucido guides the senses to continue beyond the visible and tangible into an infinity whereby something new is met; this examination never rests or settles on the drawing itself, but instead rebounds upon the visible into infinite possible worlds. The lucido becomes a passage or crossing, from the ending of one phase into the

birthing of another. This passage refers to the viewer's mental journey across an image, a transitus from sottolucido to lucido.

To further explain the nature of the sottolucidi it is necessary to recall that before the use of the carta da lucido, after a drawing was laid-out using specialized drafting instruments in pencil, with dry point or by scoring, these lines were inked to create a clear and durable image. The work horses of the architect's tool case were the ruling pen, the pricker and compasses. Physical evidence of the use of these tools is often present in the drawings and these marks and traces must be carefully understood. Ruling pens were used for drawing straight lines with a straight edge as a guide. Ink was placed between the nibs of the pen with a brush or a dropper and the setscrew was adjusted to control the width of the line. In raking light, the impressions caused by the nibs of the ruling pen are often evident. The pricker was a pointed needle-like instrument used in copying drawings and evidence of its use, expressed as pricked outlines in the drawing, are commonly found. The compass was used for drawing circles and curves, and most of them had one fixed leg with a sharp needle-like point and one interchangeable leg that could be fitted with a point, a ruling pen or a pencil holder.[5] Placing the sheet of paper against the light, the pricks caused by compasses and prickers can usually be clearly seen. In addition, one frequently finds storytelling erasures and corrections on architectural drawings marked by clearly defined thinned areas that were created with a pen knife or scraper.

Genetic Drawings

"It is pleasant to see great works in their seminal state, pregnant with latent possibilities of excellence; nor could there be any more delightful entertainment than to trace their gradual growth and expansion, and to observe how they are sometimes suddenly advanced by accidental hints, and sometimes slowly improved by steady meditation."

Samuel Johnson[6]

Genetic representations apply the material and instrumental delineations used in architectural design to reach an interpretation of the creative, tactical and powerful processes embodied in architectural factures. Genetic architectural representations are traces and expressions of the cognitive structures that are patterns of physical or mental actions that specify acts of intelligence and correspond to the stages of an architectural project development. The study of genetic representations attempts to explain architectural knowledge through "drawing knowledge", on the grounds of its history, and its material genesis by analyzing especially the origins of the drawing and the notions and operations upon which the architectural drawing is based. These notions and operations are extracted in large part from the sensorial blend generated by the sensus communis, so that they can cast light on their significance as knowledge of a somewhat higher level. However, the study of genetic representations also takes into account, wherever possible, formalizations—in particular, logical formalizations applied to poised thought structures and in certain cases to transformations from one level to another in the development of thought. The main focus is the tracing of design development in their analogous and homologous connections with the evolution of operations that takes place on both the drawing board and the construction site.

The examination of beginnings, of alternative and concurrent architectural representation, makes it possible to rethink and refine complex theoretical questions on the efficacy of architectural drawings in producing architecture. The correspondence between facture and representation is foundational for architectural pedagogy. In the past, many approaches that dealt with the tensions between these two sides of this correspondence highlighted one of them respectively. Interpreted as a duality, the facture and representation binomial has fashioned conflicting divergent results. Often, the facture, considered merely as a tectonic fact, was treated as some kind of "truth" that had to be faithfully transposed into mimesis. Recently, especially within the growing trends of digital representations, the event of a tectonic materiality is often considered as something "entirely excluded" from representation, as a retrospective fiction that results from specific cultural modes to be acknowledged or loathed. Nevertheless, if architectural representations are responsibly and effectively shaped, architects have the amazing possibility to lose themselves within their own images.

There are two factures and two representations for a total of four procedures in any given architectural project: the facture of the drawing and the facture of the building are paired with the representation embodied in the drawing and the other representation embodied in the building. Consequently identifying themselves with the emotions and the materialness of the objects to which they are referring, architects immerse themselves in their drawings materiality; as a kind of inverted transubstantiation the materiality disappears and the architectural meanings learned through these subjective immersions are then projected through two homologous creations of materialness: the one of the drawings and the one of the building. This quadripartite nature of the architectural project is the delight and the irritation of any sincere architect.

These cognitive configurations map out the expressions and the patterns recording the physical or mental actions that correspond to specific acts of intelligence ruling the development of the multiple and working together stages present in any architectural projects. The critical analysis of genetic architectural representations examines the sedimentation of architectural materiality in the weathered papers and models inscribed with pentimenti, additions, replacements, and erasures. Although it examines tangible documents such as architects' sketches, notes, drafts, models and blueprint, its real object is something much more indefinable: the motions of drawing that are not optically real, but imaginatively real.

The study of genetic representations remains concrete, for it never posits an ideal architecture beyond those documents but rather strives to reconstruct, from all available evidence, the chain of events present in an architectural process. A critically constructed genetic analysis is a continuation of the architectural imaginative act itself. The study of beginnings, of alternative and concurrent architectural representation, makes possible to rethink and refine complex theoretical questions of the efficacy of drawings in producing architecture. A critically constructed genetic analysis is the most effective and efficient way to learn architecture.

There are many documents that are part of these sets of transformation and several of them may become lost, but each one has embodied in itself the fundamental nature of the operative factures that architects have used during the processes of mediation for a specific project. These critical mediations are the actions taking place between the construction of the lines and their architectural construing. In non-digital drawings, the paper's surface is constantly in unrest with each line, erasure, retracing, and reconsideration. If the lines on a computer screen are erased there is no mix of graphite and eraser dirt, there is no risk of loosing the sharpness of your pencil or smudging the ink—smudges can occur only after a rasterizing with a Photoshop smudge tool. Hand drawings leave physical residues and pentimenti that carry inspiration and reflections. After a final computer drawing is printed, the only traces of its making are the ink marks set on the paper following a predetermined pattern derived from the algorithmic logic of fast or high definition printing and not from the real sequence of a proper architectural conceiving.

Chapter nine

Cosmopoiesis and Elegant Drawings

"You think philosophy is difficult enough, but I can tell you it is nothing to the difficulty of being a good architect."

Ludwig Wittgenstein[1]

The major conundrum in the present condition of architecture is that we do not teach or understand the discipline of architectural imagination. The main reason beyond this blindness about something which we should consider the core of the profession and its related education is that the discipline of architectural imagination is "literally" a discipline and the majority of the professors, the professionals and the students of architecture feel that to teach, and to learn, architectural imagination through defined and controlled procedures threatens their creativity. We are still suffering from the bohemian belief that architects are artists and they innately have the gift of architecture, consequently architectural studio teachings are only subtle, or aggressive massages of presumed existing talents.

Drawing architecture is a skill and like any other skill there are those who have a born aptitude for it, but it is a skill that can also be learned through rigorous practice. The most important thing to learn about drawing is about taking advantage of what your hands are doing with the chosen drafting tools, on the selected support, to put down on it the vision that you have. As I have already stated, if you can sign your name in a non-trivial way—believe me this is not so easy—you have learned enough control of a tool to make a drawing facture. What most often stops someone from drawing an architectural artifact that is not abstract, like a letter, is not being able to divide the artifact that is being drawn into lines, curves and angles. Once a person learns to think about the visible and invisible lines in the artifacts that they are drawing, he or she will be well on the way. When an architect learns to do this, anything can be drawn.

When practicing drawing, architects must be looking at what they are drawing and how the selected media work together with the paper and they must constantly compare what factual and non-factual lines they have drawn. The request for factual and non-factual lines and coloring is that architects, on working on a support, are not giving transparent images but synesthetic notations. Ranging from design drawing prepared for dining-in to construction drawing for carrying-out, non-trivial architectural drawings are the best instance of gastropoetic capabilities since they always result from contrapositions of sweet and sour lines together with fast and slow-cooked color surfaces. This synesthetic evoking in drawing becomes the real act of architectural seeing, as Scarpa powerfully stated:

> "If I want to see things, I do not trust anything else. I put them in front of me, here on paper, to be able to see them. I want to see, and for this I draw. I can see an image only if I draw it."[2]

Furthermore, a demonstration of the misunderstanding of the nature of architects' manners of working is that architectural historians study a very limited part of the artifacts that are produced by architects, they hardly present in their historical analysis a large chunk of documents necessary for the erection of buildings such as construction drawings or change orders.

Linear Translations

> "Tota res aedificatoria lineamentis et structura constituta est."
>
> Leon Battista Alberti[3]

> "People built first and drew afterward."
>
> Joël Sakarovitch[4]

As salient parts of a manifestation of culture, architecture and its drawings are assemblages of res facta (factures) not res ipsa (objects) and bear the marks, inscriptions, characters, scripts, success, glory, play, bruises and injuries of their time, place, and peoples. As living oral, written and drawn communications, architectural factures and their graphic constitutions serve not only as practicum for recycling architectural thoughts and dreams, but they become fertile settings for new thoughts and dreams that can have great consequences for the future of the people who will inhabit them.

As translators, architects perform the all-important function of bringing into the cosmopoietic spheres of architectural factures—drawings or buildings—aspects that often remain unknown. Cosmopoiesis as an act of world-making always starts from worlds already in existence and the making is a remaking.[5] Therefore, architecture becomes an elegantly conceived conjectural manifestation of translations and collations of places or structures ordered by a cultural tracing of lines.

In the practice of architecture, the cleverest segment of the process by which our constructed world comes about has always been the translation of drawings into buildings and buildings into drawings. Unfortunately, these intriguing operations have been badly disguised within the majority of current professional practices. Under the heading of production or working drawing, this segment of architecture—the drawings for the transliteration of architecture into buildings—has become a prosaic activity providing a disembodied, but professionally authoritative architectural presence. The problem with further negative connotations echoes within the educational realm. Students of architecture are frustrated by the preparation of drawings that translate their design drawings into building prescriptions and instructions. They conceive these construction drawings as a pointless disciplinary demand that merely delays the growth of their architectural capabilities.

The mystery of architecture is in the divinatory nature of the worlds of drawing and building. The conjuring up of buildings is governed by back-telling translations (transformations of the lines of building in the lines of drawing), and foretelling translations (translations of the lines of drawings in the lines of buildings). Back-telling and foretelling form a speculative chiasmus, a hypogeal structure, on which every project of architecture must be erected. Architecture is a graphic trade with an intellectual tradition that transforms buildings in drawings and drawings in buildings.

Adequate or inadequate architectural outcomes result from faithful or unfaithful and traitorous or traditional translations. Architects make cosmopoietic representations that trade "idios kosmos" (the combination of individual reality and private dreams) for "koinos kosmos" (a shared reality coalescing in dreams that all of us share). This merging of idios kosmos and koinos kosmos restricts and modifies assessments and results in a denial of the separation of past, present and future because architectural translation takes place within the interacting cosmopoiesis of drawing and construction.

The projection of an interpretative scheme on a drawing or a building is the constitutive act of the drawing or the building itself. To translate an image means to set a conjectural course of action, which is to recognize or guess what has instituted it as an image: to interpret. A translation is the result between the univocality of an interpretative scheme and the ambiguity of the image dictated by cultural identifications. Architects, by translating buildings into drawings and drawings into buildings, advance their adroitness in alternating schemes and corrections. These translations are not abstractions but successive material definitions within a continuum bounded by otherness and conformity in a culture defined by ethnicity and history.

Architectural translations are complex procedures. A simple consideration on one of the facets of the tried and tested language-architecture analogy will affirm the importance of translation for learning or practicing architecture. An adult learning another language, before being capable of formulating a thought in the new language, must learn the discipline of translation. Following a pedagogical tradition, second-language learners must translate from the new language into their native and from the native into the new. However, in the architectural discipline, the dominant didactic trends expect student-architects to conceive new architectural artifacts, without having ever properly translated any building in a set of drawings. This is like being able to think in another language without having first learned how to move from the new language to the native language, i.e. producing measured drawings of non-trivial buildings. The drawings resulting from this mono-directional way of thinking are comparable to sentences in grammelot, the gibberish language used by medieval jesters, troubadours and minstrels. It consists of a few real words, interspersed with nonsense syllables mimicking the sound utterances to convince the audience that it is a real known language. The architectural grammelot is a pedantic imitation of the graphic output of famous architects, without any comprehension of what it will be if translated in a built product. Done without the satirical and critical biases of the original grammelot, this fool-like approach avoids the richness of character and intensity of non-trivial architectural conceptions.

Thinking through drawings makes non-trivial architectural thoughts approachable. Drawings are instruments of understanding and intuition since the primary role of architects is to bring in existence what is absent. The majority of architects' representations have as their object the delineation of the absent, by making it corporeal. To draw means literally to involve oneself in a practical experience with signs.

Architects project themselves in artifacts appropriate to human experience. To draw before building is to recognize architects as agents of change because the lines of their drawings make them aware of time, life and above all the unknown others, since buildings are conceived not only for their immediate users, but also for users that cannot even be imagined. An immediate approach to construction misses or makes impossible to achieve the unspecified aspects of human change. Architecture expressed by drafted lines liberates human beings from the total conditioning produced by codified cultural, structural and functional resolutions. Not-drawn architecture operates according to tradition and usage, not by processes and questioning. Drawings are based on different modes of thinking converted into lines; the primordial element at the source of the elegant translation of architecture is a relationship of causality. The drawings developed for the construction of an edifice translate drafting factures into building factures: in essence, a different use of material reality, an elegant architectural translation, defines and demonstrates the marginal by bringing into focus the tensions between orthodoxy and heterodoxy, centrality and diversity; as such, it gives expression to "otherness" in society.

Lineamenta

The translation of lines of drawings into lines of buildings and vice versa is the essential phase of the process of imagination by which buildings are conceived and erected, since the ontogenesis of architectural lines assimilates the processes of designation that take place on construction sites. Lines are enigmas that determine architects' ability to think about the facture of buildings. An opportunity to solve the mysteries of architectural lines lies in an assessment of the use of the Latin word "lineamenta" used by Leon Battista Alberti in his *De Re Aedificatoria* (c. 1450): Lineamenta is the title of the first book of his treatise. Several critics and historians have asserted that Alberti's meaning for such a distinctive term is less broad and, at the same time, more specific than the Italian "disegno". Nevertheless, in Cosimo Bartoli's traditional Italian translation of De Re Aedificatoria, published in Florence in 1550, the word used to translate lineamenta was disegno.[6] In the first complete English edition of *De Re Aedificatoria* (1726), the text prepared by the Venetian architect James (Giacomo) Leoni was not a translation of Alberti's original Latin, but of Bartoli's Italian version. Consequently, in English lineamenta became design although John

Dee's "Mathematicall Praeface" to the *Elements of Geometrie of Euclid of Megara* (1570) translated lineamenta as "Lineamentes":

"The whole Feate of Architecture in buildyng, consisteth in Lineamentes, and in Framyng. And the whole power and skill of Lineamentes, tendeth to this: that the right and absolute way may be had, of Coaptyng and ioyning Lines and angles: by which, the face of the buildyng or frame, may be comprehended and concluded. And it is the property of Lineamentes, to prescribe vnto buildynges, and euery part of them, an apt place, & certaine n ber: a worthy maner, and a semely order: that, so, ye whole forme and figure of the buildyng, may rest in the very Lineamentes. &c. And we may prescribe in mynde and imagination the whole formes, all material stuffe beyng secluded. Which point we shall atteyne, by Notyng and forepointyng the angles, and lines, by a sure and certaine direction and connexion. Seyng then, these thinges, are thus: Lineamente, shalbe the certaine and constant prescribyng, conceiued in mynde: made in lines and angles: and finished with a learned minde and wyt."[7]

The first French translation by Jan Martin (1553) used lineamens (lineaments).[8] In a note to a modern Italian translation, Giovanni Orlandi says that at the beginning of his work of translation, he wanted to use "progetto" instead of "disegno". However, after having noticed that in later chapters Alberti himself makes a restrictive use of the term lineamenta, Orlandi decided to keep the traditional translation in disegno.[9] The most frequently quoted interpretation of lineamenta was proposed by Susan Lang.[10] She assumed that Alberti was talking about some kind of outline and concluded that lineaments must equal the plan. The glossary of a recent English translation indicates that there have been too many interpretations and the editors' and translators' reason for translating lineamenta as lineaments is the physiognomic nature of Alberti's understanding of architectural bodies. Furthermore, they have noted that Lang's limiting the notion of lineamenta to mean "outline" would not work in many of the instances, when Alberti's use of the term refers to parts of the classical orders or openings.[11]

Considering the convoluted panorama of the translation of lineamenta I would like to suggest the locution "denoting lines" to translate Alberti's term is a more appropriate choice than design or lineaments, since I am persuaded that Alberti's attention to lineamenta (denoting lines) is the recognition of a building practice traditionally accustomed to designate the future buildings' configurations and elements by pulling lines, strings and plumb lines on the site during the tracing of the plan, the setting of the erection and assembly, and shaping of building elements.

For Alberti, the art of tracing buildings on site preceded construction and drawings; accordingly, lineamenta (denoting lines) and structura (building) are related but independent. In the prologue of his treatise on architecture, Alberti argued that architecture consists of two parts, lines (lineamenta) and construction materials (materiale).

Denoting lines are the product of human ingenuity (ingegno), and generative processes (natura) portrayed in the materiality of construction.[12] Alberti verified in his practice that the use of the denoting lines needs a rational mind, whereas the handling of construction materials requires groundwork and the capability of selection. However, if the connection between denoting lines and the materiality of construction is alienated, there is no architecture. What is necessary for a mutualistic symbiosis between materials and tracing lines is the work of an accomplished architectural maker (artifex):

> "All the intent and purpose of the denoting lines (lineamentorum) lies in finding the correct, infallible way of joining and fitting together those lines and angles which define and enclose the surfaces of the building ... It is quite possible to set whole forms in the mind disregarding by no means the material, by designating and determining a fixed orientation and conjunction for the various lines and angles. Since that is the case, let lines be the precise and correct delineation, conceived in the mind, made up of lines and angles, and perfected in the culture and imagination."[13]

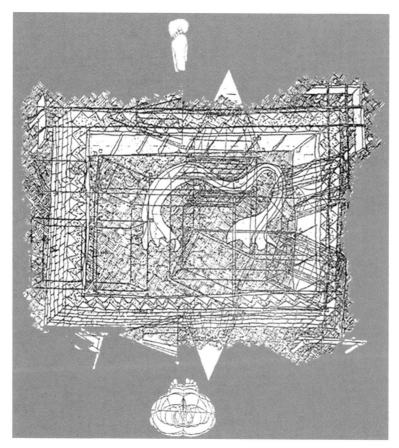

Cosmopoiesis and Elegant Drawings

Alberti's understanding of denoting lines (lineamenta) derives from the use of tracing lines, ropes, ribbons, strings or threads mostly made with flax fibers and used by the builder on construction sites during the facture of buildings. These denoting lines range from the lines pulled between different pickets and the battered boards to map out the footprint of the building, to the taut strings that, stretched at the end with weights, guide the masons in their erecting of stone and brick walls, from the plumb lines directing the builders in the making of vertical walls or vertical placing of building elements, to the colored snap lines (chalked strings used to make long, straight lines on horizontal or vertical surfaces) used to guide the layout of finishes and from measuring ropes and tapes to assess modularity, to the bending and stretching of knotted ropes to generate angles and basic proportional ratios.

Alberti—an eminent scholar of the Latin language—knew that there was a connection between flax and line as established by the Latin origin of word linea (line) that derives from linum = linen thread and textile (linum usitatissimum = flax). Evidence that measuring strings were made of flax, preferred for its stability, is also found in the Bible when, in the Vision of the Temple, Ezekiel mentions the sacral character of a mason line made with this fiber:

"He took me there, and behold, there was a man whose appearance was like the appearance of bronze. He had a line of flax and a measuring rod in his hand, and he stood in the gateway."[14]

Flax lines and fabric are sacred material that when stretched do not deform; consequently the lines are the perfect material for measuring and guiding several acts of construction.

In the final chapter of her book on Roman and Etruscan inaugural places, Palmira Cipriano, a Latin philologist, firmly rejects the traditional

9.2
Three Levels of the Roman
Templum

etymologies for templum.[15] For Cipriano, templum derives from the root "temp" that expresses not only tension but also crossing.[16] The ancient ritual establishing the site for a templum consisted of three parts: during the first part an augur traced the temple in the sky with the lituus, a ceremonial wand; during the second part the sky image is retraced on the ground with ropes; and during the third, the image was projected in the invisible underground. Tensioning lines for determining angles and transversal crossings, all consisting of flax string, delineated the temple on the ground.

A similar procedure of templum line tracing was also at the base of the inauguration of the construction site and of the drafting surfaces. A late illustration of Alberti's treatise shows a direct connection with the procedures of the templum layout. The image refers to the passage where Alberti discusses the laying out of the foundations (Book 3–2), which is done by what Alberti calls baselines (radices):

> "From midpoint of the front of the structure pull a line to the back of it, half way along it we drive a picket into the ground and through it, following a geometric construction we draw a transversal line. We then related everything to be measured to these two lines."[17]

The two taut crossing lines on the area of a future building corresponds to the two crossing lines traced by the augurs where the positive and negative connotations of the omens were measured in relation to these lines. The geometric construction suggested by Alberti corresponds also to the traditional preparation of a sheet of paper for drawing: in handmade paper, edges were uneven or not perfectly parallel, consequently it was necessary to mark two orthogonal lines crossing in the center of the paper to coordinate the tracing of accurate parallelism and angles in the drafting area.

The proposed phenomenological origin of the denoting lines can also explain a puzzling remark by Alberti:

> "They are of such a nature that we might recognize the same lineament in several different buildings that share one and the same form."[18]

If lineamenta is translated as design, the interpretation of this remark can be only that different buildings share the same design, but if the translation is denoting lines, the meaning is that different buildings can be traced by following the same procedures of horizontal and vertical layout. In his treatise, Filarete, a careful reader of Alberti, uses the word disegno referring to drawing as well as to wooden models (disegno rilevato di legname), but in a specific occasion he uses the word lineamenti:

> "I have already conceived this city with my lord and I have examined it many, many times with him. Thought about it by myself, and decided on it with him. Then I gave birth to it, that is, for him I made drawing of the foundation lineaments (lineamenti). He was pleased, but before beginning I told him what would be needed.

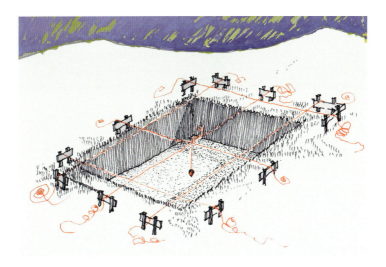

So that meanwhile I am struggling to make ready everything necessary for its foundations, I shall make the aforementioned model,
or three-dimensional drawing."[19]

This statement of Filarete regarding the tracing of urban foundations as not
dependent from the conception of the buildings is a further confirmation of
Alberti's understanding of lineaments as denoting lines.

The transformation of the use of taut lines on site to the use of denoting
lines traced on paper and vice versa reveals the cunning intelligence of architects in their divination of buildings. In the first paragraph of the first chapter of
the first book of his architectural primer, Vitruvius suggests that construction is
a meditated process of building by advancing the idea that theory is a graphic
delineation devised to explain cunningly and cleverly constructed objects.[20]

Sollertia, the act of clever judgment, is an intellectual advantage necessary to build and to interpret building. Sollertia is a fundamental asset for a
prudent, resourceful, well-educated and ingenious architect. Good architecture
is possible only when an architect is expert (peritus) and gifted with a quick and
cunning intelligence (ingegno mobili sollertiaque) (Vitruvius V,6,vii). Sollertia,
a clever internal sense, is also a cardinal virtue for criticizing, practicing and
theorizing architecture. Sollertia is a Roman notion comparable to the Greek
idea of cunning intelligence as embodied in the myth of Metis—the first one of
the many spouses of Zeus, the one he swallowed when she took the form of a
fly. Her name originally connoted "magical cunning" and was equated with the
trickster powers. When Zeus swallowed Metis, she was pregnant and became
the inner maternal genesis of Athena, changing the understanding of her faculty from "magical cunning" to "wise and prudent cunning".[21]

Sollertia is a crucial mental operation for any architect who hurries up
slowly and it is the craftiness with which architects can produce their factures.
Prudent and ingenious architects know how to meditate architecture by constructing plots and weaving plans. Sollertia/metis has its origin in the art or
technology of weaving. All the "lines" used in other crafts requiring metis

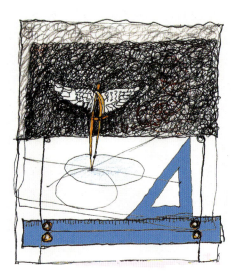

derive from the "lines" used in a loom. On construction sites, pulled between battered boards, the tracing lines mark the plan of a future building and show the textile origin of construction by appearing as a giant horizontal loom. A physical expression of sollertia is the use of a line to cut straight beams and planks. The stretched strings and plumb lines used by master masons in laying bricks during the erection of walls are all expressions of sollertia. An Italian saying "fare qualcosa per filo e per segno" is used to comment on a procedure done with order and precision, "to do/make" something by line and mark, and it encapsulates the essence of sollertia. The lines and marks used by architects within the looms of their drafting parallel bars are the clever processes by which a building comes into being on paper.

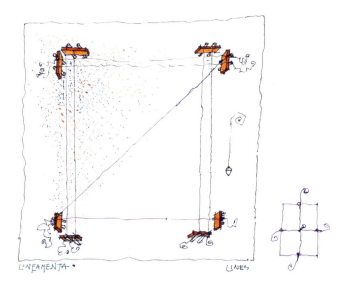

LINEAMENTA •   LINES

9.5
Site Lines

The Material Duality of Lines

"In Ersilia, to establish the relationships that sustain the city's life, the inhabitants stretch strings from the corners of the houses, white or black or gray or black-and-white according to whether they mark a relationship of blood, of trade, authority, agency."

Italo Calvino[22]

Lines are material, spatial, cultural and temporal. From a superficial reading of architectural drawings, the lines seem to describe buildings; they present to the reader a gestalt of the forces that determine constructions and uses. However, these forces are at work on drafting supports, these forces also exist outside of them and are free from time and matter. The lines describing a plan on a construction site or on a drawing are architecture's most fascinating puzzles since they make visible and tangible what is invisible and intangible to construct and to construe buildings. Lines present an entire building by simplifying its reality, but at the same time, they manifest an uncut view of the building's interacting parts by showing more of what is visible in the built reality. These lines present the invisible aspects of architecture, representing what cannot be seen once the walls are erected.

In architectural drawings, the drafted lines in the material working between supports and their facture reveal cosmosgonic events that are present in the visible building, but are in themselves invisible. In their materiality these lines should reveal a spatial and temporal sequence of constructive events, not some non-spatial and non-temporal phantasm. In the lines, the dynamic of a building is manifested in a demonstrative interpretation of the tectonic of the building; its three-dimensional extensions are represented in the material and form of a line, which we do not interpret in order to understand, but we use indexically as a guide.

The drawing and pulling of lines represents the coalescence of architectural imagining. If we assume that this architectural imagining results from an intangible super faculty that arises from the possession of a metaphysical eye capable of envisioning a future building, the enigma of the architectural drawing is a false problem. However, if we consider the extraordinary capacity of architects to conceive a building by tracing lines, the enigma becomes real. Architects can draw the lines of a building in direct sight, reconstruct the lines of a demolished structure, or devise the lines for a future building. The common denominator in all these procedures is the making perceptible what is imperceptible.

Through a peculiar procedure of de-composition, selection and re-composition, through a polysemic use of lines, architects can trace rooms, structures and building details whose functions become self-evident in the composition of the lines that will never be seen in the constructed building. However, it is essential to present the inner and outer spaces simultaneously and to reveal the temporal sequences of architectural perception. The building is represented in its entirety but there is no necessary likeness between the lines and the original.

The lines of building are neither facsimiles nor symbols; they are architectural facture. It is in this cosmopoiesis that the enigmatic beauty of the lines lays. Lines guide the oblique demonstrations of architecture, both on site and on paper. To understand the importance of their role in architectural imagining, it is necessary to remove any preconceived idea about the lines of an architectural drawing as merely an instrumental result of geometry, or as an illustration that leads to verbal and graphic prescription of usage and construction. To achieve a better understanding of the play of lines as demonstrations of architecture, it is perhaps necessary to reflect on the obsolete Vitruvian term, ichnography (ichnographia), used to indicate the drawing of a plan. Ichnography, a compound Greek word (ichnos = foot-sole, graphos = writing/drawing) is a procedure by which a representation that opposes perceptions and experiences depicts something that does not exist in the visible realm. The graphic procedure involved in translating the invisible into the visible requires a reflexive dislocation. Ichnography contains the solution to the problem. Architects can project the characteristics of a construction from the footprint of a building, as hunters, using conjectural knowledge, can identify their prey from its tracks.

Human beings have been hunters for thousands of years. Over the centuries they have learned to reconstruct the shapes and movements of invisible animals from hunting clues. Human beings learned to sense, classify, interpret such minimal traces, they reproduced them in drawings and they executed complex rational maneuvers during the hunt. Hunters have passed down their rich storehouse of knowledge through storytelling. Hunters would have been the first "to tell a story" because they were able to read the tracks left by their prey. This expertise is characterized by the ability to construct from apparently insignificant experimental data a complex reality that could not be experienced directly. In addition, the data is always arranged by the observer in such a way as to produce a narrative sequence. The reading of animal tracks is the mirror of divination: divination looked to the future by using similar interpretative procedures that had directed the interpretation of hunting clues looking into the past.[23] There were great correspondences between the hunting and divination; the intellectual operations involved—analyses, comparisons, and classifications—were identical and storytelling was the process of communication in both based on processes that designate of one thing through another. The lines of an architectural drawing, understood as a coherent sequence of events, are clearly a case of designation of one thing through another in their past, the present and the future of buildings.

By using a sequence of lines, architects generate architecture. This practice is based on processes of demonstration. Demonstrations occur both in the constructing of theoretical drawings and in the constructing of building drawings; since both are forms of realization, every architectural demonstration becomes ontological. Architects demonstrate meaningful and non-trivial architecture. This demonstration encapsulates the enigma of the labor involved in architecture. The pulling of lines on site, a projection using the compass of the human body, reveals a continuous search for human measures to bridge the past and the future of our world-making. An architectural play of lines on a support is not limited to a specific building, but becomes a projection of a cosmopoiesis based on the transformation caused by a specific drawing, the ichnography.

Architecture is the
result of transformation of traces

Nowadays, the majority of students of architecture acquire the skills of reading architectural drawing in the design studio setting. In this context, students produce different kinds of architectural drawings by themselves and learn the reading process through acts of making. History and theory courses in architecture conventionally rely on lectures, seminars and tutorial models of delivery and depend on key texts with many photographic illustrations and a few drawings. PowerPoint is also used to project photo images of buildings and architectural events and scarcely any drawings to explain and convey the teaching content. The problem with these pedagogical tools is an unnecessary and detrimental separation of visual appreciation and architectural appreciation.

A novel pedagogical move to solve this problem is to incorporate the acquisition of skills for reading architectural drawing in introductory architectural history and theory courses. By providing a structured reception of drawings made by others in other times, these courses will create the possibility to make more explicit the features of architecture reading that are implicit in the context of design studios. Drawings, as any human communication, are open to interpretation and the analysis of a drawing is framed and set forth by critical thinking. A properly taught hermeneutic of architectural drawings can critically empower students, providing them with a platform for forming their own judgments about buildings.

To read a drawing it is necessary to have a drawing literacy that could be defined as the learned ability to interpret visual messages accurately and to generate such messages based on the ability to turn architectural information of all types into diagrams, plans, sections, elevations or any other graphic form that may help to communicate the information. However, this definition does not help to understand on what a real reading of architectural drawings

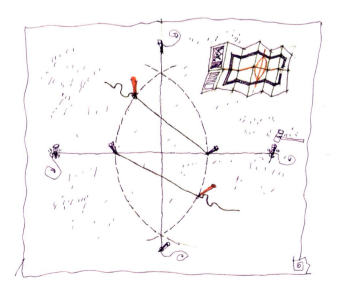

9.6
Vescica Piscis

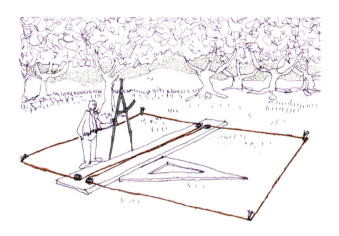

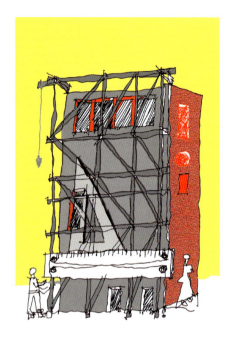

is based. What differentiates drawing from traditional systems of writing is that it posits a configuration very dissimilar from any other experience of textual arrangements. It is intricate to map out the order governing the reading of drawings because there is not any clear indication of the path that one should follow for reading them. Drawings are not linear although they are made with lines. They seem a strange tangle of communications when compared to the historical path most of the other written systems of communication have traversed. Their explicitly non-evident sorting structures may appear disordered and entropic. The reading of drawings relays, on the one hand, a traditional form of thinking based on similarity, resemblance and appearance, but on the other hand it also includes the reading of random attributes and interconnections that are not supported by traditional thinking structures.

Drawing is a kind of weaving that allows for infinite variation in color, pattern and material, and this can be learned only if they are redrawn. Drawings weave texts and textiles by presenting a structuring texture; they are webs and warps of fabrics that allow for infinite variation in color, pattern and material. It is the loom that structures the textile. For instance, the nature of the loom of the verbal text is epitomized in the laid out lines of ruled paper. In architectural drawings, the T-square or the parallel bar (the loom beam) and a set of squares (shuttles) structure the web of the drawings. The parallel bars and the squares are the immanent looms of architects weaving the plans, sections and elevations of buildings. These drafting looms not only correlate with the metaphorical horizontal looms caused by the tracing lines pulled on site, but also with the vertical warp-weighted looms generated by the scaffoldings and plumb lines: erected on sites to set up future buildings.

9.7
Parallel Bar as Horizontal Loom

9.8
Parallel Bar as Vertical Loom

The Mosaic

The tracing on the ground of the future building shows clearly the textile origin of construction. On a construction site, pulled between battered boards, the tracing lines mark the plan of a future building. A plan of an edifice is woven, just as a carpet or fishing and hunting nets. Sollertia (metis), the cunning intelligence of architecture, has its origin in the art or technology of weaving. Consequently, all the genetic lines used in architecture derive from the "lines" used in looms. The plumb line also derives from the weights used to keep in tension nets and other textiles. Probably, this phenomenological condition explains why the majority of architects used to prefer parallel bars instead of strategic versatile drafting machines, when they worked at their drafting tables. A parallel bar is just a portable loom for weaving the lines of a plan or of an elevation, by running a square back and forth as a shuttle, and meditating an architectural occasion (kairos); "the critical occasion" when the weaver must shuttle the yarn through a separation that momentarily opens in the warp of the cloth being woven.

This exercise is a drawing approach based on large drawing of sections, plans or combination of horizontal sections with vertical sections on a mosaic of paperboards, arranged on a grid. The first step is to sketch on the border of the grid the "parti" or a few graphic thoughts regarding the buildings. Then, draw the section and the plan of a small building that you are designing in a scale that will fill a mosaic made of twelve 70 x 100 double-ply Bristol Boards or similar. Twelve boards is merely a suggestion, the number of boards depends on the dimension of the building.

For the plan, pin or tape the boards to the floor and use strings and snaps lines to trace first the denoting lines (lineamenta) of the buildings,

9.9
Drawing of a Large Section

beginning with two central orthogonal axes. The next step is a drawing at the center of the mosaic of boards, a vescica piscis (see Figure 9.6 on how to make vescica piscis by using strings), to create two orthogonal axes to be used as a reference for tracing all the subsequent lines.

For the section, pin or tape the boards on a wall and begin the section by tracing the ground line and a vertical axis using plumb lines and snaps lines and a water-level to make accurate horizontal lines. To draw specific elements, the selected boards can be detached from the floor or wall and taken to the drafting table.

A variation of the exercise, especially concerning the plan, is to draw, with colored chalks and chalk dust, the plan of a small building that you are designing 1:1 on the paved area of an empty parking lot. The section should be drawn 1:1 on an external wall or on a vertical blackboard. A famous example of this drawing procedure is Le Corbusier's impromptu drawing on a large blackboard of the section of the typical patient room he had conceived for the new Civic Hospital in Venice.

Chapter ten

Traces and Architecture

In practicing their profession, architects evoke on paper or on screen images of the buildings they are conceiving for their clients so that they can decide that what the architects have conjured up for them is precisely what they want to build. Then the architects have to summon, by drawings, the same buildings for contractors who will imagine how to proceed in erecting them using what, socially, is considered the most cost-effective way. This double conjuring condition, dealing with the imagination of others, has become a stressful burden because of market conditions and societal circumstances. In the attempt to avoid such a burden, the consequences have been of two types. On the one hand, there is a group of architects who have become design-build professionals and therefore avoid the need of working with the imagination of the builder; as an additional consequence they can achieve a substantial reduction in the number of drawings necessary for the construction details by making them repetitive from building to building and consequently meaningless in specific situations. To convince their clients these design-build architects strengthen their authority by arguing that their architecture is an outcome of functional and constructively rational thinking since they know how to physically author their building. On the other hand, there is a select group of architects carrying out what they call a critical practice using visual public relations based on an over publishing of their design drawings when they are at the beginning of their career aiming to become starchitects.

Both the design-build and stardom conditions result in architects becoming authors with a consequent acquisition of authority. The result of these positions of authority is that the labor of architectural conjuring is not necessary anymore by avoiding dealing with the bodily imagination embodied in construction drawings: in the case of the design-build architects, by making these drawings unnecessary and, in the case of the starchitects, by farming them out to building management or construction firms.

The gaining of architectural authority allows illustrations to substitute demonstrations. In this circumstance the process of evoking buildings for both parties, the clients and the contractors, becomes utterly unnecessary. The consequence is that future constructions result from idiosyncratic inklings. This unfortunately justifies all the possible forms of a building production that does not belong to the imaginative universal of an imaginable cosmopoiesis, but rather is based on a fictitious personal imaginary.

The making of buildings has been solved mostly within a neoclassical and jurisprudential equation of simulation and dissimulation in a matter of verisimilarity. This is a sanctioning of a verisimilar relationship between the drawing mien and the appearance of the constructed buildings accomplished through autocratic and prescriptive sets of instructions. This verisimilarity as the appearance of being true or real has also become the legal criterion for construction. This legal resemblance makes buildings looking as they appear in the presentation drawings that had been critically acclaimed. Although it is a purely visual fulfillment, this legitimizing mimesis is carried out not only by the commercial firms, but also by avant-garde architects, starchitects and design-build professionals.

Nowadays, in almost every part of the civilized world the virtue of architects is based on their graphic documents. These documents are drawings and models and the traditional interpretation links these products to the constructed environment through the metaphorical goggles of mimesis. Different theories of mimesis have ruled these architect's documents, but nowadays they can be distilled in a simple dictum stating that the built artifact should look as the drawn expression of it. In the past, this parroting condition had been quite acceptable since the drawings and the models were quite impure, imprecise, vague, and not directly belonging to any specific moment of architectural imaging of the professionally enforced contractual sequence of architecture services. Everybody knew that the documents were not completely veracious and therefore they were to be taken with a grain of salt.

Regrettably, visual fidelity is now the key legal requirement, the dictum of likeness has become reciprocal: the building should look as the drawings and the drawings as the building. From this point of view, the illustrations of Palladio's Four Books would be rejected as false and incorrect representations, because they show proportions, angles and dimensions that are not in the built pieces. Medieval Architecture had the same lack of visual verisimilarity. Although they had been built following sets of measurement taken carefully from the prototypes, many of the replicas of the Holy Sepulchre in Jerusalem or of the Flying House in Loreto do not look at all as the originals. Nevertheless, they are accepted as candid replicas of those holy buildings.[1]

Unfortunately, the elemental conditions of representations by which drawings made before and after the construction do not necessarily look like the corresponding constructed pieces and buildings is not possible anymore. The association between authority and legitimization has completely parted documents and authors. A drafter's contract based on this process of legitimization obliges the architects to produce drawings that should not nurture any imagination. The outcome is that the reading of drawings has become an unimaginative routine; what was once a pleasant walk in the intangible vagueness of the realm of discernment and construing of factures is now a sterile exercise in the tangible precision of the realm of contingency.

The power of imagination has been ruled out by the digital machines required for the making of perspectives or photo-rendering. In the history of theoretical writings on architecture, there is a widespread agreement that perspective drawings are not proper and legitimate drawings for construction and tectonic conceiving and presentation. Yet, recently, the use of digital representations has transformed, in accepted reality, what was expressed in the pseudo-sensible statement made by Dr. Brook Taylor in 1719, who, in his famous book on perspective, wrote:

> "A Picture drawn in the utmost Degree of Perfection, and placed in a proper Position, ought so to appear to the Spectator, that he should not be able to distinguish what is there represented, from the real original objects actually placed where they are represented to be. In order to produce this effect it is necessary that the Rays of Light ought to cone from the several Parts of the Picture to the Spectator's Eye, with all the same Circumstances of Direction, Strength of Light and Shadow, and Colour, as they would so from the corresponding Parts of the real Objects seen, in their proper Places."[2]

The recognized outcome is that perspective, a mechanical product, is an objective viewpoint for casting the legitimate appearance of a building. Perspective machines, mechanical or digital, generate a trivially unimaginative and visually impaired view of the constructed world. These machines have put at rest all the imaginative undertaking of the people involved in the making of architecture. The act of reading drawings does not entail the immense labor of imaginative construction required before the invention of merely informative drafting machines. These drafting machines—electronic or non-electronic—are equivalent to those dreadful children's coloring books, authoritative instruments to teach neat exactness. The completed picture of a coloring book brings about a feeling of having imagined an image, when it has been merely a following of guidelines. With the use of coloring books and drafting machines, imagination is useless, only neatness is required.

Hybrid Drawings

> "In Latin, hybrida originally meant the offspring of a tame sow and a wild boar."
>
> Ellis Cashmore[3]

Nowadays in the age of BIM, architectural freehand drawings, usually regarded as digressing events, should become a quintessential edifying portraiture. The anaemic imitations of freehand drawings are generated with the help of fancy graphic filters after the digital construction has already taken place and cannot be a satisfactory substitute. A possible solution to the usage of these insipid drawings is the employment of hybrid drawings. A discovery of the role of marveling as embodied in hybrid drawing can turn the professionals and the professors of architecture onto a path leading towards a non-trivial architecture, true to architectural qualities rather than the quantities exemplified in the drawings, because the hybrid imagination is incongruous with the unfluctuating banality of common sense.

The Hybrid demonstrates a unique process of thinking that challenges many of the conventions currently employed by architects. "Hybrid drawing" is a locution already used in the documents used in Historic Preservation. A hybrid drawing is what you get by combining measured line drawings in vector format with photographic imagery in raster format. In AutoCAD™ software, hybrid drawings consist of DWG files with BMP, TIF, or JPG files attached to them in such a way that the resulting images reflect the same spatial conditions as the lines and polylines in the CAD drawing.[4]

The first form of architectural hybrid drawing was a mix of mechanically drafted, freehand drawings and collages. A breed of "docile" digital and "emotional" hand drawings is the present condition of hybridity. These hybrid drawings differ substantially from the neatness of photo-renderings or the over-precise CAD-drawings, and although they may appear vague and imprecise, they have the exactness of a genetic potential impressed in them. This is especially right when they are used not only during the initial design, but also during the facture of development and construction drawings, as they may help to develop ingenious and innovative judgment by suggesting diverse sensorial correlations and associations.

Hybrid drawings are powerful factures that set a correlation between form and construction, playing a crucial role in the conceiving of buildings. By tracing, signing, marking, looking, by unearthing visual analogies, remembering relevant examples, and discovering new constructs based on previously unrecognized configurations, hybrid drawing helps architects to envision and evaluate the forms and shapes they are using. These non-trivial hybrid drawings construct the past and the future buildings within a rich sensorial alphabet that results from drawing tactics of contraction and miniaturization, yielding more than drawing by handling prudent and temperate inscription of human thoughts.

The architect's involvement with the Hybrid can be traced to the mythical architect Daedalus (Δαίδαλος: cunning worker) who manufactured the device that allowed the white bull of Poseidon to copulate with Pasiphaë who gave birth to the hybrid Minotaur. Daedalus is considered the inventor of carpentry and of such things as the saw, the axe, the plumb line, the auger, and glue. A folding chair was shown in the temple of Athena Polias on the Acropolis as tangible evidence of his skill and the golden honeycomb in the temple of Aphrodite on Eryx attested to his skill in metalwork. He built many automata called *daidala* and they had open eyes, walked, and moved their arms from their sides. They had to be chained down during the night to prevent them from running away. Since then architecture has been the result of a sum of hybrid factures. However, rooted in the aseptic purity of modernity, the current circumstances are anti-hybridity. Regretfully, hybridity is seen as an inauthentic and rootless expression derived through forms of dependent thinking, whereas

Traces and Architecture

the main scope of hybrid drawings is to resist the entropy of vision by increasing the meanings and by capturing them in a network of abbreviated signs, marks and traces addressing all the senses and emotions.

Antoni Gaudí questioned the classic method and historical framework of architectural design and developed a facture of hybrid representations that probably has no parallel in the history of architectural conceiving. Within a shed erected on the construction site of the church of the Sagrada Familia, in Barcelona, Gaudí built a cunning artifact, a real facture corresponding to Filarete's disegno rilevato. He made an upside-down model using lightweight cables to represent the structural lines of the future church—a model based on the structural notion of the inverted catenary.

A catenary—a tension line—generated by hanging a flexible chain, if inverted describes a line of compression structurally optimal for masonry arches. Gaudí's cable model at the scale 1:10 is considerable in its dimension: four meters high and with a maximum length of six meters. Analogically represented by little pouches filled with lead pellets, the action of the stresses has been done in a different scale (1:10,000) suitable to the strength of the chosen cables. The resulting chain-configurations are used to determine the geometrical shapes and structural profiles of columns, pillars, arches, and vaults. In the model every part depends on the whole and an adjustment of the weight of pellets in a pouch or a modification of the hanging points of a cable leads to inclination and direction changes of all the other building elements. Even with varying weights and hanging locations, the configuration of the structure is always within the condition of being the optimal structural solution.

Gaudí's model is a pre-digital forerunner of parametric design methods. The sculptor and photographer Vicens Vilarrubias i Valls took photos of the model and, for a few of these pictures, portions of cloth placed in the model revealed the surfaces of the solid walls. Gaudí used these photos turned upside-down to draw over them the external and internal elevations, studies of details and sections of the building. The hanging and the play of weights and the graphic elaboration of the photos allowed results that were not possible with the means of representations available at the time. Gaudí can be considered one of the main precursors in the use of hybrid drawings to conceive the making of architecture.

The use of hybrid drawings gives back to architectural drawings their ontological aspect, which has been lost because of the present instrumental understanding of drawings which is firmly rooted in the erroneous notion that photographic representations must be the only ones able to sanction plausibility.

EXERCISE #7

Hybrids

As wonderful projections of buildings, hybrid drawings provide tempered and prudent factures by which architects can perform their thought-experiments (Gedankenexperiment). The stereotypical view of architectural drawing is based on a paradigm for architectural knowledge derived from a visual relationship between images presented in the drawings and the corresponding built works. The drawings operate merely as neutral and passive vehicles for the transformation of architectural thought into built implementation. In this, drawings are nothing but utilitarian imaginings convenient to present architects' imagination. Coded into this relationship is the accepted evidence of our visual sense as the only mediator of these communicative aspects of drawing.

The scope of hybrid drawings is to question the hegemonic role of vision in the execution and interpretation of architectural drawings. Architectural hybrid drawings are not created as an end in themselves; they perform a demonstration of architecture. Most notably, architectural hybrid drawings are the primary scaffold by which a virtuous imagination can be erected. This is possible because architecture begins not in thought, as other disciplines interested in architecture have often implied, but in a perceptual delineation of the chiasmus-like hybrid relationship existing between bodies and world-making.

Far from yielding less than hard line drawings or photographic renderings of pure or thoroughbred digital production, hybrid architectural drawings can be viewed as sensorial augmentation. They mirror architecture in its most powerful condition. Architecture is the result of hybrid factures, i.e. the building results from amalgams of high technology, low technology, sophisticated and naïve structures, complicated and simple systems, and refined and elemental construction events. Hybrid architectural drawings result from tactics dealing with contraction and miniaturization, conversion and suppression, yielding more by handling less. In these graphic procedures, the main scope of drawings is to resist the entropy of a normal sum of perception by increasing connotations within an architectural cosmos and by capturing architectural meanings within a network of abbreviated signs, marks and traces.

The main scope of hybrid architectural drawings is the vivid capture of a cosmopoiesis and the conquest is carried out by a denial of the 'immediate rational' by favoring the 'mediate sensual', since the latter carries the impressiveness of the essence of things. The positive power of the material mediation by hybrid signs ascribable to the designative character of drawings is instituted by merging analytical and symbolic properties, amalgamating discreteness, finite numbers, combinatory power, pictograms, hieroglyphs and ideograms, all of which epitomizes direct, prudent and temperate inscription of human thoughts.

For instance, hybrid architectural drawings can combine the eidos (cognitive form) and the morphe (sensual form) of a building in a sagacious sensorial application of the seven primary odors—Camphoric, Musky, Floral, Peppery, Ethereal, Pungent, Putrid—combining the ink or pencil 'lightweight' of visual contour of a structural framework with the odorous 'lightweight' of different structural lines hidden within the framework.

Hybrid drawings are a result of a continuous process alternating conversions and translations. Begin this exercise of hybrid drawing from the media that you prefer. A hybrid drawing can be started on paper and then edited on the computer, or it can be started on the computer and then reworked on paper and even moved back into the original medium (i.e. from paper to

10.1

The family tree of a hybrid
drawing

computer and back to paper). In these drawings, iconicity does not provide a
comprehensive account of drawing about architecture. Hybrid drawing is also
deeply involved with the creation and interpretation of signs as symbols that
participate as sensitive presences rather than sensible markers.

The drawing procedure proposed in this exercise entails a fairly good
quality printing and scanning, especially if the drawing has to be reworked
and rescanned again for many generations. Print part of the drawings or
new scan drawings on pre-existing prints or on printable transparent adhesive sheets that then can be applied to handmade drawings. Scan this drawing and introduce it in the continuing processes described above.

A final warning on this exercise, in relation to the ultimate product.
Remember that a tempting, but ultimately disappointing, answer to the
request of this exercise is to think of hybrid drawing as factures that can
be decomposed, conceptually, into two or more distinct drafting activities
or ostensible media. A drawing is a hybrid in virtue of its development and
origin, in virtue of its emergence out of a field of previously existing drawing
activities and concerns, two or more of which it in some sense combines. A
hybrid drawing is a drawing with a "past", and it is its history miscegenation
that makes it hybrid, not just the convoluted "face" that it may present as
an ultimate product.

Chapter eleven

Tools for Architectural Thinking

By reintroducing the eighteenth-century term of technography for the discipline of architectural drawings, architecture can be placed within technometry, a workable and dual system of human measures and elegant technology.[1] Technometry is a comprehensive procedure, elaborated within the blueprint for a Puritan technological encyclopedia, proposed by the philosopher and theologian, William Ames, a leading figure of American Protestantism.[2] His cultural encyclopedia—the circle of the arts—is an interpretation of the Ramist intellectual system; this Puritan system was based on encyclopedic outlines of all knowledge. Ames defined it as a measure or survey of art, namely technometry, a locution which later readers had interpreted synonymously with technology. Using the sensible context of technometry, drawings and edifices can be analyzed to discover how the faculties of building well and living well can be incorporated into the complex nature of architectural factures. Through the elegant and mediated representations, it is possible to trace the vestiges of the virtue of architecture.

"Practice and theory coincide in every art" (thesis #8) is one of the Technological Theses discussed at the Harvard Commencement Exercises, in 1687.[3] This thesis was derived from thesis #90 of the one-hundred sixty-nine propositions composing the primer written by Ames.[4] This small book is entitled *Technometria, Omnium et Singolarum Artium Fines Adequate Circumscribens* (Technometry, a Delineation of Individual and General Arts, Conformed to Their Ends); in this mini-encyclopedia, Ames outlines the arts according to their use, origin and scope, within a systematic delineation of the nature and uses of technology, as a theory derived from a contemplation of the physical environment in relationship to final causes.[5] Technometry is the measure of both rhetorical (theory) and practical arts. Technometry is the common measure ruling both "the techne of the logos" (theory) and "the logos of the techne" (practice) during the making of artifacts. In other words, technometry is the measured merging of the physical and psychical functions in a representation where reason and construction come together within the sphere of teleological hermeneutics, which produces artifacts. This coming together is based on a comprehension of the nature of the artifacts' causes that is obtained through representation.

Inherent in Ames' technometric vision is the recognition that human understanding is a representation ruled by representations. Trying to overcome the sharp distinction between the practical and the theoretical (thesis #90), this meta-discipline presupposes the existence of several disciplines and strives to find the common limit that governs them (thesis #84). Structured as an all-embracing map of human knowledge, the Greek "techne" and the corresponding Latin "ars" are the substantial footing of Ames' technological constructs.[6] Ames' technological recommendations propose an inner road for coalescing the intellectual nature located within the productive arts. Technometry is the measure for the transmutation and the integration of tangible and intangible substances and, by merging sapience and making, it befits the matrix of those crafts to transfigure inanimate matter in meaningful presences.

Technometry is not an art in itself, but rather "the precognition of the arts".[7] Accordingly, technometry is not a priori imperative of knowledge or a Platonic idea, but a preconceiving of the general faculties and uses of art, so it is possible to "represent and by representing to rule the action" (thesis #3). Before Ames' use of the notion of precognition, Vincenzo Scamozzi, the most learned among the Vicentine architects of the seventeenth century, indicates that "precognition" is a necessary condition to practice architecture. In his unfinished, but published, encyclopedic treatise devoted to the mirroring nature of architectural representation, entitled *L'Idea dell'Architettura Universale* (The Idea of Universal Architecture), Scamozzi points out that precognition, the result of an encyclopedic education, is necessary because architects work between edification and construction.[8] Furthermore, Scamozzi holds that the connection between theory and practice mirrors in the connection between architects and builders and that an appropriate use of architectural representations is indispensable to cultivate properly this connection. Representing the client, the architect cannot be the builder, but the architect rules construction with the use of well-constructed graphic representations, which mediate among the three powers governing every production of architecture: the client, the builder and the building concept.

When applied to architectural representation, the technometric notion might facilitate the figuring out of a measure for architectural edification. A well-done work of architecture should always be concerned with representing and it should be guided by appropriate representations, since the sense of measure, a correct motion, is at the very basis of any proper representation. Such representations are technographies.

Within Ames's technometric framework, technography, like calligraphy, would belong to the group of the less dignified, but eminently productive faculties, which would not be unworthy if they were practiced with natural talent rather than "artificially" (Thesis #132). In the Technometria, a striking declaration by Ames makes architecture—the faculty of building well—part of the lower but more dignified philosophical faculties, rather then placing it with the less dignified, mechanical, illiberal faculties. In Ames's encyclopedia, architecture is not presented as a trivial art, as was often claimed within the tradition of the Trivium and Quadrivium. It should be noted that Ames's favorite metaphors for explaining the precognitive dimension of technometry is the image of the architect at work with representation. "Likeness of a form is called an idea, just like the likeness of a house preexisting in the [drawing] of an architect is called the idea of a house" (thesis #4). This is making or framing (thesis #49). The essential notion is that architecture deals with the bringing into existence a construction that lies in a well-done representation generated by the architect-maker and not in the delineation derived from the requirements or specification set for building (thesis #33).

The art of measuring well (ars bene metiendi) is one of the special arts analyzed and discussed by Ames in his proposal for a technological encyclopedia.[9] The ars bene metiendi delineates the discreet parts of physical and intellectual works such as technography. Technography belongs to the art of measuring well since it is concerned with the concept of measuring. Technography is an art that becomes tangible in itself, but it is also a component of another art: the art of doing the work of nature well (ars bene naturandi). In the cosmopoietic encyclopedia elaborated by Ames, all arts derive from other arts, but the art of doing the work of nature well is a special art that does not take part of any other art and whose counterpart is the art of living well (bene vivendi). In the ars bene naturandi, architectural production arises out of an imitation of the act (an analogical procedure) rather than through an imitation of the object. All the arts that partake in the art of doing the work of nature well must follow this crucial and dynamic condition of the relationship between mind and matter to a common substratum that unifies intangibility with tangibility.

The common substratum between consciousness and matter reveals itself in the technographies of not-yet-built artifacts for the reason that they incorporate in themselves the same qualities which adumbrate the representations of still life. Technographies do not search for likeness as the basis for relating building and an architectural conception, but for a mutual measure derived from a familiar nature, which constructs both the drawing and the edifice: the essence of edification. Technographies are demonstrations related to the built world through still-life representations that contrast conventional notations of geometrical and factual construction since they deal with the representation of processes of construction. Technographies embody the Janus-like nature of technology, since they are a perfect instance of the non-separation of the techne of logos from the logos of techne in architecture. As specific acts of demonstration, technographies are based on an architectural almanac: a lexicon of technometric images.

Ames concludes the sequence of his technometric theses presenting the notions of trial-work (tyrocinium) and masterpiece (meisterstuck) (thesis #169). A masterpiece is a piece of work representing in itself the measure of the mastering of an art within a cosmopoiesis. In his analysis, Ames formulates a reference to an apprentice who, at the end of his training, has to produce a trial-work, that is to say a piece of work that must become a masterpiece marking his or her inauguration in the craft. The production of demonstrative-masterpieces is the necessary measure to avoid cacotechnics, and the proficient making of

11.1
Mario Ridolfi's Drawing as
a Technometric Drawing
Compared With the Built
Facture and a Drawing of
Krazy Kat

them is a demonstration that converts a practice into a theory and vice versa. The trial-work is not merely a trial of skills but the display of an intention that develops into a revelation marking the beginning of novel tradition. Only when this process is brought to fruition as such can the trial-work be a masterpiece.

Architectural technographies belong to the realm of this kind of masterpiece. They are inaugurations of construction not merely exact likenesses of future buildings. They are not similar images but rather they are precise analogical demonstrations of its construction since an image can never replace a demonstration. Technographies are constructions demonstrated in representation. Technographies help architects to solve one of the most difficult tasks of their profession; they give the appropriate measure of the building. They are the matrix of the edifying nature of an edifice. Mario Ridolfi, a twentieth-century Italian architect, has noted this intuitively:

> "The difficulty is in finding the just measure of the individual parts ...
> the willingness to give life to things almost to make them breathe,
> to try to make them speak."[10]

Technometry is the techno-mother that gives breath to edifices so they can speak. Technography makes buildings play a part in a common cause by finding an eidetic graphic notation for the vital measure of harmony that is necessary between the well-built parts and the well inhabiting of an edifice. Within the analogical procedures developed by technographies, the aspects of the macrocosm of architecture become again related with the aspects of the microcosm embedded in architectural drawings. Architecture results from a unique agreement of a virtue that can be understood through the formulation

of taut questions, on the one hand, to avoid the wickedness of gratuitousness and, on the other hand, to generate a definable explanation of order within a cosmopoiesis.

During the eighteenth century and the first half of the nineteenth century, the role of architectural drawings changed. Often worn out, but carefully preserved at the completion of a project, these drawing evolved from being reserved and discipline-specific documents to be read by the triad of architect, builder and client to be works of art hung in public shows and gathered by collectors and museums. The type and number of drawings created for a particular project became increasingly complex and varied, moving from the linear orthographic projections created in the eighteenth century to rendered perspective drawings of the mid-nineteenth century to contemporary photo-renderings. From being demonstrations that tell the story of the way architecture should come into being, to be read together to tell a future building as a spread of tarots, architectural drawings have turned into purely prescriptive renderings.

Drawing and Writing

In architecture, there cannot be a precise divide between drawing and writing, between the craft and skills of drawing and that of a scribe.[11] Architects are both scribes and drawing-persons. This condition was there since the beginning as identified in the historical figure of Imhotep. Imhotep lived and worked during the time of the Third Dynasty of the Old Kingdom and served under the pharaoh Djoser (reigned 2667–2648 BC). He was one of the most powerful figures of Egyptian architecture and under his guidance the famous stepped pyramid of King Djoser was erected at Saqqarah, near the old Egyptian capital of Memphis. Besides being an architect, Imhotep was an influential vizier, a high priest, a unique physician, a skillful astronomer, and, above all, a talented scribe who knew how to rest his lines; he invented the papyrus scroll, stone cladding and the use of columns in architecture.[12] Imhotep's authority lived on well after his death. In the New Kingdom he was venerated as the patron of scribes, representing wisdom and education. Surviving sculptures depict him seated in the scribal position with a scroll of papyrus open on his knees. In one of these sculptures Imhotep holds a scroll with a representation of a plan marked on it. In a papyrus from this period he is also described as the son of Ptah, chief god of Memphis, in recognition of his role as a wise councilor. During the Late Period his veneration extended to deification and he became a local god at Memphis where he was glorified for his skills as a physician and a healer.[13]

Nowadays writers are no longer scribes, they have become wordsmiths because typing and word-processing have separated the writers' bodies from the direct physical calligraphic expression of their lines. Architects have almost reached the same condition, they have become "linesmiths" by using their digital design programs. Nevertheless architects cannot afford to lose their combined role of calligraphers and storytellers because they operate by playing meaningful lines and the drawings are a thoughtful parliament of lines.

A writer can word-process a line of a text in Palatino or in Helvetica, and the meanings will not change. However, the replacement of a word with a synonym, a modification in the syntax of the sentence can make the meaning of the typed line more powerful or subtle than it was before. Lines in architectural drawing are not to be wrought by linear enhancements because they do not carry any meaning themselves, but their meaning results from their assembling and making. Rhythm, procession, and structure are embodied in the architectural lines traced on the support. As in Chinese and Japanese calligraphy, through the medium of form, the way of handling the tracing tool, presentation, and style, architectural lines convey the moral integrity, character, emotions, aesthetic feelings and culture of the architect to readers of the drawings, affecting them by the power of appeal and the joy of the "vis demonstrativa" (demonstrative force) embodied in the drawing's execution.

The Facture of Construction Drawings

An unnecessary platitude present in the literature on technical drawings and extended to the study of construction drawings is cast by the epistemic concept of scientific representation. Nowadays, the nature of construction drawings is discussed concerning their production and use in representing buildings or building elements. Consequently, drawings are evaluated on their capability of being representations of artifacts and the time when they were gauged as representations of architecture has elapsed.

Scientific norms and judgments tell us that to confuse the intrinsic properties of what it is represented with the intrinsic properties of the representation is a detrimental stance because it can lead to critical faults of evaluation. However, this is not a valid condition for construction drawings that must always share a few selected properties with the represented architectural elements or artifacts to become active representations for specific architectural events. The ability of the architect is to sort the shared intrinsic properties to make the drawing an effective representation. This assortment is the inaugural moment of any architectural facture. Construction drawings are based on a sapience of materialization by which the assembled materiality becomes the carrier of fluid and invisible thoughts. Construction drawings must not be understood as mere visualizations but as factures because they are "things made and done".

Construction drawings are magic representations that captivate their makers and readers. As factures, they transform the state of understanding in a construction and its construing through certain non-trivial kinds of media events with dense causal transaction. These representations do not just portray something—they are something in their own right since the signifying power is in their ceremonial facture and in the way this aura can be interfered from the nature of the depiction itself by a simple casting glance. To further understand the nature and power of construction representations is to relate their facture to the law of magic. Not because we should believe in magic but because it encompasses procedures attuned to a cosmopoiesis supported by a dense story line of resemblances and sympathies, analogies and correspondences. In *A General Theory of Magic*, Marcel Mauss worked out the three fundamental laws of magic: law of contagion, law of similarity, law of opposite.[14] Applied to architectural representations, the three laws work as follows:

1. law of contagion, "once in contact always in contact", for instance: a study-model of a church to be restored is made by using a couple of roof shingles taken from the original roof of the church;
2. law of similarity, "causes resembles their effects": in the topography drawing, the water-coloring of a river must be run from the spring toward the sea;
3. law of opposite, "causes that are opposed to their effects": the upside-down model made by Gaudí for the Sagrada Familia uses tension to figure out compression. These three laws of representations possess a signifying power because of an aura that inspires awe and reverence that will lead to richer factures of edifices and buildings.

Architects have been collectors of drawings from Vasari to Rafael and from Inigo Jones to Henry Ogden Avery, just to mention a few. Nowadays, there is a notion that there is no need to collect original drawings, reproductions are adequate. As Mario Carpo has demonstrated, the printing press has slowly made the reading of original drawings, an investigative and essential learning tool, seemingly obsolete. In the transfer of medium, important dimensions have been lost. The reproduced drawing has lost its original cosmopoietic nature. The printed collections of plans, cross sections and elevations of architects' monographic publications are undeniably a very effective atlas, but they do not carry the cosmogonical demonstrations of their making any more.

Architectural drawings are not objects; they are never-ending processes of reading and inscribing because the reading of drawing is, in itself, a creative process. The major problem for understanding the implications in the reading

of architectural drawings is the general understanding that visual perception is equated to the operation of a camera. Like the lens of a camera, the lens of the eye focuses an inverted image onto the retina. This analogy breaks down rapidly, however, because it fails to reflect the cognitive function of the visual system, such as our ability to perceive an object as the same under strikingly different visual conditions that cause the image on the retina to vary widely.

The degree to which the processes of reading and inscribing are creative and not passive has only recently been fully appreciated. Earlier considerations about visual perception were greatly influenced by the British empiricist philosophers of the seventeenth and eighteenth centuries, particularly John Locke and George Berkeley, who thought of perception as a simple process of assembling elementary sensations in an additive way, component by component. The view that perception is not by components but totality, that it is active and creative and involves more than just the information provided by the retina, was first emphasized in the early twentieth century by the German psychologists Max Wertheimer, Kurt Koffka, and Wolfgang Köhler, who founded the school of Gestalt psychology. The Gestalt psychologists argued that the brain creates three-dimensional experiences from two-dimensional images by organizing sensations into a stable pattern (a Gestalt) that is constant despite variation in the information received.

The reading of drawings has a history. It is not a procedure that is constantly the same any time, anywhere. We may think of it as straightforward process of mentally picking up information from a marked surface. However, if we sensibly consider the process that is taking place we will notice that the information encoded in the marks must be sifted through interpretative schemes belonging to cultural configurations that change enormously from region to region from time to time. It is extremely difficult to understand how reading takes place; it belongs to the area of cognitive studies. I suspect that there are no serious studies of how architectural reading takes place. This is because of the burgeoning assumption that architectural representations ought to be an objective specification of construction.

To understand the phenomenology of reading and drawing architecture, every architectural drawing must be seen as a result and part of a divination

11.3
Visual Phenomenology: Clouds

11.4
Visual Phenomenology: Birds

11.5
Visual Phenomenology: Beds and Folds

activity. Drawings are divinations describing future edifices, graphic prognostications that are then knowingly translated in a building through specific descriptions. In the Latin language, the idea of description is not separable from the idea of scriptura, as Dario Sabbatucci, an anthropologist and professor of History of Religions, suggests in his auspicious interpretation of divination as writing and reading of the world.[15] Romans understood descriptions as translations of objects in graphic narrations capable of depicting them. A powerful form of semiosis, divination is the description and script of a cosmopoiesis, a writing and reading of a world-making taking place on a piece of paper or in the sky. Divination is generally considered disapprovingly because it is thought of being based on a semiotic fallacy, a misjudgment of the pragmatic effect of signs and their semiotic object relation. However, the portrayal of divination, as imaginative reading and writing, disallows the negative interpretation of the idea of divination.

Divination puts itself in two manners in front of the world: on the one hand, there is a world to be written and, on the other hand, a world to be read, but both are worlds to be imagined.[16] Architecture is a reading and writing of the constructed world and architectural divination is done by casting figures of the constructed world. The divination paradigm has been understood in two different ways: one implying the mad seer and the other the wise magus. Accordingly, there are two ways to practice architecture: one by the mad architect, and the other by the wise architect. The mad architect is labeled as a gifted designer, whereas the wise architect is a magus. The mad architect is a mantic seer, because as Plato states:

"Prophecy is a madness … Mantic [mantike] and manic [manike] are really the same and the letter 't' is only a modern and tasteless insertion."[17]

A magus is the architect that through a composition of images, signs and ideas sets the future of construction. For an architect-magus, to think is to speculate with representations, and the art of conceiving buildings is a syncretic art and architectural artifacts do not receive meaning from the things that signify, but rather from the condition that generates the signifying. The drawings of the architect-magus are drafted, relating visible signifiers with invisible signifiers. They are what Krzysztof Pomian calls semifori; objects which are valued or praised not for their functional utility, but for the meaningful wonder they create, a wonder that can be only explained by reference to the union of the sensual perceptions.[18]

Dreams

Architecture, an extensively graphic divination activity, is the noblest prophecy because it is an elegant transaction of both the construed and constructed world of a culture and their proper existence is in the oneiric. Architectural dreams are maieutics and the reading and writing of architectural drawing are acts of midwifery. The delivering intelligence of architecture is based on

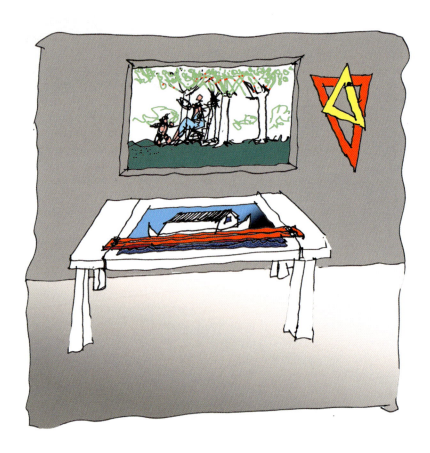

influential constellations of a cosmopoiesis, making the built and drafted worlds something to be read and written.

A false division in two different graphic procedures dominates the present condition of architecture. On the one hand there are the so called design drawings; on the other hand the construction or production drawings. The making of design drawings is considered the most prestigious act of the profession, an artistic effort that carries a vision. Nowadays in these drawings a rhetoric based on a desire of imitation is the dominant tendency to conceive buildings. These drawing are not based on factures but they seek coveted professional authority through imitation. The designer has no authority, but the subject of its imitation—the Laugier's original hut, the style etc.—has authority and as result by congruity the design drawings then become authoritative documents where the designer is the only properly identified author. Construction drawings, drafted by many hands, are considered merely protective legal documents. In this set of drawings, a rhetorically visual and mono-directional translation is the mode of production. The professors and the professionals of architecture regard this part of graphic transactions as perhaps necessary, but indeed an unbearable and prosaic part of the architectural enterprise to be left whenever possible to building management. It is simply a management problem to make sure the building looks like the drawings. This is not translation of drawings in buildings, it is merely a look-alike contest.

Translation is recognized as necessarily repetitive, as it aims to match form and substance in a different language. Translation is not imitation, but artful morphing of factures. Nevertheless, in the past, these documents of translation, between designing and building, were the most poetic ones since they were based on delightful factures. In these translations the relationships among the signs on paper and the buildings are not based on formal causality but efficient causality of knowledge. Non-trivial construction drawings are signs of entrancement. They are the crucial means to go from the extramundane of building drawings to the mundane of building on the site.

Chapter twelve

Disegnare Designare

In discussing or analyzing the notion of design, many writers think that by recognizing its etymological derivation in the Italian word "disegno", they have made the necessary explanatory correlation. Undeniably, during the Renaissance, with the discovery of the powerful role of the visual arts, the word "design" entered the English language. In Renaissance Italy, disegno assumed its contemporary sense of artistic or geometric composition and the social sense of purposeful planning.[1] In French, these senses are expressed by two words: "dessein", meaning "purpose" or "plan", and "dessin", meaning "design in art". In English, however, as in Italian, both senses are combined in the single word. Design involves making patterns out of matter and thoughts and the spontaneous recognition that something has been designed, i.e. was intentionally made. Ending with these considerations in their etymological quest, these authors do not ask why Italian speakers in the vernacular deformation of Latin did not pick up a Latin word obviously related to the pictographic arts, since the Italian disegnare stems from the Latin designare, meaning to denote by some indication, contrive, devise, point and appoint. In Italian vernacular, the use of the word disegno did not originate in painting and sculpture, but in ground measuring and in construction sites as the following excerpt from a thirteenth-century Florentine narration indicates:

> "Sent the surveyors to measure the land of Cartage, drilled in the ground the boundary poles that were drawing/designating (disegnavano) it."[2]

By the fourteenth century, the idea of disegno is related to a construction site, as indicated in the following line from a Senese Chronicle:

> "The drawing (disegnio) of such a church was made where nowadays San Pietro a Ville is, and it was done then when he was canonized."[3]

The facture of a drawing and the facture of a building are analogous as both are edifying constructions in this other Florentine text:

> "That such a church should be built (edifichare) and made following how it was built (edifichato) the drawing (disengnio) or real model (rilievo) that is walled up in the house that is called Opera and it is near the campanile."[4]

The drawing of lines is the fundamental step of the architectural facture both on construction sites and on drafting supports. In his commentary on a translation of Vitruvius, Cesare Cesariano compared the white page on which projects are drawn to a field covered with mud, pastry dough or snow. On it, metaphorically, the architect walks back and forth, designating with his feet the angles and the lines of future buildings.[5] In 1966, Scarpa used the footprints left by people to formulate his conception for a new paving in the square fronting of the cathedral in Modena. He was staying in a hotel facing the square and very early in the morning he was drinking his coffee and looking out of the window of the room. Overnight, a light snow had covered the square and the view of the trails marked by the people going to early mass caught Scarpa's emotional imagination. He based his drawings for the layout of the stone parterre on his reading of early morning human traces.

Scarpa's use of short-lived footprints to determine a permanent solution illustrates the corporeal nature of the lines projected on plans. The experience of lines of life is made tangible by non-trivial architectural elements. In conceiving architecture through drawing, body and mind merge. In an amalgamation of senses, architecture takes place within experience, which come to life through drawing factures. As a phenomenon, this process can be observed, noted and reinterpreted to provide insight into drawing knowledge and the nature of architectural understanding.

All the senses are implicated in drawing factures. The making and reading of drawings affect us by manipulating our senses: architects see, smell, hear, touch and taste the drawing. The drawings are based in time and space; they come from deep inside, from the common sensorium, and materialize on a surface through the interaction of hands, tools and surfaces.

The Role of Touch

> "In perception we do not think the object and we do not think ourselves thinking it, we are given over to the object and we merge into this body which is better informed than we are about the world ..."
>
> Merleau-Ponty[6]

Vision, among the different sensory modalities, is by far the most extensively studied both by psychology and by neuroscience. About fifty years of neuroscientific investigation have clarified many aspects of vision, from the transduction processes carried out at the interface between light stimuli and receptors in the retina, to the different stages along which visual images are processed and analyzed by the brain. However, the sense of touch plays a curious role in our dealings with the external world. Everything we see, we simultaneously also recognize as a tactile object, as something which is directly related to the human body. Also, linguistic expressions, such as "keep in touch", figuratively expressing the wish of being related or in comunication with someone, indicate a fundamental role of the tactile dimension for social cognition.[7]

To find their way in the built environment, many think that they rely essentially on vision. They think that through vision, they are able to recognize different buildings, structures, to locate them in space, and to record and understand their functions. Architectural interiors and exteriors are photographed from good points of view during tourist visits, picture postcards are bought as mementos, magazines and books on the history and criticism of architecture are filled with illustrations in black and white or in color. Undoubtedly, our sense of sight gives us much information about the inside and the outside of buildings: their masses, the colors, the profiles, the openings, the proportions, and plays of light and shadows give character to the facades by enhancing details that are discovered little by little by focusing and zooming on the different parts and building elements. Nevertheless, non-trivial architecture does not have only visual concerns and what pure vision presents to us is not necessarily architecture's fundamental nature. A cosmopoiesis involves more than the mere vision of objects. Instead the body accumulates and appropriates objects, temporarily including them within its scope or limit. Such objects are acquired and used by the body as part of its projects, in an active engagement with world-making.

Because illustrations and marketing of the architectural experience are reduced to sight only, the understanding of the perceptual experience of architecture is distorted by the understanding that the optic condition is the only parameter. Unfortunately most of the dominants trends in conceiving buildings and the elaboration of architectural presentations fall within the same distorted realm. Too many professionals and students conceive their architecture only visually, by tracing plans, cross sections and elevations; they draw the envelops of spaces and places determining the appearance of surfaces by photo-rendering effects frozen in time ... always during a "nice looking day".

Many years ago, I found myself in disagreement with the dean of the school where I was teaching because he refused a blind student admission to study architecture, arguing that architecture is all about vision. As a protest I wrote a short philosophical tale about Capo Maestra, a girl who was born blind but who had the dream of becoming an architect.[8] A common but false notion of the nature of blindness had apparently guided the decision of the dean. It is not easy to refuse the idea that being blind is like being in a total absence of light. Most people think of blindness as a state of blackness, absence and deprivation. We suppose that there is a gargantuan gap in the consciousness of a sightless person, a permanent feeling of incompleteness. Where there could be light, there is no light. The born blind people do not experience blindness as a disruption or an absence. This is not because touch and hearing get stronger to compensate for the failure to see; it is because the sightless individuals do not experience their blindness at all.

In my tale, I pointed out that, unable to gain entry to a school of architecture, Capo followed audio transcriptions of the writings of Vitruvius, Alberti, Filarete, and L.I. Kahn. From these works she understood that the meaningful dimensions of architecture always originate in architecture's representations, which are mostly haptic demonstrations. In her haptic perception she knew that drawing is not beyond the capabilities of the blind because of three basic provisions. The first provision is an emphasis on substance and shape properties rather than on form. The second is based on the integration of successive sensation, and the third is the ability to take advantage of the mobility offered by the hands and the body. Capo was able to draw tactile pictures by embossing wet paper with the representation of metaphorical devices expressing the thought of an object rather than the object itself.[9]

Capo understood the differences in the processing of perceptual information between the blind and the sighted, and used them in her drawings. They were the result of emotional lines that can be tactically described and inscribed by the blind but are also evocative of visual perceptions. The result was a unique synthesis of technological procedures merging extramundane constructs and mundane unfoldings: in Capo's drawings the plans and cross sections as perceived by vision and as perceived by touch were integrated because her "drawing fingers" became her body and, as Cesariano suggests, walking back and forth on the paper, those fingers designate the parts, the angles, the lines and the aspects of future buildings.

The action of drawing is a problematic operation because it put architects through a conceptual condition of blindness in the way architecture is communicated to the sheet. Perceptual experience of architecture acquires meanings

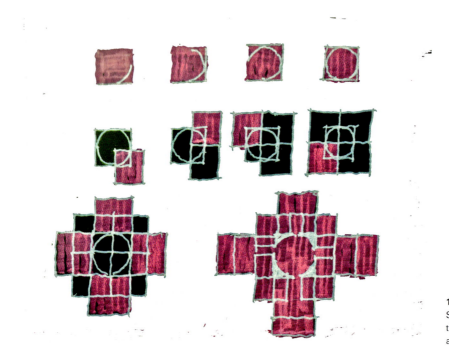

12.1
Sequence of the Drawing of the Plan of Palladio's Rotonda as Geometrical Composition

Disegnare Designare

and reality through sensimotor knowledge. The perception of architecture is not something that comes to us, but it is something that we get by acting. Architecture makes itself available through physical movement and interaction. Perception of architectural artifacts acquires content through our bodily skills and total sensorial involvement. What we perceive is determined by what we do and by what buildings make us do. We enact our perceptual experience of architecture; we act it out.

The showing of photographic pictures of architectural artifacts has been one of the most deleterious events caused by the media selected for the teaching of architectural history. This choice has also tainted architectural criticism and seriously damaged professional presentations of designs. I remember the first classes of architectural history I attended a long time ago; the school did not have a slide library and the professor made a superb use of the blackboard. She sketched plans, sections, elevations, details, meanwhile referring to the small black and white picture in the textbook in front of us and we students attentively copied in our notebooks her often wonderful and always sensible sketches. The key here was not the visual nature of the finished sketch, but the performance of the act of drawing and the active conditions of copying them which was the understanding of architectural rules not the final visual image in itself.

With the passing of years, architectural teaching evolved in projecting slides—even with four projectors at the time—and now PowerPoint presentations are further reinforcing the passive visual condition of architectural learning. This has generated a sensually impoverished perception of architecture, despite an overwhelming presence of visual sensations. The result of passive ocular dominance is an incapability to integrate sensory stimulation and perception with patterns of movement and thoughts. An unkind experiment that was performed by a physiological psychologist with two kittens from the same litter can be used to explain the problem of teaching architectural history without performing a drawing of the key parts, plans, sections, details of the building presented in class. In this experiment, one of the kittens was harnessed to a carousel, the other was placed in a little cage connected to the carousel at the opposite side of the first kitten and suspended in the air. The harnessed kitten could walk (only in a circle, but was in charge of moving), whereas the other kitten was passively moved around, getting the identical visual stimulation as the harnessed kitten. However, the result of the experiment showed that only the self-moving kitten developed a normal depth perception and the perception of the tridimensional pattern of the surrounding environment.[10]

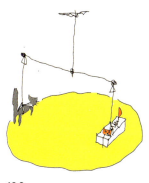

12.2
Kittens Experiment

EXERCISE #8

Blind Drawing

The definitive solution to an architectural concept is the result of a set of progressive transformations, an investment of time that the architect has devoted to drawing, researching, redrawing, and so on.

Closed in its perfect form and in a status of architectural equilibrium, any architectural project seems the immediate expression of its own internal necessities, nevertheless this expression remains the mediated product of its genesis. Many documents are part of this set of transformation and several of them can be lost, but each one of the drawings carries, embodied in itself, the fundamental nature of the operative concepts that the architects had used during the process of mediation of their architectural ideas for a specific project. These critical mediations are the actions taking place between the construction of the lines and their construing.

Make a plan, a section and an elevation to be read by a blind person.

Do not make a model, but rather draw by using raised lines and minimal textures to make the drawings meaningful. Architectural notations use a certain way of representing their tactile cosmopoiesis. Jagged lines might be used to communicate about something that's hard and flowing ones to show something that's soft and yielding. When John M. Kennedy, a perception psychologist, set out to test this very metaphor, he found that all his subjects, blind or sighted, read jagged lines as "hard" and flowing ones as "soft". Even though, as Kennedy points out, the real forms that our eyes and hands perceive are never that clear-cut: a polished stone, for all its hardness, doesn't have a single jagged edge and a soft maple leaf is nothing but zigzags.

Remember also the exercise of the drawings done using foodstuffs as a source for an odorous aura and try to apply what you have learned from it to these sequence of drawings.

Mano Oculata

An amazing photomontage by the Russian architect El Lissitzky (Lazar Markovich Lissitzky) entitled *The Constructor* (1924) shows a self-portrait on which the image of a hand holding a compass has been overprinted. The overlapping of the two images is done in such a way that the right eye of El Lissitzky's is emerging within the palm of the hand. This image of a hand holding a compass first appeared as an illustration of the hand of God in a 1919 book designed by El Lissitzky. The hand and compass, as a drawing, turned up in an advertisement conceived for the Pelikan Ink, and, as a photo, published as a cover for the magazine *Arkhitektura VKhUTEMAS*.[11]

Several times in his photomontages, El Lissitzky revives, in modern configuration, classical allegorical topoi and devices. In the case of *The Constructor* the reference is to the Renaissance emblem of the "mano oculata"(eyed hand) as it was presented in a vignette used in Mario Bettini in his encyclopedic collection of mathematical curiosities, published in 1642.[12] El Lissitzky's reinterpretation of the emblem tells us that insight is revealed through drawing tactile activity. Between the action of the hand, and the hand's relationship to the rest of the body, the judgement of the compass—Michelangelo's seste del giudizio—and the drawing surface, another form of architectural sense of vision is available.[13]

Seeing is a remote sense. It tells us about distant parts of our environment by receiving rays and waves. Seeing is also touching at distance, for example,

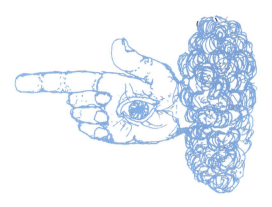

12.3
Indexical *Mano Oculata*

the haptic vision is a form of tactile vision; here the eye is used as an organ of touch; haptic images invite to come close to the image. The word "haptic" is derived from the Greek term "hapthai", meaning touch, an emotionally loaded sense, about the communicability and possibility for shared cultural experiences.

In *Traité des Sensations* (1754), Etienne de Condillac illustrates his post-Lockean theory of the senses with a philosophical tale of a marble statue, which gradually gains knowledge about the exterior world by way of a sequential revelation of sensory input.[14] While the sensations of smell, taste, sound and colors endow the statue with a sense of being and consciousness, it is only through touching that Condillac's statue becomes certain of external objects. The pivotal concept is that smell, taste, hearing, or even sight cannot yield the idea of an object and of an external world unless something is touched. Colors, sounds, odors, and tastes are mere sensations or states, not yet referred to external objects. Before external causes can be substituted for their sensations, the statue must be endowed with the most important of all senses: the sense of touch.

Touch alone can reveal to us the objective world, by giving us the ideas of extension, form, solidity, and body. Even sight cannot suggest them. Persons born blind cannot, upon receiving their sight, distinguish between a ball and a block, a cube and a sphere, until they touch these objects. Only after having touched things, we turn to the impressions received by the other senses, such as colors, sounds, tastes, and smells, to objects existing outside of us, Hence, touch is the highest sense, and the guide of the other senses; it is touch which teaches the eye to distribute colors in nature. Touch is passionate and gives an immediate communication with internal, or external bodies.

Tools and Instruments

Through valid haptic interactions with physical tools and instruments, architects have conceived and developed rich representations and have coordinated constructions of amazing architectural possibilities. By grasping and manipulating their drawing instruments, architects developed enlightening manifestations of architectural conception. Drafting and measuring tools are extensions of the

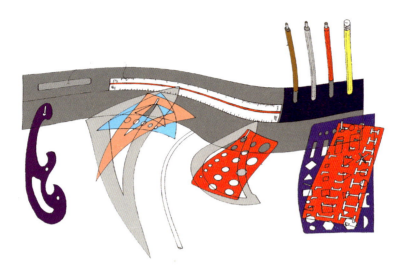

architect's body. Indeed, architects ought to learn to sense the world through pencils, squares and many other drafting tools and when they develop these capabilities properly, they would not even be conscious of the tools as such, but directly of what the tools touched, by merging tangible and intangible and by letting the drawing processes rule both the presentation and the construction documents.

Long before the invention of personal computers, our architectural drafting precursors manufactured a variety of specialized physical artifacts to draw geometric shapes, to compute and measure the passage of time, and to predict the movement and influence of planets and weather. We can find these true technological jewels made of brass, silver, steel, and oak located behind security glass within the cases of museums where they cannot be touch or grasped. The rich affordances of these traditional drawing instruments inspired many architectural achievements. The majority of these historical tools have disappeared from schools, laboratories, and design studios and have been replaced with the most generic and general of the drafting appliances: personal computers.

Embodied theories of conceptual representation propose that the human sensorimotor system may serve to embody abstract ideas.[15] Precisely, if "ideas are objects" then "understanding is grasping".[16] In the process of drawing, the grasping of tools plays a major role in developing architectural ideas. The haptic condition of a traditional pair of compasses and a beam compass are totally different, although both generate circles; one relies on a body analogy, "legs", and the other on a building analogy, "beam", but when the tools are grabbed two different set of ideas can be developed. The tools are filters of architectural perception. Through grasping and manipulating these instruments, users of the past have developed enlightening manifestations of architectural conceptions. Through valued haptic interactions with real physical tools and instruments, architects have developed rich representation, and amazing architectural possibilities.

Joining the world-making richness by grasping drafting tools is an essential condition of architectural factures, because the physical grasping develops drawing tactics through both haptic interactions based on the manipulation of tools and the tacit learning due to the peripheral senses becoming aware of the rules embodied in the movements of the tools themselves. In current drawing procedures, most of these drawing tactics cannot be discovered because of the diversity and the chasm between the mouse and typing input and the output in screens or 2D and 3D printing.

Architects live between two realms: a physical and a virtual environment. Despite their dual citizenship, the absence of seamless couplings between these parallel existences generates a great divide between the worlds of electronic bits and physical atoms. At present, we are torn between these parallel, but disjointed spaces. The invention of new architectural tools can lead to novel demonstrations of architecture. They have to be prosperous not prescriptive instruments, but manifestations of architectural thinking.

The Knife and the Pen

The drawing pen is a knife that enables architects to cut through the bodies of buildings—that is, the tool with which they write the history of their buildings. Architectural writing and reading are always architectural cutting. Claudius Galenus of Pergamum, know as Galen, a Greek physician born into an architect's family, stresses the homology between dissection and the combination of writing and reading in his description of the origins of anatomy.[17] He places the origin of medicine in anatomy itself:

> "It was then superfluous to write a treatise like this one, because since their childhood, from their parents the pupil had learned dissecting as they did for reading and writing. The ancients practiced adequately anatomy, not only the physicians, but also the philosophers. There was no need to worry that the procedures of dissection could be forgotten since they were learned during childhood as the art of writing."[18]

The knife sections the body and organizes knowledge, which is then written in treatises by the pen. In architectural drawings, the pen is a knife, a stiletto that becomes the stylus with which architects can pierce both bodies of buildings and bodies of drawings:

> "Meanwhile I was publicly commenting on the books of the ancient physicians, I was proposed to comment on Erasitratus' book, The Movement of the Blood. Following the tradition the stylus [grapheion] was nailed in the scroll and marked that part which advises on phlebotomy."[19]

Manfredo Tafuri, an architectural critic and historian who knew how to draw, applies the same critical procedure in describing a method consonant with the aims of the "historical project" in architecture:[20]

"Operating on its own constructions, history makes an incision with a scalpel in a body whose scars do not disappear; but at the same time, unhealed scars already mar the compactness of historical constructions, rendering them problematic and preventing them from presenting themselves as the 'truth'."[21]

Dissection is the task of knowledge since, as Foucault says, "knowledge is not made for understanding; it is made for cutting".[22] The process of cutting is at the basis of our understanding of representation as an anatomical demonstration. This concept will become clear through a comparison of two drawings of the twelfth century: one is an anatomical drawing kept at the Bodleian Library in Oxford and the other is a representation of the Monastery of Canterbury. The Medieval anatomical drawing shows a human body in a dissecting frog-like position, a configuration that many corpses assume during the dissecting. The circulatory system of the veins is traced within it, in a phenomenal transparency. The drawing of the Monastery of Canterbury displays a homologue representation: the buildings are laid out frog-like and the water system connecting them is traced in transparency, as in the anatomical drawing.

Knife and pen are the tools used by Aristotle in producing his scientific taxonomy entitled *De Partibus Animaliurn* (The Parts of Animals). Aristotle unified into a common science dispersed kinds of knowledge generated by the empirical methods of various trades such as fishing and hunting. During the sixteenth century, emulating Aristotle's taxonomic method, the humanist Francesco Maria Grapaldo wrote a book entitled *De Partibus Aedium* (The Parts of Buildings). The book is a categorization of a built world achieved through the dissecting of many classical literary texts. Grapaldo is represented on the frontispiece holding a knife and a pen.[23]

A prodigious development in anatomical research took place during the sixteenth century and Andreas Vesalius's *De Humani Corporis Fabrica* (The Edifice of the Human Body) is the epitome. According to Vesalius, anatomical investigation unveils the harmony between the use and function of the diverse parts.[24] Furthermore, for Vesalius, the duty of the anatomist is to demonstrate the number, location, figure, property, and composition of those parts.[25] Anatomy is not only considered to be the process of taking a corpse apart, but also a way of reconstituting it as body in an anatomical theatre. The reconstitution of the body of architecture was at the core of Renaissance architectural investigations; the "tacquini di rilievo" (survey-logs) produced by humanist architects in measuring the architectural ruins of Rome. The drawings of the architects were equivalent to the drawings of the anatomists. These architects filled their notebooks with drawings of anatomical fragments of classical buildings. Their graphic annotations were not merely records of historical pieces and patterns, but, rather, carefully done bodily studies of parts of buildings. Autopsies of classical edifices, they were a direct visual exploration, as the word autopsy indicated in its original Greek meaning. These graphic logs were the basis for writing the story of future architecture by listing the numbers, locations, figures, properties, and compositions of classical building elements. Vesalius's *Fabrica* demonstrates the central role of anatomical representation in the constitution of medical and human knowledge. Anatomical representation is also at the core

12.5
Collage of Vesalius' and
Rusconi's Anatomical Images

of the *Dieci Libri di Architectura*, a work by Giovanni Maria Rusconi, an almost forgotten architect of the sixteenth century, who made a beautiful set of illustrations for a text never completed. Rusconi completed his drawing work in 1553, a decade after the publishing of Vesalius's *Fabrica*. The illustrations were then printed posthumously in 1590. Consisting of one-hundred and sixty elegant woodcuts, Rusconi's illustrations reveal basic evidences on the construction practices of the sixteenth century. Representation of the architectural orders are mixed with depictions of the construction details, materials and materials preparation, and working phases accompanied by brief explanatory descriptions.

Rusconi's drawings present the same facture of Vesalius's anatomical illustrations. The Vesalius anatomical figures are not inert corpses—they move in a beautiful landscape displaying a great dignity. They stroll at the feet of the Eugenean hills, located between Padua and Venice. Following an established tradition, these anatomical figures are shown through successive stages, and, as they become stripped first of their skin, then of their musculature, they conform with the surrounding natural landscape gradually made barren by the passage of the seasons from spring to winter. In Rusconi's drawings, we witness the same representational procedure: the bodies of buildings are exposed through successive stages of dissection as they become stripped of their plastery skins to show the structural skeleton. A striking instance is Rusconi's use of the dissection sequential process to show the processes of derivation of many classical details.

Dealing with abdominal viscera in Book V of the *Fabrica*, Vesalius did not show his anatomical demonstration within real corpses. Instead, his anatomical findings were represented within the remains of famous antique sculptures. Rusconi followed the same procedure: he showed the 'viscera' of buildings within the ruins of antique edifices. Rusconi's drawings were trying to raise the role of construction documents into monuments of architectural science, just as Vesalius was trying to raise anatomical understanding above the world of objectified human violation. For Vesalius the bodies of his anatomical illustrations are not residual dead matter containing only the potential to be described, organized, and disciplined, but rather they are representations of embodiment of human culture. Similarly for Rusconi, building details are not lifeless building stuff to be designated, classified, but rather eco-niches of human embodiment fostering architectural imagination.

In the current state of anatomical investigation, physicians have exploited a new kind of knife and a new system of representation—a bloodless knife that can write the stories of the human body on the electronic screen. Medical imaging makes observable that which is hidden in the body. Physicians probe through bodies performing painless, benign vivisections; they use sonography, angiography, tomography, etc., with new digital knifes that allow non-invasive electronic vivisection and displays of anatomic structures.

In architecture, the use of true "electronic vivisection" of buildings and models as a base for generating construction drawings is poisoned by the practice of imitating established representations—an imitation that does not model processes but only mimics products. In drawing buildings, the substance and the form of the contents and physical expressions are not two separate aspects, but they are embodied as one in the built object.

An assessment of the parallel medical imagining can be the springboard to foster a better mastery of the role of architectural imagination. The bodies of architecture surround our bodies; architecture and the human body are one in front of the other and, between the two, there is not a frontier, but a contact surface. The use of imaging tools should offer a way of writing and reading architecture, an imagining which can feed architectural imagination by rearranging into a meaningful whole the shattered world in which we live.

Chapter thirteen

The Light of Drawing Imagination

An active member of the Neoplatonic School of Chartres and a follower of sensible Salernitan dietetic principles, William of Conches, a Norman scholar born toward the end of the eleventh century, gives us a fantastic description of the metabolic nature and origin of the light of imagination.[1] Conches drew from Galen the conception of food being changed from matter into light by a sequence of conversions. The first conversion occurs in the liver where the digested matter becomes natural virtue, which then trickles through the heart where it is changed into spiritual virtue. Finally it exudes within the brain where it transmutes in a luminous wind.[2]

In architectural dreaming, this wind, the pneumatic light of human imagination, edifies our minds and visions of building. This luminous wind powers the dual act of constructing images and construing meanings within a tectonic environment. If we consider windy architectural drawings, the luminous effect sets in motion architectural imagination. Architectural drawings deal with two

13.1
Dreaming Architecture

kinds of light: a light that we see and a light that makes us see, and this latter radiance is generated by the action of the spent light of the ink, the graphite, the charcoal left by pens, pencils, crayons, and any other drafting media on the luminous surface of paper.

Louis I. Kahn has sensitively called "the gift of light" what takes place in the act drawing; he recognizes the power of marks on paper to give luminosity, a result of the contrast between the lightness of paper and the darkness of the lines drawn on it. Kahn searched this effect in all his diagrams and sketches presenting his conceptual chiasmus of "silence light and light to silence".[3] For Kahn, light was not only an instrument of our perception of things, but the very source of matter itself:

> "You were made from light and therefore you must live with the sense that light is important. Without light, there is no architecture."[4]

Both materials made with byproducts of firelight, the India ink and the charcoal, are expired light capable of becoming carriers of inspired illuminations:

> "I sense Light as the giver of all presences, and material as spent Light. What is made by Light casts a shadow, and that shadow belongs to Light. I sense a Threshold: Light to Silence, Silence to Light an ambiance of inspiration, in which the desire to be, to express, crosses with the possible."[5]

The byproducts of firelight deliberately evoke or induce sensory joining in which the real information of one sense is accompanied by a perception in another sense through a cross-modal mapping device. This is virtual synesthesia or synthetic synesthesia: the selected drawing media becomes an inducer and the result is a going beyond mere information, but it becomes a source of impetus for imagination. To have imagination entails much more that having a functioning organ of vision: it is essential to know how to construct the image through all our senses.

13.2
Indirect Representation of Light

To Make Sense in Drawing

To truly appreciate the synesthetic hypothesis that I am going to make about Scarpa's drawing imagination you should imagine that you are reading this chapter sitting at one of many cafés scattered along the Zattere waterfront in Venice, during a pleasantly warm mid-summer night, while enjoying a few multicolored Popsicles and a portable CD-player is playing Luigi Nono's piece entitled, "A Carlo Scarpa, Architetto, ai suoi infiniti possibili".[6] In these cross-modal associations—Venice smells, colored sweet ice, microintervals music—the elicited sensations are both emotional and noëtic, and the phenomenon of synesthesia makes virtual perceptions work together with normal sensory perception, rather than replacing one perceptual mode for another.

Synesthesia can give radical insights into the multi-modal nature of Carlo Scarpa's drawing and teaching by merging the delight of res extensa with the

The Light of Drawing Imagination

judgment of the res cogitans in cross-sensual emotive constructs. Scarpa made use of drawing even when following logical or other rational procedures of critical thinking could easily solve the problem at hand. In his drawings the roles of reason and emotion are reversed. Creativity is an experience, not an abstract idea, and a mind that incessantly analyzes rationales impedes that experience. The drawing surface and its working together with the drafting media are Scarpa's essential expression of his synesthetic experience as inauguration of architectural imagination. By practicing synesthetic mediations or appropriations Scarpa sees architecture in a different light, an interior light. He uses the data acquired by one sense during the facture of drawings to project perceptions in another sense in future architectural artifacts. This synesthetic act of projection is the fundamental nature of Scarpa's conceiving of buildings.

Scarpa's concerns in material substances and their transformations and transubstantiations in the built world can be recognized through a synesthetic understanding of his drawing procedures. Scarpa is using his drafting media and skills to solve and test, through subjective synesthesia, objective inter-modality and inter-media problems of architecture. The "making sense" of a projected architectural object becomes an integral, indivisible, simultaneous process by which a construction will sound, look and feel good as colored markings resonate, appear and test good in the drawings. This happens because in the reality of the constructed world the distinction between "sensation", "perception" and "emotion" are mere cognitive abstraction.

A substantiating musing about the powerful role ascribed by Scarpa to the act of drawing by merging sensorial perceptions and emotional notations is that if we go along for a moment with the professional separation between subjective informal preparatory drawings and objective formal construction drawings, the logical conclusion is that formal construction drawings being objective should have been easily codified. Nevertheless, architects have had an incredibly hard time in agreeing on construction notations, a predicament which probably extends back to the Biblical Babel Tower, turris confusionis, and its architect Nimrod's rave, "Rafel mai amech sabi almi", meaningless to anyone but himself.[7] Each office, each architect has an individual system of notation. After a confusing beginning, Western musicians have mostly agreed on a system of notation, but architects have not been able of doing so in spite of the many unification and standardization attempts made by governments and professional associations. The reason is simple, the process of figuring out "sound edifices and structures" is in reality a synesthetic process because a normative cannot give a satisfactory response to the question of the subjective condition of synesthetic perceptions.

Synesthetic drafting acts within the conditionality of architectural perceptions and judgments and their applicability to others. Since their beginning, architectural drawings have evolved within specific manifestations of non-verbal thinking and tacit knowledge, realized by either involuntary or purposeful comparison of the impressions of different modalities, drawing from structural or semantic and, most of all, emotional similarity. Drawings become aural-aromatic-chromatic-visual substitute for flavoring buildings. The mixing of factual lines and non-factual demonstrations is that architects, in their tracings, are not making transparent notations, but synesthetic images.

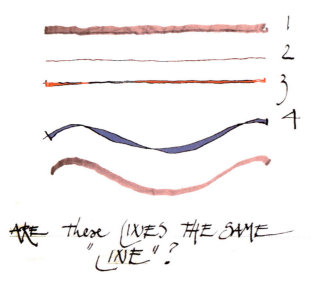

The most commonly known synesthesias are the chromo-graphic and the chromo-aural. A little known allegoric description of the phenomena is told in *Gargantua and Pantagruel,* a prominent book in Carlo Scarpa's library. An interpretative reading of the Rabelaisian allegory may make clear the synesthetic nature of architectural drawing. In the Fourth Book, Francois Rabelais tells that, while traveling the Nordic Seas, Pantagruel and friends hear startling sounds, but cannot find the source. The boat captain explains that they have reached the border of the Frozen Sea where at the beginning of winter there was a terrible battle between the Arimaspians (One-Eyed-People) and the Nephalibates (Cloud-Dwellers) and the clatter that they are hearing is generated by the thawing of the frozen sounds and cries of the battle:

> "Here, here, said Pantagruel, here are some that are not yet thawed. He then threw us on the deck whole handfuls of frozen words, which seemed to us like your rough sugar-plums, of many colors, like those used in heraldry; some words gules (this means also jests and merry sayings), some vert, some azure, some black, some or (this means also fair words); and when we had somewhat warmed them between our hands, they melted like snow, and we really heard them, but could not understand them, for it was a barbarous gibberish. One of them only, which was pretty big, having been warmed between Friar John's hands, gave a sound much like that of chestnuts when they are thrown into the fire without being first cut, which made us all start. This was the report of a field-piece in its time, cried Friar John."[8]

In describing the *glace et lumier* ciphering of the sounds, this English version is reasonable—the translator used heraldic color replacement—but not accurate; the expressions used by Rabelais to describe the substantial look of the

frozen sounds are "des motz de gueule, des motz de sinople, des motz de azur, des motz de sable, des motz dorez". Pantagruel is handling and thawing not merely verbal sounds but meaningful frozen colored orders of things, as something made in a medium (air waves) and converted in another medium (heraldically colored ice); a consubstantiation that makes visible and palpable the sound configurations as the material form of iced-up sounds.

Investigating the mapping of a structure, originally composed in one medium, onto another structure in another medium is the fundamental undertaking of Scarpa's architectural drawings. To create, view, or interpret an architectural drawing is not usually acknowledged to involve multiple senses since vision is considered the only sense needed to accomplish these tasks. Produced first with concerns for specific physical events, these drawings explore synesthetically all the sensory necessities of architecture.

Infused with an "invisible tincture" Scarpa's drafting elaborates a thoughtful architecture. On paper, he created rooms for thoughts, meanwhile planning for human order and disorder. Through a drawing and blending of formal and informal notations, and carefully drafted lines and freehand lines, he traces raw thoughts that he then constructs or deconstructs through a variety of formal, conceptual, and physical actions performed on paper that anticipates the yet to come conceptual and physical events of the building. To make sure that architectural ineffability and immaterialities are not, will not and were not subordinate to pure visual formalism, Scarpa's drawing aims at a balanced concentration of drawing substances. Scarpa's drawing factures in their transformations and consubstantiations reveal vital differences between what buildings are in themselves (their substance) and their perceptible qualities or characteristics (their accidents). The architectural substance underlies visible, tangible, measurable qualities. A substance in itself is not evident, materially quantifiable, or measurable because it has no extension but its accidents are quantifiable and the appearances of architecture include all those outward characteristics that can be perceived by the senses of sight, taste, touch, smell and hearing. Scarpa achieved "architectural accidents", by guiding drawing accidents within synesthetic conversions.

The first thing that architectural students—generally third and fourth year undergraduates—about to take Scarpa's design studio learned through the school's grapevine was that a major change had to take place in their "drawing habits". They would no longer be required to present their work traced in china ink and rendered with shadows made with retini (transferable or adhesive half-tone screens) on carta da lucido. This was the dominant presentation method required by the Milanese architects teaching in Venice (Ignazio Gardella, Franco Albini and others). These drawing were considered a necessary condition to show a pseudo-professional efficiency at that time when the cyanotype duplication of drawings was assessed as the most efficient procedure for architectural exchanges of communications. The implicit requirement of Scarpa's studio was that non-duplicable drawings were to be traced on Bristol board or similar material using a full range of colored pencils and pens. The first attempts by the students were too often drawings with blue skies, red bricks, green grass and gray concrete, black poché and terra-cotta parterre. Unfailingly, these drawings dissatisfied and frustrated Scarpa, who after examining and carefully touching them, used to urge his assistants to explain to the students that the colors used in the drawings were not to suit a process of material identification or to give three-dimensional pseudo-effects of the building, but to make architectural ideas present and morphed with non-visible phenomena and colored with meanings.

The ongoing quarrel on the use of colors between Scarpa and the students was the analogical relationships between pigments on paper and colors in the constructed world. The colored drawings of the students where based on photographic and photometric definition of hues and tints whereas Scarpa's drawing factures were performed within a phenomenological and anagogic understanding of the use of colors. The red of a waxy pencil, the red of a brick and the red of an India ink could be identical under a photometric comparison, but if applied in a drawing, according to Scarpa, they are dissimilar colorations carrying different cognitive and emotional natures, and opening a view to what is beyond. In a synesthetic perception, the marks of those reds cannot substitute each other, especially if they are simultaneously perused and felt by running the fingers over the drawing surface.

Although Rabelais never reveals who won the battle of the Frozen Sea, in Scarpa's use of drawings, the Cloud-Dwellers, the perceivers of nuances, are the winners against the perspectival or photographic rulers, the One-Eyed People. In the inaugural address of the 1964–65 IUAV Academic Year, Scarpa stated:

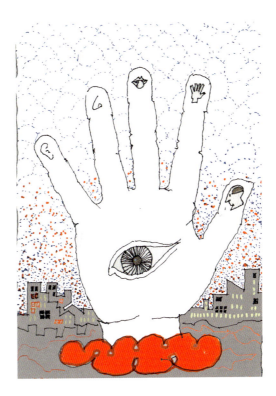

"What I want to say is that the sense of space is never given by a pictorial order but always by physical phenomena. Modern art has enabled us to see certain phenomena with new eyes and to make discoveries of primary importance about natural facts."[9]

For Scarpa, drawing factures were a never-ending alternation between the representable and non-representable. Consequently, the drawn surface had to be made an anagogic shimmering manifestation of architectural desire instead of being precipitated in a transparency by which the drafted representations were not through or within the drawings but merely photographic appearances denying any reflection of architectural perceptions.

"Photographs are of no use: a drawing is useful. Take a photograph and a drawing. I understand the drawing better. A bad photograph is a public act of falsification. The human eye is better than the camera, because it is mobile, and a camera though you cannot reproach it for anything regard to it does not state anything true, everything is false; or else, if it is a great photographer who is taking the picture and he seizes a particularly illuminating angle of view, and it is the artistic instinct of the photographer which is involved instead of colors, pencil or pastel strokes."[10]

Architectural drawings are metaphors, not in the literal meaning, but factually they are a carry over, a moving of sensory information from one modality to another modality, from one set of emotions to another set of emotions. Photo-rendered drawings are merely stylistic deceptions; they are comparable to the cardboard and plaster cakes arranged on bakery shelves or the trays of plastic sushi displayed in Japanese restaurants' windows. They look good to a photo-graphic eye, but they are not projecting any valid quality of the real food since the accidents of cutting, baking, cooking or tasting are not consubstantiated into the casting and coloring of plastic or plaster.

Photo-rendering wastes everyone's resources, as, in time, they have to be replaced by procedural representations conveying the past, dealing with the present and casting the future, because in the architectural imagination there are no dead ends, but rather a continuous set of connections. If an anticipated or discerned percept gets in the connective system, it flows through a different sensorial path and the crossing over generates interferences and interfacings which makes the devising of new buildings possible by using parallel sensorial realms. In other words, if we were to dream again of being at the Zattere, our popsicles would let us know the whispers frozen in their heraldic colors.

EXERCISE #9

The Single Drawing

The drawings developed for the construction of an edifice are strictly a process of transmutation by which the facts of an architectural project become the reality of any building. Through an act of construction, a sharp transmutation takes place and drawings develop into transfigured buildings. Freehand draw-ings are tense modes of representation equipoised between magical-associative (symbolic) and logical-dissociative (allegorical) forms. In magical-associative representations, the symbol and the symbolized merge, and in the logical-dissociative, a relation of disjunction operates between the symbol and its object. Because of these magical-associative representations, what Aby Warburg said in his famous lecture on the serpent ritual can be applied to architects:

> "They stand on the middle ground between magic and logos, and their instrument of orientation is the symbol. Between a cul-ture of touch and a culture of thought is the culture of symbolic connection."[11]

Trained to use the interaction existing between paper and pencil, between touch and thought, architects elaborate conceptual and cognitive represen-tations of designs. With the iterative act of freehand drawings, they mediate between the sensible and the intelligible, between the visible and the invisible parts of architecture. Their freehand drawings, vivid materialization of touch and symbol, become charts of a cosmos suggesting an ordered system of ideas between tracing and envisioning.

Homologous to a Beaux-arts analytique, but less prescribed in structure, this exercise is based on a technique that presents multiple scales and multiple projections on the same drawing board. It is a technique that allows explora-tion and process development while providing, at its completion, a cogent end

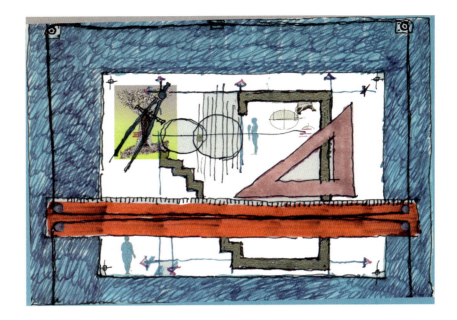

product. In many cases, these drawings are detail-oriented and focus more often on parts than on a view of the whole. Rather than describing a set of specific dimensions, these analytique techniques lay out a set of guiding construction principles for builders. Specific ordering principles help the builder to resolve joints and contradictions.

For this exercise, the drawing is restricted to a single sheet of paper for the entire development. All work is to be developed on one surface including sketching, study of precedents, technical detailing, and all this is done, using at the same time, multiple drawing scales. An abbreviated description of this drawing exercise might include the following steps:

1. Use only a single sheet of 70 x 100 drawing paper (double-ply Bristol board or similar).
2. Start by transferring a few small topic-appropriate images (line-work transfers better than photos) to the board perimeter with a xylene transfer marker.
3. Draw some light construction lines of existing conditions of the site at a scale that takes up approximately 1/5 of the board. Use darker pencils and inks only after you are sure about your decision.
4. While all work must be done on the board, sketches can be done in notebooks and can then be transfered to the board at a reduced scale.
5. Collage can contribute to the evolution of the drawing, but use sparingly as it is opaque and difficult to draw over.
6. Thin translucence paper can be glued over so that a palimpsest of lines, tones, and images accrues over the time of the facture of the drawing.

7. Light erasures are allowed but the notion is to maintain bits of everything drawn visible.
8. Instead of erasure, a light translucent gesso layer can mask modifications.
9. Colors should be used, but not in a natural way; no green grass, no blue water, no red bricks.
10. The drawing should be scanned periodically at high definition and part of it should be cropped and modified in Photoshop, or similar graphic programs, and used in collages for a final presentation.
11. Remember that you can also use the verso of the sheet, especially if some of the inks or colors bleed through and can be incorporated in the drawing.[12]

Chapter fourteen

Cosmopoiesis and World-Making

"In dreams the visual structure of thinking and the icons dissolve as abstractions and move back into the realm of illustration."

Otl Aicher[1]

In an architect's dream, architectural factures become demonstrations, meaningful and useful to other architects. Nietzsche pointed out that dreaming that you are dreaming is not the same thing as the pure and simple dreaming.[2] By "rediscovering the truth in the mythopoietic, preserving, the universality of dreaming ... and the continuation of the dream", effective tactics can be worked out that generate effective architectural factures.[3]

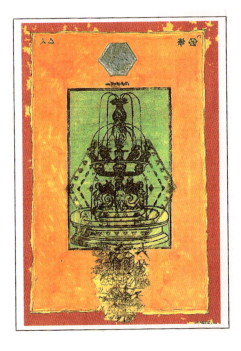

14.1
Dream Land of Architecture

One of the most famous illustrated books in the world, with its 172 wood-cuts and a pioneering typographic composition, the *Hypnerotomachia Poliphili, ubi humana omnia non nisi somnium esse ostendit, atque obiter plurimascitu sanequam digna commemor* appeared as an anonymous text in Venice, in 1499.[4] Hypnerotomachia is a composite term of three Greek words generally translated as the "strife for love in a dream". Poliphilo, the hero of the story, is also a composite Greek term and might mean "lover of Polia", or lover of many things.

The work, ascribed to a friar, Francesco Colonna, tells of a dream within a dream. After spending a sleepless night because of a lover, Polia, Poliphilo finally falls asleep at dawn. He dreams of falling asleep and finding himself submerged into a dream world where he traverses several landscapes containing ancient ruins, magnificent buildings, all represented in the book by enchanting woodcuts and by punctilious descriptions. These verbal and visual illustrations give durable and subjective value to a built environment that has only a doubtful or ephemeral objectivity.

Dreamscapes, as metaphors, are fundamentally important for architects. In an actual dream, dreamers may dream to be in a room that does not have any walls; nevertheless they know definitely that they are in a room. It is a demonstration and the "dream" is a hypothetical design of the unknown; thus, it is a substantial tool for acquiring knowledge. The dream is a rhetorical procedure, that sets the labyrinth of imagination where architects wonder about the material and hypothetical possibilities of things.

Alberti gives us an autobiographical example of how this act of architectural imagination takes place. In a passage quoted by Girolamo Mancini, Alberti attests that, not being able to sleep, he forces himself in a dream-like status, where he designs tremendous building machines and unusual building details:

> "During the night especially when the anxieties (stimoli d'animo) keep me restless and awake I am used to survey and build in my mind an unheard-of machine able to lift and to carry, to consolidate and to erect (statuire) tremendous and inestimable things. Sometime being deprived of these images, I created or built in my mind few well-composed edifices, with their Orders arranged in several columns, with unusual capitals and bases, and with proper ties and a new grace in cornices and entablatures."[5]

This "soporific" work of imagination is a constructive fantasy moving from a confused state of anxiety to a clear image of a construction embodying the human condition within monstrous expressions of building details. A latent theorization embodied in the Alberti passage is that the dream of architecture produces imaginative class concepts, i.e. demonstrative representations conceived under the aegis of Hypnos, the god of sleep.

Dreaming alters the notion of the imagination, within which all perceptions are ascribed to one consciousness. Dreaming challenges the limits of this consciousness by remaining outside the standard awareness, producing perceptions that are an in-between condition. The position of being in between or being located on a threshold is the condition of pending thoughts. Architectural thinking is all based on pending thoughts; both the Italian verb pensare and the French penser derive from the meaning of hanging or suspending something to give the subject time to consider it, an all-important phase in the process of thought. Architectural drawing is a facture combining action with thinking, the act of drawing gives architects the pause, in a dream-like state, to think about what they are drawing, which is pending in the drawing facture.

Pause—Pending Drawings

During the use of today's mass-marketed digital modeling, drafting, and designing tools, there are no tasks that require more than a negligible conscious attention. The monotonousness of the long processes of hatching, cross-hatching, scribbling, and stippling have been removed and replaced by the click of the mouse. The never-ending running of a wash to render a sky or a parterre is done in no more than two clicks. Even the randomness and complexity of graphic scumbling—the "brillo pad" technique—that uses layers of small calligraphically scribbled marks that, by varying the direction and shape, add more effective depth of perception than mere scribbles, is now digitally generated. The result is efficiency. Yet, it eliminates part of the original experience. No longer is there time for a mind to wander, no more a daydream appears during the rendering of the surface of a facade with whirling, scribbling, or cross-hatching shadow. The time to dream over a drawing has been efficiently, almost surgically, eliminated.

In a professional culture obsessed with efficiency, to daydream over a dull and repetitive task is derided as a lazy habit or a lack of discipline, or considered an inferior, useless kind of thinking. Nowadays, the time spent in hatching, cross-hatching, scribbling, and stippling is dismissed as a sign of procrastination, non-productive, wasteful time. However, recently, neuroscientists have begun to understand the role of this kind of dreaming that they have labeled daydreaming in a different way. They have discovered that daydreaming is an essential trait of the human mind, so essential that it can be considered as our default mode of thought. The findings suggest that daydreaming—which could occupy as much as one third of our waking lives—is an important cognitive state where we may subconsciously move our attention from the immediate task to sort through important problems.

Every time we slip effortlessly into a daydream, a distinct pattern of brain areas, known as the default network, becomes active. Studies show that this network is most engaged when people are performing tasks that require little conscious attention, such as routine driving on the highway or reading a tedious text. Although such mental trances are often seen as a sign of lethargy—we are staring haplessly into space—the cortex is very active during this default state, as numerous brain regions interact. Instead of responding to the outside world, the brain starts to contemplate its internal landscape. This is when new and creative connections are made between seemingly unrelated ideas.[6] Neuro-scientists argue that daydreaming is a crucial means to achieve creativity, a thought process that allows the brain to make new associations and connections.[7]

When architects daydream their brain's architectural function is at work. Instead of focusing on immediate specificity—such as the tectonic configuration of a window detail or dealing with pure functional issue of ventilation—when taking time in cross-hatching the section of the walls surrounding the window or stippling the glass panel, the daydreaming mind of architects is free to engage in abstract thought and imaginative ramblings. As a result, during this period of relaxation, architects are able to imagine things that are nonexistent, retrieve memories, contemplate "what if" scenarios, and come up, for instance, with a new solution for detailing the window element.[8]

Another powerful graphic form for architect's default mode of thought is doodling. A doodler switches into a different space and time, where union of body and brain in daydreaming sublimates the stress or boredom of a situation. A doodle is a type of freehand drawing made while a person's attention is otherwise occupied.[9] They are simple drawings that can have meanings, shapes, or just irregular abstract forms. Doodling gives the impression of a scribbling with no specific semantic context, performed while an individual is involved in another activity. To see and enjoy doodles as facture, one should appreciate their incidental character, the naturalness of gesture, and the intimacy of personal notes. The lure of doodles, especially in architectural hybrids, also includes the frequent co-presence of drafted lines and freehand tracing on a drawing surface—drawings that point to the ease and grace with which a doodler makes transitions between drafting and doodling meanwhile answering the phone or having any kind of conversations not related to the drawing under facture.[10]

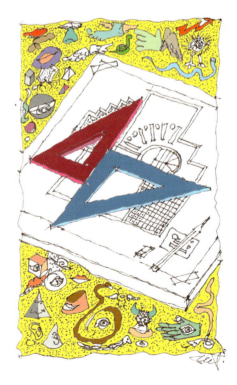

14.2
Doodling

With the digital drafting programs, doodles, scribbling, and hand-lettering have disappeared, gone forever. Clearly, the digital constructs provide for an abundance of side notations. Nevertheless, those notations cannot take advantage of the time and space influence that doodles have: to let one be somewhere else without really going away, but always present on the same page, in the margins or in the vacant spaces between the main parts of the drawing.[11] In architects' drawing factures, the presence of these side-pictures (marginalia and doodles), and space-filler textures for delineations and depictions (scumbling, random hatching, etc.), has a major role in the unconscious perception of the drawing itself. Doodling may be something that architects make and read because it helps to keep them on track, rather than being an unnecessary distraction that they should try to resist doing. Doodling aids concentration and perception of what is being drawn during its execution because it aids memory and cognitive performances.[12]

The best manner for understanding the role played by these graphic fillers in the perception of architectural factures is to refer to the earliest studies of unconscious perception. Unconscious perception is a set of processes by which we recognize, organize, and take account of subliminal stimuli and presences in our environment. What we sense with our sensory organs is not necessarily what we perceive. We create mental representations of objects, properties, or spatial relationships also on the basis of subliminal sensory information. When looking at drawings, architects may not perceive what does exist, and sometimes they perceive things that do not exist.[13] In these graphic fillers there can be hidden—intentionally or unintentionally—stimuli too weak to be consciously detected that can nevertheless powerfully affect the understanding of the architecture presented in the drawings.

A study conducted by Knight Dunlap, an American psychologist, showed that the Muller-Lyer arrows gestalt illusion could be induced by "stimulation of such low intensity as to be imperceptible".[14] In the experiment, the task for the participants was simply to indicate which line segment appeared to be longer. For segments without the faint additions, the participants showed no bias in judging either the left or right segment as being longer. However, when arrows were added, with a visual intensity below the level of conscious perception,

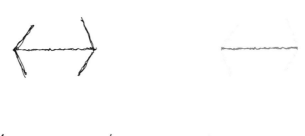

14.3
Regular Muller-Lyer Arrows

14.4
Low Perception Muller-Lyer Arrows

placed in opposite directions, at the end of clearly visible segments as required by the standard format of the gestalt illusion, the participants were more likely to indicate the segment with the arrow that pointed in as the longer one. Dunlap's conclusion was, "We have evidence for the belief that under certain conditions things of which we are not … conscious have their immediate effects on consciousness".[15]

A demonstration of the immediate effect on consciousness that could be evolved from the presence of doodling in the drawings is in the diagrams illustrating some of the texts written by Giordano Bruno, the heretic philosopher, burnt at the stake in Campo dei Fiori in Rome, at the beginning of the seventeenth century. Bruno filled up with hearts, moons, stars, ivy leaves, flowers and geometric decorations the diagrams illustrating his mathematical and geometrical treatises. This kind of detailed ornamentation is very unusual for a printed work of geometry in any period of Western history. A comparison with the other geometric treatises printed during the fifteenth and sixteenth centuries shows that such overwhelming use of this kind of ornamentation in geometric diagrams is unique to Giordano Bruno.[16]

Bruno thought of his geometric diagrams as cosmopoietic links between the construction of the realm of mathematics to the construing of the realms of metaphysical and physical understanding, and, in doing so, made his mathematical and geometrical diagrams a figurative discourse. His geometry is articulated on the verge of Dante's suggestion of a possible synesthetic crossmodality: "visibile parlare" (visible speech).[17]

In seeing Bruno's geometric diagrams it is easy to think that the ornamentation is purely decorative, added by xylographers to decorate the visual aids with rhetorical embellishment to make them less nonfigurative. The nineteenth-century editors of Bruno's work have cleaned the diagrams of all the space filler decorative effects and reduced them to meaningless, crudely odd and mundane geometric proofs.[18] The reality behind these alleged embellishments, however, is quite different. Bruno had cut most of his diagrams for his texts himself. Bruno's use of fleurons, entrelacs and flourishes show a translation in printed form of a marked degree of acute sensory perception to heighten the synesthetic capacity of the readers to grasp the supra-mundane aspects of his geometry.

Daydreaming and doodling operate within special conditions of time; as previously mentioned, the ancient Greeks had two conceptions of time, as expressed in the two gods, Chronos and Kairos.[19] Chronos marks a chronological or sequential time, and Kairos marks a time in between, an undetermined stretch of time during which something special happens. Chronos has a quantitative nature—it is a taskmaster—whereas Kairos has a qualitative nature and alters destiny. The very essence of the god Kairos—called Opportunity by the Romans—the youngest child of Zeus, is illustrated by Callistratus in one of his descriptions of famous statues representing the gods:

> "Opportunity was a youth, resplendent from head to foot. He was beautiful to look upon as he weaved his downy beard and left his hair unconfined for the South wind to toss wherever it would. He closely resembled Dionysus; his forehead glistened and his cheeks, reddening to youthful bloom, were radiantly beautiful, conveying to the beholder's eye a delicate blush. He stood poised on the tips of his toes on a sphere, and his feet were winged. His hair did not grow in the customary way, but its locks, creeping down over the eyebrows, let the curl fall upon his cheeks, yet the back of the head of Opportunity was without tresses, showing only the first indications of sprouting hair."[20]

The wings on Kairos's feet suggest swiftness, and that he goes rolling on through all eternity. As for his youthful beauty, it suggests that good looks are always opportune, and that a beauty that has withered has no part in the nature of opportunity. The lock of hair on his forehead indicated that he is easy to catch by these very locks as he approaches, yet when he has passed by, he can no longer be seized by his locks because the back of his head is shaven: the moment of action has expired, if opportunity is not acted upon immediately, as it presents itself, it is lost forever. To miscalculate Chronos is inconvenient. To ignore Kairos is inexcusable and deplorable. When we are daydreaming and therefore lose our sense of time passing, we are in Kairos's time; here we are totally absorbed in the moment, which may stretch out over hours. Describing or capturing a Kairos moment is fluid and beyond expression, because Kairos rules the unquantifiable time of daydreaming, during which our ability to adapt and to take advantage of changing, contingent circumstances is heightened.

As a facture, daydreaming constitutes and substitutes objects, the perfect tool for our mental motions. Because of its connate capability to alter and create perceptions, daydreaming is not only a way for conceiving the steps of architectural making in the drawing mode, but it is also the real way for reading the drawing of architecture. No other procedure allows the transmutation of the composition of lines describing a future building into an assembly of meaningful structures, rooms, and details. The merging of imagining and imaging into the same activity makes readable the architecture within a cosmopoietic framework.

Architects with their dreams and daydreams do not open the pearly gates for their modus operandi to enter everyday life; on the contrary, they raise the everyday to a higher plane of understanding, releasing the emotional contents of a physical reality. The types of representational media and techniques of depiction that architects use have a direct and lasting effect in the architectural interlocking of the subtle substance of the cosmopoietic framework that configures physical reality through the dream stuff, converting buildings into physical fabrics interwoven with dream stuff.

Verso Dreaming

The Architect's Dream is the title of a canvas by the American painter, Thomas Cole, commissioned by the prominent American architect, Ithiel Town, in 1839 and completed in 1840.[21] This architectural reverie presents a dreaming figure and a grand architectural vista showing edifices from the remote past. This oneiric composition stands out on a stage-like view, framed between heavy velvet curtains. The vista presents an architectural continuum on the sunny side of a Mediterranean inlet showing a hazily Egyptian pyramid dominating the skyline over an Egyptian temple. Two Greek temples are located in front of a retaining wall which is reinforced with pilasters and a hanging garden, and a round Roman temple on top of the wall. A Neo-Gothic church rises out of the forest on the dark side of the inlet.

At the center of the painting is placed a huge monumental column inscribed with the artist's name and the name of the patron. On the top of the column, in a post-prandium slumber, a melancholic architect rests languorously on a set of huge architectural treatises and folios of drawings—too much food for thoughts. He is looking backward and he is holding the drawing of the plan of a temple unfolded toward the audience. This blessed individual is a peculiar anchorite who, by living on the summit of such a column, exercises his architectural stamina to pursue the dream-light necessary for the conception of edifying edifices.

Dreaming architecture is a connoisseur craft for making meaningful drawing factures. In his Scientific-Natural Studies of Freiberg, Novalis (1772–1801) has indicated that the "peristaltic movement of the brain" originates dreams and defined daydreaming as a beatific circumstance.[22] This insightful statement opens up an amazing line of inquiry on the association between imagination, dreaming and the food for thought which can guide us through the dreamland of architectural drawings to figure out how and where the digestion and absorption of buildings and edifying events takes place. The importance of architectural dreaming lies in a thorough enlightenment of a person's awareness wonderstruck by the possibility of association built in the images. Through dreaming, any person can enter in any building. Mostly non-verbal structures, dreams are a way for thinking by using representations. Dreams are the way by

which myths are created. Oneiric images show the prospect of possible translations, conversions by which images can be manipulated through dimensional
combinations, scale changes and analogical aspects resulting in the creation
of new forms and understandings. During reveries, images are dominant and
a demonstrative semiosis takes place. During dreaming, everybody learns the
subtle art of representation since a dream is always a representation of being
awake or asleep. Dreams are not irrational instruments; they are efficacious
tools for penetrating the rigor of reason by enlightening the imaginal aspects
of human thinking.

The light of dreaming that Pavel Florensky, a Russian mystic and a sophisticated academic, has musingly theorized will be the clue guiding the following
considerations on dreaming architectural drawings.[23] Oneiric images show the
possibility of transformation, a translation that makes imperceptible the perceptible, since a dream is the first step toward an understanding of the emotional
nature of perceptions. Florensky sees dreams as something on the threshold
joining and separating the perceptible sphere of the real with the imperceptible sphere of the imaginable. The dreams are our sensing and making sense
of perceptions. They are the inverse perspective for the translation of the real
into the imaginal.

Florensky sees the dreams of the night as psychological, but the hypno-
pompic dreams, the awakening dreams, are the ones accomplishing the conversion from the sphere of the real into imagination. Under the aegis of Kairos,
a dream, in itself, can last a short instant in time, but the corresponding time
in the dream can last from seconds to millennia. Dreams are gates open within
the barrier separating the imaginal from the real. During dreaming, the speed
of the vector of time can be infinite and its direction can be inverted by moving from the future to the past. This inversion of time is essential for Florensky's
understanding of the role of dreams as analogous to the icons hanging on the
iconostasis since both dreams and icons open small holes in the iconostasis
enclosing the realm of imagination. The dream inversion corresponds to the
inverse perspective of the looming orthodox icons attached at the iconostases
of the Orthodox churches. For Florensky, dreams and holy icons partake of the
same ontology: they have the same causal inverse time, since dreams are fluid
holy icons and holy icons are congealed dreams.

Florensky gives an instance of the causal inverse time of the dream as an
opening in the wall enclosing the imaginal by telling the story of an individual
who dreamed of being involved in the French Revolution. Then, after intensely
prolonged and complicated adventures, this early morning dreamer finds himself in front of a Revolutionary Court. At the end of the proceedings, he is
sentenced to death by guillotine and he wakes up with a cold iron bar of the
bed-head pressing on the neck.[24] This inverse vector taking place in dreams is a
demonstration of how tempus fugit backward in the imaginal sphere.

> "In the dream, time runs, and runs fast, toward the present, inverse
> from the awake consciousness. We are brought on the plane of an
> imaginary space, by which the same event seen from the plane of
> the real space is seen imaginably as it was taking place in a teleo-
> logical time."[25]

There are two cogent aspects of icons that turn the vector of perception incorporated in them into inverse constructions of time. One aspect is the inverse perspective and the other is the gold of both background and "lumeggiature". The gold correspond to the innate light of the dream and the inverse time to the inverted perspective typically used in the orthodox holy icons. Illumination can both refer to intellectual or religious happenings and to the production of decoration or illustration of manuscripts, the two being closely associated. The gold functions directly with a minimal external light and potentializes internal light: it allows you to view illuminated drawing in dim light and also to have enlightenment. The gold leaf of the illuminations imparts a three-dimensional quality that modifies to the viewer time and space location.

Inverted Perspective

The representations of space in Byzantine and Medieval art as a reversed variant of perspective had several different sources; the terms "inverted" or "reversed perspective" were used by two art historians at the turn of the nineteenth century as expressions to name these deviances from perspective as based on central projection through a plane. Byzantine iconographic scholar Dimitry V. Ainalov (1900) used "reversed perspective" as a name for a stylistic trait connecting Russian Orthodox icon painting with the Early Christian tradition, and understood it as resulting from mistakes caused by the artists' inability to make correct foreshortening.[26]

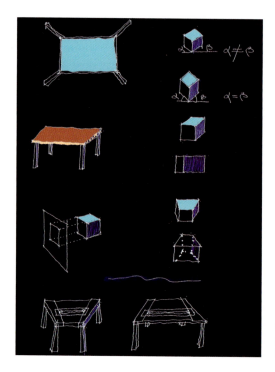

14.6
Summary of Different
Perspectival or Oblique Views

Cosmopoiesis and World-Making

A German art historian, Oskar Konstantin Wulff, suggested that, in the inverted perspective (der umgekehrte perspective), the image is oriented toward the viewer who is in essence inside the picture itself.[27] For the inner viewer the representation then follows the laws of normal perspective. For Wulff, a psychological cause is the reason for the occurrence of reversed perspective. As cause, he argued for the notion of "empathy", as described by Theodor Lipps in 1903.[28] Empathy is not a result of reflection, but an aesthetic primitive reaction before the understanding of unspecified presence as a thing.

In a remarkable essay, dedicated specifically to the inverse perspective, and in his lectures at the VKhUTEMAS (Russian acronym for Higher Art and Technical Studios) was the Russian state art and technical school founded in 1920, Florensky points out that through the inverse perspective we are looking within the imaginal sphere of human cognition.[29] In the essay, Florensky is attempting a demonstration of the existence of the inverse perspective through mistakes that can be seen in many of the perspectives before the affirmation of the so called costruzione legittima and in a few others done after the legitimization of the monocular view that took place during the Italian Renaissance.

Florensky, to demonstrate how the perspective of the costruzione legittima fails to recognize interior light as a necessary component of representation, analyzes the sequence of four famous incisions from Albrecht Dürer's *Painter's Manual* showing the few mechanical aids to be used for drawing a costruzione legittima.[30] The first illustration of the sequence shows a bedroom where an artist is making a perspective portrait—probably a legitimate likeness—using a portable perspective machine. A table on which is vertically set a frame containing a glass plane or a sheet of almost transparent oily paper constitutes the core

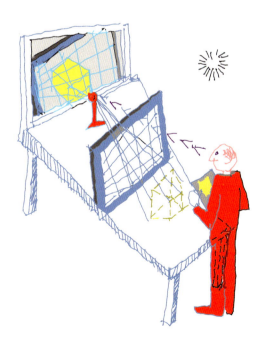

14.7
Super Lucinda

FIGVRA .II.

of this portable machine. In front of it, an adjustable contrivance holds the drafts-man by the nose in the required position for a fix point of view. This machine is an emblematic rendition of the rules governing the costruzione legittima.

The second illustration has often been misread and misapplied by ver-bose-gazers in love with a contraption called the "lucinda"—a square frame within which a grid of strings divides the space in 36 squares. The illustration in question shows a working table upon which lays a female model, while the draftsman is viewing her through a lucinda and he is getting ready to draw her on a piece of paper already traced with the same grid of the lucinda. The eye of the draftsman is trained on the wanted spot with the help of a miniature obelisk. In this apparatus there is already a quadratura an indication in nuce of a coordinate system that will eliminate sight from the site of perspective drawing.

The third illustration shows a bedroom—quite a dim space—where an artist is reproducing an urn on a transparent oily sheet held in a frame that stands between the artist and the urn. He looks at the urn through the oiled paper using an optical pipe attached to a ring on the wall behind him. The artist's eye is still part of the process, and moves deliberately following the tracing of lines by looking inside the narrow pipe, but the eye is not the hub of the construction lines anymore. The real center of this perspective is located in the ring secured on the wall to which the optical pipe is attached.

The fourth illustration, the most specific of the series, shows a very narrow room with a pair of artists and a pair of windows. One window is open and the other is closed; one artist is standing and the other is sitting. At the center is a huge working table holding a lute and a special kind of perspectival apparatus made by combining a lucinda with movable orthogonal arms and with a turning frame holding a drafting sheet. The perspective delineating string is connected with a ring in the wall and it is kept in tension by a counterweight, meanwhile a wand, held and maneuvered by the standing artist to delineate the contours of the lute, is connected to the other end of the string. Using the coordinated device of the lucinda, the sitting artist records one by one the "digital points" necessary for the construction of the image. The points are then pricked on a sheet of heavy paper stretched on a movable panel. No human or divine vision is needed in this perspective construction. The two fellows could be as well two visually impaired artists making a Braille rendition of the lute. Synthetic geometry has been replaced with analytic geometry. With their machine they can reproduce any three-dimensional object in a jiffy and probably with fewer distractions than visually able artists executing the same task.

A powerful commentary on Dürer's drawing machines is also a canvas done by a Sicilian architect observing a surrealist practice in the arts of painting and stage design. Entitled "Colloquium (Conversazione)", Fabrizio Clerici's oil painting shows all the drawing machines presented by Dürer sublimated in a super-drawing machine located within a perspective box. The surrealistic characters presented together with the super-drawing machine are a mask and an eyeball. The eyeball represents the sublimated eye of the draftsman and the mask is the object to be represented. Beyond the mask is placed a mirror that reveals the inverse side of the mask, demonstrating the condition of the rendering of faces with inverted perspective in Byzantine and Eastern Icons, which look at the backs of masks. The presence of the mirror delegitimizes the view of perspective and projects the potentiality of this super-drawing machine as a key to opening the gate of the realm of drawings that are real within a different tangible materiality.

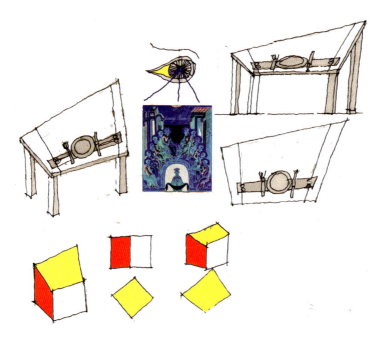

Icons

In some Byzantine and Russian icons one finds both nearby objects and buildings in the background depicted in very accentuated inverted perspective. This
practice and other ways of providing visual effects are important in these icons,
for they have significance in metaphysical terms. However, many art historians
in the eighteenth, nineteenth and twentieth centuries maintained that there is
no significant rationale beyond these inverted perspectives. For these art historians, painters, especially during the medieval times, were simply unable to represent on picture planes "reasonable" representation of the visually observed
objects, because they didn't yet know or understand how to apply the optical
laws of visual perception. These laws are necessary to produce a perfect image
that is almost identical to what we could see through the frame of a window. In
many pseudo-perspectives—such as herringbone, multifocal and axial—visual
irregularity and absurdities were skillfully concealed by the painters. The painters who did inverted perspectives did not even make attempts to avoid or to
conceal the evident geometric inconsistencies or absurdities.

Contradictory visual situations often arise, although we are not usually
consciously aware that this is happening. The viewing of a three-dimensional
rendering of a building is one of the most obvious examples. While admiring
a rendering of a building, the pattern of binocular disparities specifies that you
are looking at a flat two-dimensional surface. However, the shading, highlights,
texture gradients, and perspective variations are more parsimoniously consistent with a three-dimensional interpretation.

It is not possible to translate the perceived shapes of a building into a
two-dimensional surface of a drawing without distorting some of them. Those

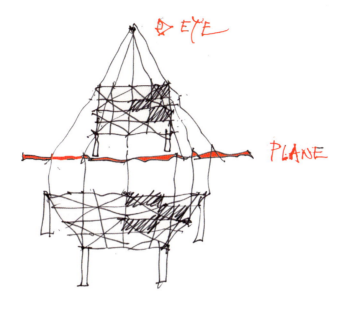

who draw, no doubt, understood this insoluble challenge a long time ago; the result was that in different cultures dissimilar rules were adopted for the depiction of objects by deciding which distortions should be accepted, avoided or minimized. This may account partially for the fact that many architects exercise the "right to distort" selectively in their drawings and sketches what they see or conceive. Distortion is the alteration of the original shape (or other characteristic) of an object and the distortion reverses the flow of architectural space, creating a disorienting, anti-naturalistic sense of space.

The aim of this exercise is to draw the perspective of a building, building element or the interior of a room first using an inverted perspective done as watercolor and with the sky or space around (ceiling in the case of the room) rendered with silver mirror-like-paint and then to draw a plan, section and elevation of it in CAD as if the inverted perspective is a traditionally correct representation of the building or the building element.

For instance, if you have drawn a surface as a possible parallelogram in the inverted perspective, the translation in the orthogonal representation should be a skewed trapezoidal surface. Lines that in the inverted perspective should be horizontal or vertical—because of our cognitive understanding—but, out of orthogonality in the inverted perspective rendition, must be represented out of perpendicularity and horizontality in their translation in the orthogonal drawing. The second part of this exercise is to take the orthogonal drawing and draw its object in an isometric rendition where the plan and the roof or the base, the top part of the building element or the plan and the ceiling of the room are both present as horizontal planes and connected to the visible vertical planes.

Imaginary Points

In 1922, having completed his book *Imaginary Points in Geometry*, Florensky asked Wladimir Favorsky, an engraver and xylographer, to prepare a cover for it. When Favorsky's finished the image for the cover, Florensky realized that the xylography demonstrated a particularly significant representation of the merging of real and imaginary and accordingly he decided to add a new chapter to facilitate the understanding of the recto and verso disclosure taking place in the print. In his explanation, he investigates the two-sidedness of the "incarnation of the abstract in a visible material point" and, furthermore, he points out the value of the ambiguous duality of perception that takes place in our perception of the world.[31] Some parts of it are visible and others are "visible in abstract" because of touch or other perceptual indicators. For Florensky, the crucial evidence demonstrated by the xylography is the existence of two worlds, a perceptible one and an imperceptible one and how they can exist on the same surface.

In architectural drawings consciousness deals with this duality of perceptible and imperceptible, split between the image of what has been directly perceived and the image of the indirectly perceived, through the intermediary of sensations. In these conditions of receptivity, there are two elements or two layers of elements, similar in content but significantly dissimilar in their position in our consciousness, and, thus, incapable of coordination, mutually exclusive. We should think of the sheet of paper as an infinitely thin space for images, something in the nature of a transparent film. This film is not yet, in its own right, either side of the figurative surface but the whole surface with both sides and all its thickness, however infinitesimally small this may be. The architect brings this surface into being. The next thing the architect has to do is to demonstrate clearly both sides of this film-space in all their qualitative tonalities.

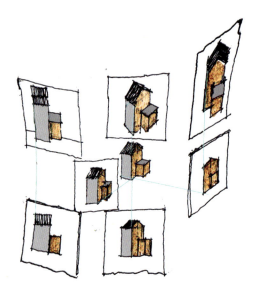

14.11
Axonometries and Obliques

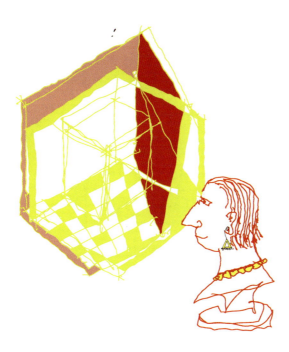

The architectural works and drawings produced by El Lissitzky (Eleazar Markovich Lisitskii) carry on in the graphic realm the same demonstration of two worlds existing on the same support. Florensky and Lissitzky were part of the same intellectual circle, both taught at the VKhUTEMAS. Trained as an architect, Lissitzky used quite often axonometric and isometric representations in his work. Prounen are a series of axonometricly arranged architectural looking abstract shapes executed by El Lissitzky from 1919 to 1924. Ambiguously, Lissitsky saw Prounen as an interchange between painting and architecture. The word Proun (pl. Prounen) is an acronym derived from "proekt unovsia" (project of UNOVIS), or from "proekt utverzhdenya novoga" (project for the confirmation of the new).

In drawing the Prounen, El Lissitzky took the pure, reduced geometric shapes produced by the Russian Suprematist Crusade and gave them an ambiguous materiality and broader cosmological array of functions. Prounen also offered infinite possibilities for the creation of new dualities in actual construction work. They contain the seeds of Lissitzky's famous horizontal skyscrapers project (1924) but also the recto and verso possibilities that were fully presented in the drawings done for his solo exhibition, the Proun Room, at the Kestner Society in Hanover, in 1923. The Proun Room is a chamber articulated with Prounen in two and three dimensions, and the lithograph showing the layout of the room is titled print no. 6, Proun Room from the Kestnermappe Proun, published in 1923. The print portrays the space in a collapsed isometric representation that shows the walls and the Prounen. These ambiguous axonometric representations used by El Lissitzky are factures projecting architectural events onto multiple planes of time and space. Lines in an axonometric drawing are always parallel and never converge onto a vanishing point.

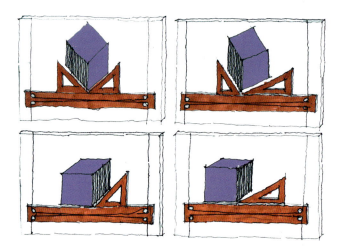

Axonometric projection gives us a counter-perspective. One point perspective centers one viewer at the time and inscribes the viewers into the space of the picture. Axonometric drawings, with its rejection of the horizon line and vanishing point, allows the viewers to situate themselves in any place on the two sides of the image.

In these axonometric representations, the apprehension of architecture deals with embodiment. It makes sense that axonometric drawings should be the locus of the creative embodiment of architecture because they are objects standing between two natures, the recto and the verso, the floor and the ceiling, the outside and the inside, situated on the border between direct and indirect perceptual apprehension. In these drawings, architecture is represented in a subjunctive mode since construction constitutes an activity that cannot be

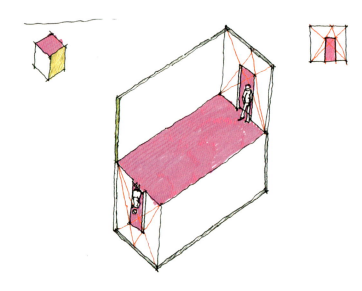

14.14
El Lissitzky meets Serlio

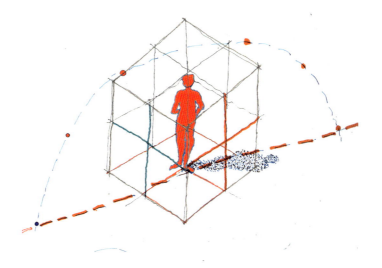

subordinated to another enterprise. Verso and recto drawings make perceptible what otherwise will not be perceptible from the recto point of view—the traditional binomial locution "recto and verso" if changed to "verso and recto" makes clearer the inversion of the procedure. As predictive models, verso and recto drawings are parched basis for tectonics. Constructing and construing verso and recto representations is a hermeneutical procedure depending on prior knowledge of possibilities since we can only recognize what we make. Drawings are often cited in discussions of architectural invention, but they are rarely broken down into their components as graphic tools that: 1) connect, 2) reconstruct, and 3) identify phenomena in telic mode. It is an act that establishes meaning through rich tectonic conglomerations of solid and dream stuff. The hermeneutics depends upon personal responsiveness, somatic engagement, cognitive analysis and a telic conception.

EXERCISE #11

Verso-Recto

Any architectural drawing traced on a piece of paper is a three-dimensional machine, although by viewing drawings on computer screens, in book and magazine reproductions or on the wall of art galleries we think that they are merely two-dimensional objects. A sheet of paper is a three-dimensional apparatus, a condition that is too easy to forget. Every sheet has two sides and a thickness, and because of the paper's materiality and its reaction to liquid media something interesting often takes place between the two sides.

In the jargon of the art historian, the front of a work on paper is called recto, while the back is the verso. The terms recto and verso to designate duality of images on a folio did not originate in the world of drawings, but came from the language used to describe manuscripts and books. In a book, open in front of you, the page on the right is the folio recto (right leaf) and the page on the left is the folio verso (turned leaf), recognizing the turning of the preceding page.

The semiosis of these terms is loaded with cultural values as they are applied to drawings. The Latin word rectus means right or straight, whereas versus, regardless of being merely an assessment movement, stands as a negative otherness meaning that what is on the versus is less important, however these significations have no value in the architectural drawings, perhaps the verso in architectural drawing is the constructive side, becoming a verso/recto drawing.

The development of the recto/verso condition is closely related to the use of paper. Introduced in Europe only in the late thirteenth century, paper was not in widespread use in the West until the fifteenth century. Obviously, its primacy as a support for drawings was not established instantaneously, and the medieval practice of drawing on wax or plaster-coated wood tablets continued well into the sixteenth century. While the tablets were convenient for working, the drawings made in this way were by nature ephemeral, as the tablets were always eventually smoothed or re-plastered for re-use. Other pre-paper drawing supports tended to encourage the obliteration of drawings once they had outlived their use. Parchments, made from animal skins, were strong enough to withstand scraping, and so tended to be re-used until repeated scraping wore the support away. This re-use through scraping and re-drawing belonged to the tradition of palimpsests. Since paper will not stand heavy erasures nor scraping, drawings executed on it could not be removed and consequently the need for the use of the other side.

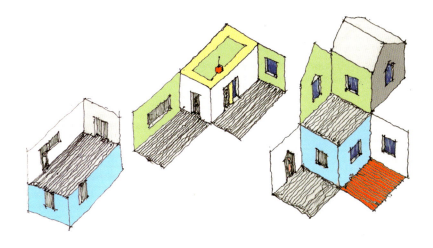

This drawing approach is essential for the making of a proper architecture responding to the unknown other. By producing a chiasmus of theory and practice, the verso/recto condition ushers us into a different realm from which we are to take back mysteries to our own particular realm. The cosmopoiesis of a verso/recto conceiving is to alter consciousness by conjuring up a proper architecture responding to the unknown other by consubstantiating the invisible into the visible.

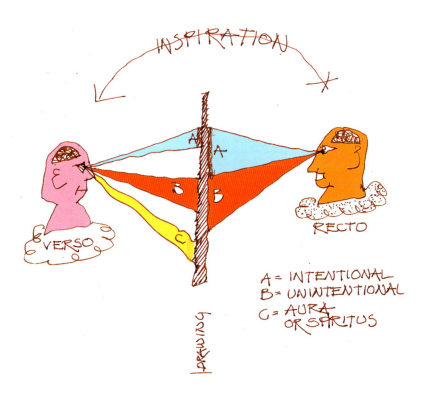

Select two sheets of one-ply porous paper that will allow ink markings to bleed through to the other side.

On the first sheet of paper draw with colored ink or a marker a section of a building on the verso, then turn it around and draw the elevation of the same building, taking advantage of the bled-through markings in any way you will see fit (see in the appendix what Scamozzi says about the quality the color and the bleeding of the ink).

On the second sheet of paper draw a plan of a building on the verso and its reflected ceiling plan on the recto, following the same instructions as above.

When the drawings are almost completed, oil the paper to make it transparent (you can use linseed oil, walnut oil or even regular olive oil). You can also use a clear varnish for this purpose. Be careful not to overdo it otherwise it will never cure. Allow the paper to dry, then complete and modify the drawings by using media that can work on varnished or oiled paper.

The initial coordination between the drawings on the two sides can be achieved by piercing tiny holes.

For many centuries paper was impregnated with materials that had a similar index of refraction such as linseed oil, poppy-seed oil, starch, varnish, etc. Today starch, mineral oils, and synthetic resins are used to raise the transparency of paper. From the middle of the nineteenth century, paper was made transparent through treatment with acid, mainly sulfuric acid. Through the effect of the strong acid, a coating of colloidal cellulose is produced on the fibers that is insoluble in water, fills out the pores in the paper, and makes the paper translucent.

Other ways to perform verso/recto drawings is to use a good light table or to use a very heavy tracing paper.

Historias Complures Noverit

"On September 26, of the year one thousand two hundred and sixty-four, at dawn, the Duke of Auge climbed to the top of his castle's tower, to consider for a moment the historical situation. He found it rather obscure."

Raymond Queneau[32]

There is insufficient awareness for the cogency of the multifaceted semiosis and intelligences taking place within the architectural making of drawings because they are always considered and presented as ancillary components rather than being probed as the most important architectural means. They carry embodied in themselves the essence and transformation of architectural theory. In elaborating a theory of architecture or in devising norms and codes, drawings are produced first and texts may be written later. The theoretical statements are derived from reading the sequential factures of architectural drawing. The ideal mentors for this transhistorical reading should be able to sketch plans and sections, meanwhile explaining the tales or novels of architecture.

In his prescription for an architect's education Vitruvius says "historias …
noverit", that is usually translated as "knowing history" but in reality the hypothetical future "noverit" does not mean to merely to know but is also akin to innovative
telling of events, that is to be able to generate new architectural storytelling.

The making of architecture is not a unitary and sequential project, but
rather a plurality of mostly irreconcilable interpretations, a chaotic situation of
contesting interpretations. In the work of the architect, there is no neutral space
between interpretations on which a debate between them can be conducted;
there are no neutral criteria to arbitrate between interpretations. Consequently,
from a heterodox point of view, architects should develop the skill of dreaming ahistorically—recto and verso—their storytelling following the paradigm of
critical path set by Raymond Queneau in *Les fleurs bleues*, in 1965.[33]

The story of *Les fleurs bleues* begins in 1264, with the aggressively feudal
Duke of Auge on the top of his castle in Normandy. After a couple of pages, the
reader meets Cidrolin, a peace-loving citizen living on his barge moored on the
outskirts of Paris, minding his own business—in 1964. The story unobtrusively
jumps 175 years ahead every so often, which means that for a while it stops off
in 1789. After a while, the reader realizes that the Duke and Cidrolin are each
dreaming of the other, and when they finally meet on Cidrolin's barge in 1964,
they realize it as well. *Les fleurs bleues* is an alternate merging of recto verso telling of micro-history between the extraordinary and the infraordinary.

Dialogic micro-stories of the extraordinary and the infraordinary are at
the base of assimilation of the processes of architectural conceiving. They bring
together the facture of a monumental public bath with the facture of a bath-
room in a public housing. The historical thinking of architects is based on a
discerning imagination. Their use of history for conceiving architecture does
not have a cognitive aim for a rational explanation of the past but with the use
of tectonic story telling they have a complete different set of cognitive aims
aiming to dialogue with human consciousness back and forth.

As a refined manner of fabrication, storytelling sharpens the virtuous
vision of architects by way of an exercised imagination. Any kind of historical knowledge is constructed rather than perceived through senses. George
Berkeley's diktat "esse est percipi" (to be is to be perceived) challenges the
metaphysics on which history, most of the time, had put its foundation, and
Giambattista Vico's dictum "verum ipsum factum" points in the direction of a
knowledge construction made by interlacing consciousness and making. Thinking of the power embodied in Vico's motto in influencing a school where fictive
drawing factures are made, Scarpa had it carved on the main entry gate of the
Tolentini (main seat of the IUAV), illuminating with gold leaf the acronym of
the school hidden in it by playing with the absence of the letter "U" within the
classical Latin alphabet:

VERVM IPSVM FACTVM = ISTITUTO VNIVERSITARIO
ARCHITETTURA VENEZIA.

This graphic play between Vico's dictum and the IUAV acronym is a perfect little
demonstration of the power of a micro-story to deal with the extraordinary and
the infraordinary moments and aspects of making and of humanistic culture.

The teaching of architectural history has as its primary goal the recollection of a factual recognition of the past; students must recognize buildings shown to them in slides, but why? What is useful in knowing that Santa Maria Novella is the church that, in the slide, used by the professor for teaching and then for the final test, has a blue car parked in front of it and that San Miniato al Monte is the one with a woman wearing a red jacket in its foreground? Recognizing them, without the easy use of memory props, but by understanding the tectonics, the geometry, the parti and the other architectural processes is not just useful but necessary to penetrate into and recapture the cosmopoiesis of the past and integrating it in a present cosmopoiesis, a discerning imagination that cannot be derived only from illustrations. Architectural history and imagination, therefore, have to be combined in a virtuous manner to generate novel architectural fictions. In other words, the storytelling of architecture based on the dynamics of drawing should help architects to shape, fashion, form, mould, arrange, put in order in what they represent, imagine, conceive, fabricate and devise because in the human movement embodied in the drawings they taste the sapience of the movement to be embodied in future building.

Postface

Architectural drawings are not traits of ideas, or operational fictions; neither are they empirical givens. They do not set constitutive or transcendental categories; or expressions of syntax, or language games, not even abstractions from ideas of order. Architectural drawings are forms of being, expressions of complex states of mind and experience. More precisely, the drawings that architects produce are fragments derived from a multiplicity of thought and serve varied epistemological functions.

The dominant explanation of architects' work affirms that architecture is knowledge and that edifices are done, first, by building complete images within the head, and later those images are chirographically drafted on paper or typographically fed in a computer. This explanation overlooks the reality that the architectural discipline belongs to another order than the order of explicit knowledge. Architecture and architectural drawings are about factures and tacit knowledge. Architecture belongs to the order of making, since architecture fits into the mercurial sphere of formativity, a manner of making that allows architects to perform a drawing, finding at the same time the way of devising drawing factures that lead to building factures. From the beginning on the drawing table to the end during its consumption, architecture is established on factures and embodiment and likewise all the in-between translations and transmutations in different drawing and construction media are established on the same duality. The realm of architecture ranges from a discerning drafting of lines, surfaces and volumes to a sapient construction of walls, rooms, quarters, streets, borough, cities and countryside contributing to the neural formation of individuals and society sense.

In drawings, architects become *spontaneously* able to represent knowledge that was previously embedded in effective conceiving procedures. Because of their drawing habitus, architects can conceive a building by recalling some episode from the past or by summoning up a train of thought governed

by implicit schemas and constraints. Only when architects develop cognitive awareness are they able to represent that episode in a form that allows them to insert new events, or alter it to provide new architecture.

In more general terms, the union of mind and body exploits knowledge that is already stored (both innate and acquired), by representing tacit procedures as explicit structures. Drawings provide architects with the means to consider this experience of representation. Tacit drawing skills allow architects to review an activity, recast them in other drawings, and use them to probe long-term memory, recall related drawings, integrate new knowledge with the old, and explore and transform it.

The transition from tacit knowledge to deliberate cognition is not easy. The embodiment of tacit knowledge is a natural part of drawing development, even if it is muddled and incomplete. Reflective understanding alone may be inadequate to drive the drawing process: bringing tacit knowledge into conscious awareness is no guarantee of being able to understand or control it. We have no everyday vocabulary to describe our mental processes to ourselves, but architects can slowly draw them. The increased mental burden of trying to reflect on one's own thinking can cause cognitive overload and this,

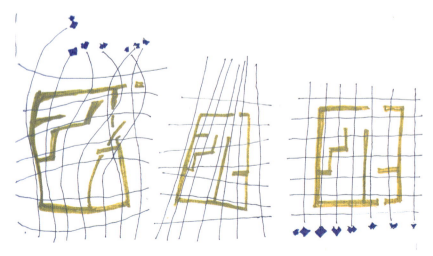

15.2
Deformations in Plan

176

Postface

combined with the attempt to work on incomplete ideas of building, can lead to a drop in the general quality of drawing. It is at this point that it is necessary to develop a drawing habitus, a coherent framework of plans, operators, and drawing modalities that can guide the process of knowledge by integration and transformation.

Architectural concerns in matter(s), material substances or material beings and their transformations and transubstantiations in the built world can be recognized through a learned synesthetic view of the drawing procedures. In drawing, the stimulation of one sensory modality reliably causes a perception in one or more different senses. With the possibility of drafting fat graphite lines, sharply thin India ink lines, waxy-red-colored pencil lines or gleaming gold marker lines, an architect can use any of them to draw a plan, a section or an elevation and the represented architecture should not change. The standard belief is that the selection of one media or another depends purely on the taste of the architect and has no influence on the represented architecture; perhaps the drawing will look different with different media and supports, but the built edifice will not change. If this condition of drawing is true, why are so many architects so particular in the selection of pens, pencils, charcoals, markers and papers to draw or sketch their architectural projections? It would be simpler and more efficient to use just one unified medium. A complex phenomenon hides beyond this behavior; architects are using architectural drafting media and skills to test and solve through a subjective synesthesia the objective inter-modality and inter-media nature of architecture. The "making sense" of a projected architectural object becomes an integral, indivisible, simultaneous process by which a construction will "sound good", "look good" and "feel good" in a multi-medial making of drawings.

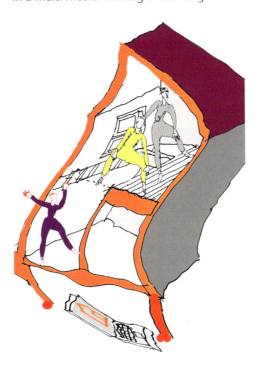

15.3
Deformations in Section

In the reality of the constructed world the separations between "sensation", "perception" and "emotion", are thinking abstractions. A German philosopher, Alexander Gottlieb Baumgarten, started the modern understanding of aesthetics; his original idea was the formulation of clearly confused concepts.[1] Using Baumgarten's powerful oxymoron with a little twist it can be stated that synesthetic drawings are clearly a confused representation of architecture, which is once more the process of figuring out "sound edifices and structures". It is in reality an individual synesthetic process because neither the normative nor the arbitrary can give satisfactory answers to the question of the conditionality of our perceptions and judgments. Synesthetic drafting acts within the conditionality of architectural perceptions and judgments and their applicability in relation to others' consciousness.

Embodied theories of representation resolve the relationship of the human sensorimotor system with the drafting tools as a way to embody complex architectural proposal. The sensations generated by the grasping of tools take part in a major role in developing the drawing. In drawing, the elicited sensations perceived by synesthetic approach are emotional and noëtic and the conclusion is reached when the lines rest in an emotional balance. As long as the searched-for result is not achieved, the drawing cannot rest; the battle lines and the drafting materials are changed until the intended nuances of synesthetic perception are achieved. Its reality and vividness are what makes architectural drawing so motivating in its violation of conventional perception of what a building should look like. Architectural drawings then move sensory information from one modality to another modality, from one set of emotions to another set of emotions.

Architects deal with drawings in a slow simmer: they stew, braise, bake, roast and toast. These are forms of deep cerebration, yet each one of those actions carries its own distinct gourmet or metaphorical cooking sense. The eye, the nostrils, the tongue, the ears and the skin are the vital gates through which human beings receive the nourishment of otherness and through those gates take place the amazing process of architectural thinking. Both cuisine and architecture are powerful expressions of a philosophy in the flesh that is dealing with the role of the embodied mind. Coming into architectural ideas is slow cooking and slow eating. The insatiate appetite of architects is not only for raw facts but also for elaborated translations of thoughts in matter and of matter in thoughts.

Complicated as it is to critically disentangle the purposes of architecture and cooking, it is a clear demonstration of the efficacy and elegance of human conceiving since we very easily understand these different functions when we experience them in context. In dealing with the res cogitans, we purely think, but in our sensual transacting with the res extensa we guess, suppose, surmise, assume, and speculate. This is the ability of forming an opinion based on inconclusive evidences. A subtle but important difference exists between the deterioration of evidences and the setting of opinions that are a fast boil of ideas. During the drafting of a building and its constructive details, an architect elegantly discerns and savors architectural objects by planning their causes.

Architectural sapience has a discriminating estimative character; in other words, it is a sensual reaction. A sensual reaction occurs immediately on

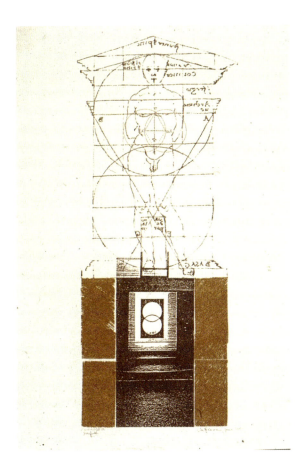

stimulus contact, before reflecting on the warrant for any evaluation. Rather than valuing a product after the fact, architects savor it during its making and in so doing they would sensually respond through the evaluative component of their architectural experience. By thinking about the built pleasure waiting in the future, architects set the path of its making in the present. The material at hand used for the translation is a figuring out of sensual images and the resulting delight is the catalyst of the architectural imagination.

Architectural imagination is one of those critical faculties of the human mind that resists any adequate definition. To describe it as creative, conscious, intuitive or insightful ideas elaborated through a graphic media is quite inadequate, because each of these terms will remain fuzzy under a deeper scrutiny. One might argue that a definition is unnecessary, since a tacit understanding of this phenomenon exists, and one can safely assume that everyone who knows how to live well can be engaged in thinking in architecture. If they can savor the art of living well they can delight in architecture since architecture results from the permutations taking place between the art of building well and the art of living well. A demonstration of the power of this merging is the case of those individuals who having lived in worthy architecture cannot go back to live in worthless buildings. Comparably speaking, an individual that has tasted the quality of a real pizza sold along the streets of Naples cannot go back to fast-food pizza because the art of living well came together with the art of eating well during the course of a pizza mastication.

Embodiment stresses the continuity and the motivating character of the relationship between architectural bodily experience and cognition. The neural and cognitive processes that allow us to perceive and move around also generate our conceptual mode and way of reasoning. Thus, to understand architectural reasoning we must understand the details of our sensorial system, our motor system, and the general mechanisms of life within architecture. In summary, reason is not, in any way, a transcendent feature of the world or of the disembodied mind. Instead, it is shaped crucially by the physical characteristics of our human bodies, by the remarkable details of the neural structure of our brains, and by the specifics of our every day functioning in the world.

A world-making, architectural cosmopoiesis, mirrors a drawing cosmopoiesis, both these kinds of cosmopoiesis require a body, meaning that embodied systems actively induce information structure in sensory inputs and outputs. In non-trivial architectural drawings, sensual perceptions and projections are all part of a cognitive cluster that parallels the cognitive cluster of nourishment. Speaking of food and buildings as the material embodiment, it is important to identify the ways meaning is manifested through their factures.

Inter-sensory associations are the basis of the art of cooking and eating as described by Filippo Tommaso Marinetti in his manifesto about Futurist cuisine. He advocated synesthetic banquets based on "sculpted meals": flavor enhanced, colorfully scented, and tactile food sculptures that will form perfect simultaneous meals. He calls for the abolition of the knife and fork for eating since they can give misleading pre-labial tactile pleasure and to enhance tasting

15.5
Possible Result of Farfa's
Stomach Drawing

he advises spraying artificially obtained food aromas and spreading them around with the help of electric fans.[2] The searched effect is a world in which the senses amalgamate; where sounds are seen and words and aromas have color; where the number eleven can be smelt; and the color gold tastes sweet. Futurists promoted a light responsive body, and acutely sensitive to synesthetic experience. Laughter was the digestive enzyme of the Futurist body, a body trying to discover new sensorial conditions.[3] "White and Black" is a recipe elaborated by the futurist poet Farfa (Vittorio Osvaldo Tommasini):

> "A one-man-show on the internal walls of the Stomach consisting of free-form arabesques made of whipped cream sprinkled with lime-tree charcoal: contra the blackest indigestion and pro the whitest teeth."[4]

Envisioning the mouth and the stomach as metabolic surfaces to draw on, not vessels to fill up, is the aspiration of Futuristic cuisine.

The drawing media are the essential components of the synesthetic experiences leading to the conceiving of buildings. Investigating the mapping of a structure, originally composed in one medium, onto another structure in another medium is the fundamental function of architectural drawings. Architects produce drawings concerned first with the exploring of specific physical events through drawings that create and explore synesthetically all the sensory necessities of dwelling. Drawings are imbued with invisible spices used by architects to link and to elaborate thoughtful architectural morsels. On the space of the paper, through drawing, architects are able to generate non-trivial thoughts to be served up in buildings.

A.1
Scamozzi's Frontispiece of his Treatise,
L'idea dell'Architettura Universale

Appendix

Scamozzi on tools and drawings

Vincenzo Scamozzi,
L'idea dell'Architettura Universale,
Venezia: published by the Author, 1600.
Translation from the First Book, Chapter 15, p. 49 and followings

On the instruments needed by the architect, of drafting materials, of models: instructions on how to make them well

Since many [architects] believe that the art of drawing well is based on the quality and the beauty of the instruments, they have strived to obtain ebony rulers, dividers, squares, and magnetic compasses made of gilded brass or even silver. Made by master artisans and very expensive, Princes and Lords, who collect them because of their beauty, more appropriately own these instruments. Yet, in the end, the people holding these instruments in the highest importance are mistaken because, in proper drawing, what really matters are the beautiful inventions, the grace of the forms and the liveliness of an experienced hand.

Although we know that nothing we have made could not be improved or made more perfect, many have become persuaded that we were using exquisite instruments, and having seen that they were plain brass ones, they became puzzled. That's why every individual should use [instruments] that best serve him, the ones his hand is accustomed to use and that suit his purpose.

We praise, and we have found through our own observation, that rulers must be made out of pear-wood, or apple-wood or jujube-wood (zizyphus) or rowan-wood (sorbus) either the domestic or the wild type, since they are noble woods, easy to work and stable during the changing seasons. These rulers should be four or six fingers wide, their length in accordance to the size of the drawings. Rulers could also be fashioned out of yew-wood (Nasso), or out of pernambuco-wood (Verzino), or even out of violin-wood, all of them being beautiful and aromatic. The rulers should be thin and absolutely straight, and on one edge they should be sharply squared to allow the marking of ink-less lines, [which should be] engraved either with the point of an ivory stylus, with the tip of a sharpening blade, or even with the tip of a blunt needle making a gentle impression on the paper. The points of compasses are not to be used for this purpose, because they wear out and become ruined, and in the end may tear the paper. The other edge [of these rulers] should be beveled on both sides for one third of the thickness. This will allow to trace ink lines without smearing the paper, and also will let to trace two or three lines without moving the ruler, and the draftsman's eye should be directed on the inside of the pen, not on the outside. Thick rulers are heavy, and make it hard for the pen to be precise, while with thin rulers, the ink easily oozes onto the paper and stains it.

Rulers or the wide alilade or diopter (linda) give very good results.[1] One of them being that, when held with the squared off edge up [away from the draftsman] they keep the sheet of paper nicely flattened down and even. For this reason we use them more than many other types, and across the middle of the ruler we mark an orthogonal line that is used to put down in an instant all the lines of the drawing intersecting at right angles. The other good result is that one can hold and move such rulers very easily with his left hand fully open and laid palm down; [maneuvering them] with four fingers; that is the index and the little fingers apply pressure and push the ruler forward, whereas the middle and the ring finger bear on the ruler and pull it back according to the need, all of these things that cannot be done with a ruler that is either narrow or slippery, as are those made out of Ebony or Ivory or similar materials; the ones made of metal can soil the whiteness of the paper. The number of [necessary] rulers depends on the architect's will, and on the length, width, and diversity of the drawings, and for that reason we have used two, three, or even five foot long rulers.

The compasses must be made of brass, rather than other material subject to rust; lightweight and thin legged, but sturdy and not shaky, as in the French manner: but they should not feel heavy to the hand, they should be held lightly between the first two fingers of the right hand [thumb and index]; and in regard to how many [are needed] ordinarily three are sufficient, that is one large, one medium and one small: having a large number of compasses is confusing, and it is easy to mistake one for the other. Their tips should be thin, and shaped in such a way as not to perforate the paper, which is a rather ugly thing [to see], and each compass should have an incision cut lengthwise along the inside of one of its tips; in such a way that, when dipped in ink, it would work like a pen when drawing portions of circles, arches, or other things of this kind. They must have rounded heads, or even better eight faced heads not too big; to allow the thumb and the middle finger of the right hand to turn the divider this or that way and to hold it still when needed with the help of the middle finger.

With regard to squares, the large ones must be made of pear-wood, or of other noble and well-seasoned wood, and the small ones made of brass, both types must be thin, and reasonably wide and constructed with great precision. We first square up the sheet of paper tracing parallel lines lengthwise and widthwise then we divide up the lengths and the widths of the plans using the rulers and strips of paper. Usually we lay out every big and important drawing without any further use of squares, because it is much easier, instead [using a square] many times we use a half of a sheet of thin paper [diagonally] folded crosswise twice. These are the proper instruments of the architect, and if he wants to use others, such as magnetic compasses and similar objects, he can do so if he pleases, for his own amusement and pleasure, but they are not necessary.

The quills must come from local goose, easily workable, clear, transparent and of medium thickness, because the ones that are thick are very difficult to handle when drawing, they also tend to split more than usual whenever more pressure than needed is applied, particularly those imported from Holland. They should be sharpened with rather long cuts in the fashion of an Eagle's claw, with a medium-thin tip which is to be slit with a very thin cut since they need to be sturdy enough to trace lines although when needed it is possible to trace extremely fine lines using a slightly dull penknife.

However, the quills used to outline and to draw capitals and similar objects must be somewhat softer and workable; [they are] better for tracing gracefully the double lines needed in the hatched areas. We praise this sort of quills because they are supple and do not wear off because they are not stiff and do not get dry all of a sudden. Also they do not deteriorate the ruler's edge as the pens made of brass or silver or metal generally do; nor do they cut the paper. At the most, only three kinds of quills are needed, one somewhat thick, one medium, and one thin.

The Ancients frequently used Parchment paper, a membrane obtained from the hide of young animals. We find especially in Gellius (book 19, chapter 10), shown by that Architect many sorts of Baths drafted on Parchment paper that was something truly refined to see, such as we strive sometimes to do, especially when it comes to truly exquisite things.[2]

Because many times we have received inquiries about the way we prepare the paper we use for drafting, we will oblige with some information. In regard to paper, one must principally consider thinness, density, whiteness, and smoothness, as even Pliny (book 13, chapter 12) says: therefore these qualities must be diligently obtained; whether the paper be of the Royal, Imperial, or Papal size, or of any other size: whether it is coming from Fabriano or from Lion in France or any other place where it is made of better quality; in order not to waste time and labor in vain, when in the end, as it often happens, the drawings do not turn out well. If the paper is fine and beautiful, it will be sufficient to rub it with a white, thin sheet of paper folded up like a letter; it must be rubbed this way several times lengthwise and widthwise; but if the paper is somewhat rough, then it must be evenly rubbed in every direction with a cowry shell (porzeletta di mare), or with ivory burners, or with a boar's tusk; but first, said paper must be positioned well stretched between two other sheets of very thin and very fine paper, in this way it will become even and delicate; but no markings from the rubbing should appear.

Whenever the paper is even rougher (as is the case more often than needed) then many sheets of such paper must be put one on top of the other and all of them together put in between other sheets of paper and must be well beaten. Afterwards it must be squeezed in a press, as bookbinders do, and left there for a few days. We have always prepared our paper in this way, and we have kept it for years to be used for our drawings: and with every passing day it became better; and it is quite suitable for washes. And all affectations should be avoided, like those often fancied by many professionals, such as some glossy papers and some that are polished, which even the Ancients disliked, as Pliny (book 13, chapter 41) tells us, at times even decorated with all sorts of colors. All of these artificial disguises ruin the noble arts and they are better left to the cobblers.[3]

In the process of drawing, care must be taken not to heavily impress the paper when tracing lines with iron or brass tips, nor the sheets of paper should be folded often; since, as all other materials, they tend to lose their stiffness and their strength, so that handling them over time they weaken and become easy to tear.

A definite rule cannot be given regarding ink, contrary to the opinion of some; because good quality ink can be found in a few cities. Although it can be manufactured properly with excellent Rumanian wine, or white wine, and it must be quite clear (because it absorbs the substance better), and with the crinkled Gall growing in the peninsula of Istria, somewhat crushed and left infusing in the wine within a glass vase exposed to the Sun for ten days, during the summer heat, stirring it every day. During winter time it can be heated often on hot embers; after that the liquid must be drained and to it one must add the right amount of Sulfate from Cyprus, or from Rome, which must be soft and smooth and finely sifted; it should not be the raw kind from Germany, nor the refined kind (because it cannot be used for washes) then it must be left resting for a day or two, then it must be sieved again through a piece of tightly woven wool fabric; and poured in a tightly closing glass container, so that its quality cannot evaporate. For drawing, freshly made ink is better than the one made months earlier, therefore (it is advisable) to just keep the gall-steeped wine at hand and to add the sulfate to make a fresh batch when needed. When using the ink, add a little of clear and crumbly Arabic gum, which gives the ink body and luster. Among very ancient memories we have found this recipe: … Una sit galla, mediata sit Gumma, Vitrioli Quarta, superaddas octo Falerni; Noctibus ista tribus simul confecta serene, Sepius hanc missa, & demum colata repone, Sic Atramentum tu scriptor, conficem crudum.

Even if we are considering that the old ways are better, and the dosage is of 30 ounces or one pound of wine, 2 of gall, 3 of sulfate, & 1 of gum, nevertheless, depending on the quality of the ingredients, there can be great variations [in the grade of the ink]. The excellence of the ink, something we have always pursued, is recognizable from the purple hue of its washes, which gives such elegance to the drawings, and from the fact that the slight markings appearing in the back of the paper are of the same color, which is a sign of the ink quality, instead of an ugly yellowish color, or reddish or even rusty; and the Inkwells must be made of glass, bone or some other enameled material, and must contain silk sponges, or Cyprus cotton wool those must be turned upside down every day, and the inkwell themselves should be well covered to protect the ink from air and dust, to keep it from being polluted and ruined. In addition to that, the sulfate corrodes all metals, causing the ink to lose the brightness of its beautiful color, and that's enough of this.

In order not to leave anything behind that might result useful to men of virtue, we will also reveal a memory device to easily remember the instruments belonging to the architect, which are also borrowed by other arts: the vowel letter A looks like an open and standing compass, with its screw in the middle to tighten it or widen it, and also like the level used on construction sites. The vowel E and the letter F look like the pen used to trace two or three lines simultaneously. The letter H represents the pantograph used to transfer the sites in drawings. The vowel I the ruler, also called alilade or diopter. The letter L the square; the letters M & N represent the movable rulers, or those that can be folded to measure corners; and the vowel O looks like the magnetic compass with the markings of the winds used to take down the aspect of sites. The letter T looks like a double square; the letter V represents the open divider in an upside down position; and lastly, the letter X represents the movable square used to draw all sorts of angles.

The use of models goes back to ancient times. Vitruvius mentions them in several places, and so does Cicero writing to Marcus Celius. It can be said the Model is like a messenger & explicit subject of the object that is going to be built: it is an Archetype as much as it is example, or model, as Martial says, and also Pliny Cecilius writes to Anthony; and as the drawing is a linear part of the process which we consider theoretically and as well as mathematically; so the model is a part which is a sensorial and acting demonstration.

Models must be made for public or private works of great importance: this is to the purpose of having right in front of your eyes a proportioned body, corresponding to the shape of the work which has already been determined to be built. In the model, it must be possible to see the length, the width as well as the height of all parts, and also of the walls, of the floors, of the vaults and the roofs which pertain to the building, and how the entrances and the courtyards and galleries, and the stairs and the halls and the parlors and other rooms correspond to each other; (they also must show) the quality of the openings and their proportions, to the right and to the left: so unified as separate from the body; and finally, in case the architect has passed on, it must be possible to see [from the model] what his intentions are, at least in a general fashion, so that no parts should be removed or made worst [later]; as in such cases usually happens, because of the scarce understanding of its successors, or because others on purpose want to make something different.

The model of Saint Peter's Church in Rome, which we have seen many times, an invention of Antonio San Gallo and made by his pupil Antonio Labaco, was 22 feet long, 16 feet wide and about 13 feet tall of our [Vicenza] feet, representing only a thirtieth part of the entire work. The cost of this model in labor and wood, came to 4184 Roman Scudi, additional 1500 Scudi were later paid to the architect.

Models can be made in different ways; but the easiest and least expensive ones are made of wood, and of modest dimensions; such as the oncia, the palmo, the piede or the braccio, divided in at least three or at the most five parts, can be used as scale for the small foot of the Model.[4]

Boards of pinus cembra (Alpine Fir) or Filarea (Mulberry) or linden must be prepared, well seasoned and quite smooth and planed to the right thickness; on the surface of these boards one must draw the heights and the lengths and all the partitions of the façade, of the sides and of the back; as well as those of the interior parts, with all the doorways, main and secondary, and the windows and other things belonging [to the building]; after this work is done, the boards must be diligently cut by the master cabinet makers, and then they must be assembled properly and glued together in the grooves; and starting from the outer elements or from the interior progressing towards the outer parts, then all work must be put together: as long as it is possible to see all the partitions of the rooms and of the staircases and all the other parts.

Afterwords, the columns and the pillars and their cornices must be applied in relief to the outer and inner surfaces wherever they are needed, and the same must be done for all the other ornamentations, and the floors the vaults and the ceilings must be built, but in such a way that is possible to remove them or to open them up and out of the way in order to allow the view of all interior or exterior parts, both in general and in detail. Such kind of ornaments could be done in maple-wood & other fine woods that are very white, so to imitate marble and other white stones, Pear-wood, yew-wood (Nasso), pernambuco-wood (Verzino), jujube wood and service tree wood, and other woods can be used to imitate stones of various colors; or otherwise can be painted, all the walls, & the floors, and the vaults, & the roof: all of it to imitate the way the building itself will appear.

We had some models of rather large size and considerable cost built for us and they were made so well and finished with such fine details by the clever masters of Vicenza, that it was possible to understand everything distinctly, and one could see clearly the parts of the pedestals, columns and ornaments, down to the single elements. One of these models was the one made for the Most Illustrious Procurators in Saint Marc Square, designed and commissioned by Us to show part of the edifice (Fabrica), and that model displayed the magnificence of that work and was held as unique and extraordinary, since nothing of the kind was ever done before or after in that city. No less reputed was the model representing of all the buildings surroundings the two Squares, that is, Saint Marc Square and the one opposite the Palazzo Maggiore (Ducal Palace), with everything that they include. [Said model] was eight foot long and five foot wide: and after Most Excellent Senate viewed it in a plenary session and determined to commission to us the completion of the buildings according to our invention and arrangement.

It is very appropriate to caution that the models must be seen in the same conditions of quantity, quality and clarity of natural light in which the built work will have to be seen; never to be viewed in enclosed rooms, nor at night-time in the lamplight: save from exceptional cases, because in such conditions no right judgment can be given regarding how harmoniously the rooms come together, and the enfilades running in both directions form one end to the other: how the openings meet and the luminosity of the sources of light, which must reach all spaces. Models must never be made using cardboard or other thin and flimsy material because such thinness cannot rightly represent the thickness of the walls and if it is done that way, all the parts would result so small that the model itself would be of little or no benefit, even not considering all other imperfections and problems.

We are accustomed to say, and rightly so, that inventions, & drawings traced on paper, and for the most part also the Models in relief, no matter how they are made, the ones and the others are only inanimate, soulless bodies, therefore they need the voice of the Architect, or of other person of science and value to express in words and to demonstrate in reasoning what they really are, to give them soul and speech. Because in this way people become excited and inflamed and decisions are reached concerning important and great ventures. It is just so that we spoke to the most Serene Doge Grimani, while we explained the above mentioned model of the buildings of the most Illustrious Procurators in saint Marc Square. We can say that Models are like nestlings so small; it is not possible to see if they are male or female, but when they become big, they become recognizable as eagles or as crows, because of this fact the Patrons can be easily mislead through the appearance of the Models.

Notes and References

Preface

1   Peter F. Drucker, *Peter Drucker on the Profession of Management*, McGraw-Hill Europe; 1st edition, Sep 1, 2003, p. 185.
2   Ludwig Wittgenstein, *Philosophical Occasions*, J. Klagge and A. Nordmann (eds.), Indianapolis: Hackett Publishing Company, 1993, p. 133.
3   Nelson Goodman, *Ways of Worldmaking*, Indianapolis: Hackett Publishing Company, 1978.
4   Giuseppe Mazzotta, *Cosmospoiesis: The Renaissance Experiment*, Toronto: University of Toronto Press, 2001.
5   John Matthews, *The Art of Childhood and Adolescence: The Construction of Meaning*, London, 1999.
6   André Castelot, *L'histoire à table, 'si la cuisine m'était contée...'*, Paris: Plon, 1972.
7   Paracelsus (Aurelius Philipus Theophrastus Bombast von Hohenheim) an alchemic cook that founded the discipline of iatrochemistry, or medical chemistry. Paracelsus, *The Hermetic and Alchemical Writings of Paracelsus*, 2 vols, vol. 2, London: James Elliott, 1894, p. 151.
8   Martin Roland, *Lexicon alchemiæ sive dictionarium alchemisticum, cum obscuriorum verborum, et rerum Hermeticarum, tum Theophrast-Paracelsicarum phrasium, planam explicationem continens*, Frankfurt, 1612.
9   Willemien Visser, "Use of episodic knowledge and information in design problem solving", *Design Studies*, vol. 16, pp. 173.
10 Ernesto de Martino, *Sud e magia. Introduzione di Umberto Galimberti*, Milano: Feltrinelli, 2004.
11 Fattura and Jettatura were philosophical questions in Naples. Nicola Valletta, *Cicalata sul fascino volgarmente detto Jettatura*, Roma: Canesi, 1961.

1 Architectural Iconoclasm

1 Deborah K. Dietsch, "Applying to the crowds: Model homes project perfection right down to the fake food", *Washington Post*, June 12, 2003, section H, pp. 1 and 5.
2 Gunter Dittmar, Kenneth Rogers and Emmanuel Ginis, "Architecture and Depiction Design Quarterly", *City Segments,* 1980, No. 113/114, pp. 4–7.
3 Luigi Pareyson, *Estetica, teoria della formatività,* Firenze: Sansoni, 1974.
4 *Ibid.,* p. 195.
5 Friz Neumayer, "The Work of Material Stuffs: Regarded Superficially", *Material Stone*, Cristoph Mackler (ed.), Basel: Birkhäuser, p. 10.
6 The etymology of the name, *grimoire*, can be traced to the Middle English *gramaire*, to the Old French *gramaire*, and ultimately to the Latin *grammatica* that comes from Greek *grammatike tekhne* (art of letters), with a sense of both philology and decoration. The Greeks took the Phoenician letters and used them to create their own script. These Greek letters gave rise to both the Latin and Runic scripts. The Greeks called these letters *gramma*, from stem of *graphein* (to draw or write) but *gramma* also meant pictures. An individual with knowledge of these letters and drawings, and how to use them was called *grammatikos*, and Owen Jones, an English Victorian architect, was a tacit *grammatikos* when he created his masterpiece: a stunning work of chromolithography entitled: *Grammar of Ornament* (first edition 1856), London: Studio Editions, 1986.
7 Michael Polanyi, *Personal Knowledge*, London: Routledge, 1962.
8 *Ibid.,* pp. 93–94.
9 Michael Polanyi, *The Tacit Dimension*, Chicago: University of Chicago Press, 1966, p. 4.
10 Pierre Bourdieu, "Postface", in: E. Panofsky, *Architecture Gothique et Pensee Scolastique,* Paris: Edition Minuit, 1974, pp. 135–167; English translation in: Bruce Holsinger, *The Premodern Condition: Medievalism and the Making of Theory*, Chicago and London: University of Chicago Press, 2005, Appendix II, pp. 221–242.
11 Ursula Mulder and Alma Whiteley, "Emerging and capturing tacit knowledge: a methodology for a bounded environment", *Journal of Knowledge Management*, 2007, vol. 11, no. 1, pp. 68–83.
12 Alva Noë, *Action in Perception*, Cambridge: MIT Press, 2006.
13 D. M. Mendelowitz, *Drawing*, New York: Holt, Rinehart & Winston, 1967, p. 11.

2 The Cosmopoiesis of Architectural Drawings

1 Charles Fourier, *Le Nouveau Monde Amoureux*, vol. 7, p. 130.
2 Peter Collins, *Changing Ideals in Modern Architecture, 1750–1950,* Montreal: McGill-Queen's University Press, second edition, 1998.
3 Ruth Cowen, *The Extraordinary Life of Alexis Soyer: Victorian Celebrity Chef*, London: Weidenfeld & Nicolson, 2005.

4   Alan Davidson, *Wilder Shores of Gastronomy: Twenty Years of the Best Food Writing*, Berkeley, CA: Ten Speed Press, 2002.

5   Carlo Petrini, *Slow Food: Collected Thoughts on Taste, Tradition, and the Honest Pleasures*, White River Junction, VT: Chelsea Green Publishing, 2001.

6   Vattimo introduced the notion of weak thought in the late 1970s. The idea was developed in a volume of essays entitled *Il Pensiero Debole* edited by Vattimo in collaboration with Pier Aldo Rovatti. Vattimo also discusses the notion in: Gianni Vattimo, *The End of Modernity: Nihilism and Hermeneutics in Postmodern Culture*, Baltimore: Johns Hopkins University Press, 1991.

7   Beatriz Colomina, "Architecture production", in Kester Rattenbury, *this is not architecture*, London: Routledge, 2002, pp. 207–221.

8   Ignasi de Solà-Morales, "Weak Architecture", in Sarah Whiting, ed., *Differences: Topographies of Contemporary Architecture*, Cambridge, MA: MIT Press, 1996, pp. 57–71.

9   Laura Maragnani, *Franco Fava, Leggende e storie milanesi*, Milano: Meravigli, 1981, pp. 121–122.

10   Walter J. Kilner, *The Human Aura Whitefish*, Montana: Kessinger Publishing, 2003.

11   Franco Mongini, *Headache and Facial Pain,* Stuttgart: Thieme, 1999, pp. 223–227.

12   Walter Benjamin, "The Work of Art in the Age of Mechanical Reproduction", in *Illuminations*, New York: Harcourt, Brace and World, 1968, pp. 219–253.

13   *Ibid.*, p. 251.

14   Antonio Averlino Filarete, *Treatise on Architecture*, ed. J.R. Spencer, New Haven and London: Yale University Press, 1965; Antonio Averlino Filarete, *Trattato di architettura*, Firenze: Biblioteca Nazionale, MS. Codex Magliabechianus (M), II, I, 140, text edited by A.M. Finoli and L. Grassi, introduction and notes by L. Grassi, 2 vols, Milano: Il Polifilo, 1972.

15   A.R. Luria, *The Mind of a Mnemonist*, New York: Basic Books, 1968.

16   Richard E. Cytowic, *Synesthesia: A Union of the Senses*, New York: Springer Verlag, 1989, p. 40.

17   Recently many publications have connected architecture with neuro-phenomena: Harry Francis Mallgrave, *The Architect's Brain: Neuroscience, Creativity, and Architecture*, 2010. The neurologist Semir Zeki has called for the creation of a neuroaesthetics to investigate how the brain perceives and relates to the visual arts. Another art historian John Onians has recently published his book, *Neuroarthistory*, to fashion a major neurohistory of European art.

18   Bulat Galeyev, "Synaesthesia is not a psychic anomaly, but a form of non-verbal thinking", http://prometheus.kai.ru/anomal_e.htm, accessed August 21 2009.

19   Richard E. Cytowic, "Synesthesia: Phenomenology and Neuropsychology: A Review of Current Knowledge", *PSYCHE*, 2(10), July 1995, http://psyche.cs.monash.edu.au/v2/psyche-2-10-cytowic.html

20   Ayub K. Ommaya, "Emotion and the Evolution of Neural Complexity", WESScom: *The Journal of the Washington Evolutionary Systems Society*, 1993, 3(1): 8–17.

3 *Festina Lente*

1   Folco Portinari, "The Slow Food Manifesto", November 9, 1989, in Carlo Petrini, *Slow food: the case for taste,* New York: Columbia University Press, 2001, pp. xxiii–xxv.
2   Milan Kundera, *Slowness,* Scarborough ON: HarperCollins Canada, 1996, p. 1.
3   "Festina Lente" or hasten slowly is one of the many emblems presented in the "Hypnerotomachia Poliphili ...". Aldo Manuzio the printer of the book adopted it as the mark for his printing house; the visual part of the emblem is a combination of a dolphin and anchor.
4   Carl Honore, *In Praise of Slow: How a Worldwide Movement is Challenging the Cult of Speed,* Toronto, Canada: Random House, 2004. pp. 216, 218.
5   Johanna Drucker, "Digital Ontologies: The Ideality of Form in/and Code Storage—or—Can Graphesis Challenge Mathesis?" Leonardo, vol. 34, no. 2, April 2001, pp. 141–145.
6   J.J. Gibson, "The Theory of Affordances", in R. Shaw and J. Bransford (eds), *Perceiving, Acting, and Knowing: Toward an Ecological Psychology,* Hillsdale, NJ: Lawrence Erlbaum, 1977, pp. 67–82.

4 Drawings as Loci for Thought

1   Saul Steinberg, *All in Line,* London: Penguin Books, 1945.
2   Filarete, *Filarete's Treatise on Architecture,* facsimile and translation J. Spencer, New Haven and London: Yale University Press, 1965, fol. 40r.
3   Bruno Latour, "Visualization and cognition: thinking with eyes and hands", in Knowledge *and Society: Studies in the Sociology of Culture Past and Present,* 1986, 6: 1–40.
4   Umberto Eco, *The Aesthetics of Chaosmos: The Middle Ages of James Joyce,* translated from the Italian by Ellen Esrock, Cambridge, MA: Harvard University Press, 1989.
5   Pierre Bourdieu, *The Logic of Practice,* book 1, chapter 3: "Structures, Habitus, Practices", Stanford: Stanford University Press, 1990, pp. 52–65. Pierre Bourdieu, *Outline of a Theory of Practice,* Cambridge and New York: Cambridge University Press, 1977.
6   Pierre Bourdieu, "Postface", in: E. Panofsky, *Architecture Gothique et Pensee Scolastique,* Paris: Edition Minuit, 1974, pp. 135–167; English translation as an appendix in: Bruce Holsinger, *The Premodern Condition: Medievalism and the Making of Theory,* Chicago and London: University of Chicago Press, 2005, Appendix II, pp. 221–242.
7   Pierre Bourdieu, *op. cit.,* p. 53.
8   Ludwig Wittgenstein, *Philosophical Investigations,* New York: The Macmillan Company, 1965, remark # 129.
9   Richard Sorabji, "Aristotle on Demarcating the Five Senses", *The Philosophical Review,* vol. 80, no. 1 (January 1971), pp. 55–79.
10 "Conversazione tra Gullaume Jullian de la Fuente e Amedeo Petrilli", in

Le Corbusier: Il Programma Liturgico, eds Giuliano & Glauco Gresleri, Bologna: Editrice Compositori, 2001.

5   The Pregnancy of Drawings

1   René Daumal, *Mount Analogue: a novel of symbolically authentic non-Euclidean adventures in mountain climbing*, Boston: Shambhala, 1992. p. 9.

2   James Joyce, *Finnegans Wake*, London: Penguin Books, 1999, p. 297.

3   David Summers, *Judgment of Sense*, passim, and p. 205, n. 20.

4   James Joyce, *op.cit.*, 1999, p. 284.

5   Antonio Averlino Filarete, *Trattato di architettura*, Firenze: Biblioteca Nazionale, MS. Codex Magliabechianus (M), text edited by A.M. Finoli and L. Grassi, introduction and notes by L. Grassi, 2 vols, Milano: Il Polifilo, 1972, p. 7v.

6   Bernard Maupoil, "Contribution à l étude de l'origine musulmane de la géomancie dans le Bas-Dahomey", *Journal de la sociéte des africanistes*, vol. 13, pp. 17–18.

7   Leibniz, *Discourse on Metaphysics*, Manchester: Manchester University Press, 1953, p. 10.

8   George Stiny, *Shape: Talking about Seeing and Doing,* Cambridge: MIT Press, 2006.

9   Bethe Hagens, "The Divine Feminine in Geometric Consciousness", in *Anthropology of Consciousness*, the American Anthropological Association, 2006, vol. 17, Issue 1, pp. 1–34.

10   Plato, *Timaeus, Critias, Cleitophon, Menexenus, Epistles,* Loeb Classical Library No. 234, Harvard: Harvard University Press, 1929.

11   For a discussion of tectonic precision see: Marco Frascari and Livio Volpi Ghirardini, "Contra Divinam Proportionem", in *Nexus II: Architecture and Mathematics*, ed. Kim Williams, Fucecchio, Florence: Edizioni Dell'Erba, 1998, pp. 65–66.

12   Ernest Irving Freese, "The Geometry of architectural Drafting, 7—Some Detective Work", *Pencil Points*, February 1930, p. 101.

13   Vitruvius, *On Architecture*, 2 vols. ed. and trans. by Frank Granger, reprinted 1983, Cambridge MA and London: Loeb, 1931, vol. II, p. 3.

14   For the relationship between footprints vestigia and ichnographia see: Indra Kagis McEwen, *Vitruvius: writing the body of architecture*, Cambridge, Mass.: MIT Press, 2003.

15   For the story of the life of Monge and the evolution of descriptive geometry see: Boris Hasseblatt's course site, Savants; http://www.tufts.edu/~bhasselb/135/savants.pdf

16   Baptized as Giuseppe Lodovico Lagrangia, born in Turin January 25, 1736.

17   Quoted by Docci, Mario and Riccardo Migliari, *Scienza della Rappresentazione*, Roma: NIS, 1992.

18   James J. Gibson, "The ecological approach to visual perception in pictures", in *Leonardo*, 11:3, 1978, pp. 227–235. Also in James J.Gibson, *Reasons for Realism*, ed. E. Reed & R. Jones, New Jersey & London: Lawrence Erlbaum

Association, 1982; James Gibson, "A prefatory essay on the perception of surfaces versus the perception of markings on a surface", in *The perception of pictures*, Volume I: Alberti's Window.

19 Michel Serres, "Mathematics and Philosophy: What Thales Saw", Hermes: Literature, Science, Philosophy. Baltimore: Johns Hopkins, 1982, pp. 84–97.

20 Michel Serres, "The Origin of Geometry", *Hermes: Literature, Science, Philosophy*, Baltimore: Johns Hopkins, 1982, pp. 125–134.

21 Charles Sanders Peirce, *Collected Papers* , 8 vols, Harvard: Harvard University Press, 1931–1960, CP 5.171.

22 *ibid.*, CP 2.777.

23 My language, in describing the analytical solution, probably will disgust a mathematician, but I am sorry I am a geomatrician.

24 I am using the concept of affordances as put forward by the perceptual psychologist J.J. Gibson to refer to the actionable properties between the world and an actor. J.J. Gibson, "The theory of affordances", ed. R.E. Shaw & J. Bransford, *Perceiving, Acting, and Knowing*, Hillsdale, NJ: Lawrence Erlbaum Associates. 1977; J.J. Gibson, *The Ecological Approach to Visual Perception*, Boston: Houghton Mifflin, 1979.

25 Aristotle, *Posterior Analytics*, I, 13, http://classics.mit.edu/Aristotle/posterior. 1.i.html, accessed October 11, 2009.

26 Using the analytical method, someone can also calculate the rate of healing by using a function which starts with the wound's area, A, and decreases exponentially with the passage of time. The match is remarkable for all points along the curve except at the end. The mathematical function approaches the x-axis asymptotically, which means that it never reaches the x-axis, or better it meets the x-axis at infinity. However, healing doesn't comply with the generality of the equation. At some point, the wound closes and A goes to zero or time goes to zero by making the wound a fistula.

27 Livio Volpi Ghirardini, Arturo Calzona, *Il San Sebastiano di Leon Battista Alberti*, Firenze: Olschki, 1994.

6   *Nullo die sine linea*

1 Manfredo Massironi, *The Psychology of Graphic Images: Seeing, Drawing, Communicating*, Psychology Press, 2001.

2 "Littera gesta docet, quid credas allegori. Moralis quid agas quo tendas anagogia." Attributed to Augustine of Dacia was previously considered by Nicholas de Lyra.

3 The proper Latin translation for the Greek "anagoghe" is "sursumductio" and can be found in writings of Isidore of Seville, Venerable Bede or Rabanus Maurus.

4 Patrice Sicard, *Diagrammes médiévaux et exégèse visuelle : le Libellus de formatione arche de Hugues de Saint-Victor*, Bibliotheca Victorina 4, Paris: Brepolis, 1993.

5 Edwin A. Abbott, *Flatland: A Romance of Many Dimensions*, London: Seely and Co., 1884. Reprinted New York: Dover Publications, 1992.

6   Robin Evans, "Translations from Drawing to Building", *AA Files* 12, 1986, pp. 16–22; Robin Evans, The *Projective Cast: Architecture and its Three Geometries*, Cambridge, Massachusetts: MIT Press, 1995.

7   Federico Zuccaro, a painter-architect of the third generation of Mannerists, working in a pre-baroque Rome. Zuccaro subdivided the disegno into two categories, *disegno interno* and *disegno esterno*. Federico Zuccaro, *L'Idea de' Pittori e Scultori e Architetti*, Roma: Marco Paglierini, 1768, p. 68.

8   Reyner Banham, "A Black Box: The Secret Profession of Architecture", *A Critic Writes: Essays*, ed. Mary Banham, Paul Barker, Sutherland Lyall and Cedric Price, Berkeley: University of California Press, 1996, pp. 292–299.

9   R.G. Miner and D.B. Thomson, "BIM: contractual risks are changing with technology", *Consulting-Specifying Engineer*, 40 (2), 2006, pp. 54–66.

10   James Vandezande, "In the trenches with BIM", 2004. http://www. aecbytes.com/viewpoint/2004/issue_7.html, accessed March 30, 2010.

11   Nuria Pelechano, Jan M. Allbeck and Norman I. Badler, "Virtual Crowds: Methods, Simulation, and Control, Synthesis Lectures on Computer Graphics and Animation 2008, Lecture available on line at http://www.morgan-claypool.com/doi/abs/10.2200/S00123ED1V01Y200808CGR008.

7   Architectural Consciousness

1   Douglas Rushkoff, *Coercion: Why We Listen to What "They" Say*, New York, Riverhead 1999. pp.69–81.

2   Antonio R. Damasio, *The Feeling of what Happens: Body and Emotion in the Making of Consciousness*, W. Heinemann, 1999.

3   Pierre Bourdieu, *The Logic of Practice*, Stanford: Stanford University Press, 1991, pp. 72–73.

4   Luigi Pareyson, *Estetica, teoria della formatività*, Firenze: Sansoni, 1974, pp. 41–42.

5   Unfortunately, sapere and sapore are not anymore cognates in imaginative thinking. Virgil of Toulouse, grammarian of the VI Century, has beautifully shown the connection between sapere e sapore. Virgil of Toulouse, *Virgilio Marone grammatico: Epitomi ed Epistole*, ed. and trans. G. Polara, Naples, 1979.

6   David Summers, *Real Spaces: World Art History and the Rise of Western Modernism*, London: Phaidon, 2003.

7   Scarpa as Carlo Lodoli and Socrates did not write down their theories, unfortunately Scarpa did not have a Plato or a Memmo to put his elegant thoughts on paper.

8   Scarpa quoted by Philippe Duboy, "It was long Ago", *Daidalos*, December 15, 1990, p. 8.

9   Scarpa rejects the *pro forma* professional exam administrated by the Italian Government after the WW II. His clients, associates, crafts persons, called him "Professore", rather than "Architetto".

10   G. Vasari, "Proemio delle Vite", *Le Vite de' piu eccellenti pittori, scultori e architettori nelle redazioni del 1550 e 1568*, ed. R. Bettarini and P. Barocchi, 2 Firenze Testo, 1967, p. 14.

11 *Ibid.*, p. 15.

12 Federica Goffi, *Renaissance Visual Thinking: Architectural Representation as Medium to Contemplate 'True Form'*, paper presented at Lincoln University http://www.lincoln.ac.uk/home/conferences/human/papers/Goffi-Hamilton.pdf

13 John Onians, *Neuroarthistory*, New Haven and London: Yale University Press, 2007.

14 Mary Douglas, *Purity and Danger: An Analysis of Concepts of Pollution and Taboo*, London: Routledge and Kegan Paul, 1966, p. 115.

15 Giambattista Vico, *Keys to the New Science: Translations, Commentaries, and Essays*, ed. Thora Ilin Bayer and Donald Phillip Verene, Ithaca: Cornell UP, 2008, # 405.

16 Gerald M. Edelman, *Second Nature: Brain Science and Human Knowledge*, New Haven and London: Yale University Press, 2006, p. 24.

17 Genevieve Stebbins, *François Delsarte: Delsarte system of expression*, second edition, –1887.

18 George Lakoff and Marck Johnson, *Philosophy In The Flesh: the Embodied Mind and its Challenge to Western Thought*, Basic Books, 1999, p. 555.

19 Oliver Sacks, *The Man who Mistook his Wife for a Hat and other Clinical Tales*, New York: Harper & Row, 1987.

20 Paul Schilder, *The Image and Appearance of the Human Body*, New York: International University Press, 1950.

21 Phantom limbs are a necessary presence following leg or arm amputations. For instance, a phantom appears when a leg is surgically removed and the individual vividly feels the presence of leg to the point that he or she may forget the amputation and fall down.

22 From an interview with an architect; quoted by Rob Imrie, "Architects' conceptions of the human body", *Society and Space*, 2003, vol. 21, p. 47.

23 The "counterpoid" is a term invented by Jean Louis Barrault, as part of his general theory of mime. See Jean Louis Barrault, *Reflections on the Theatre*, London: Rockliff, 1951.

24 Julien Offray de La Mettrie, *Machine Man and Other Writing*, Cambrige: Cambridge University Press, 1990.

25 Jan Dorcy, *The Mime*, New York: Robert Speller & Sons, 1961, p. 34.

26 *Ibid.*, p. 35.

27 Marcel Mauss, *General Theory of Magic*, London: Routledge, 2001.

28 See Jean Louis Barrault, *op. cit.* Also see Paul-Louis Mignon, *Jean-Louis Barrautti le theatre total*, Paris: du Rocher, 1999.

29 Bernard Tschumi, *Architecture and Disjunction*, Cambridge, MA: MIT Press, 1996, p. 123.

30 *Ibid.*, p. 110.

31 M. Johnson, *The Body in the Mind*, Chicago: University of Chicago Press, 1987; G. Lakoff, and M. Johnson, *Philosophy in the Flesh*, New York: Basic Books, 1999.

32 Nigel Thrift, "The still point: resistance, expressive embodiment and dance", in M. Keith and S. Pile, *Geographies of Resistance*, London: Routledge, 1997, p. 127.

33 S.L. Foster, *Reading Dancing: Bodies and Subjects in Contemporary American Dance*, Berkeley: University of California Press, 1986.

34 M. Sheets-Johnstone, *The Phenomenology of Dance*, New York: Books for Libraries, A Divisionof Arno Press, 1980.

8   Architectural Brouillons

1   Paul Valery, *Cahiers*, 15: 480–81; *Cahiers/Notebooks*, "Poetry" 2: 219.

2   Bloch et von Wartburg, *Dictionarie: étymologique de la langue française*, Paris: P.U.F., 1968.

3   Carlo Ginzburg, *Clues, Myths and the Historical Method*, Baltimore: Johns Hopkins University Press, 1989.

4   Luigi Pareyson, *Estetica, teoria della formatività*, Firenze: Sansoni, 1974.

5   For a history of drawing instruments see: Maya Hambly, *Drawing Instruments 1580–1980*, London: Sotheby's Publications, 1988.

6   Samuel Johnson, *Selected Poetry and Prose*, Berkeley: University of California Press, 1977, p. 407.

9   Cosmopoiesis and Elegant Drawings

1   Quoted in Andrew Ballantyne, "The Pillar and the Fire", in *What is Architecture?*, ed. Andrew Ballantyne, London and New York: Routledge, 2002, p. 7.

2   Quoted by Sergio Los "Introduzione", in Manfredo Massironi, *Vedere col Disegno*, Padova: Marsilio, 1966, p. 17.

3   Leon Battista Alberti, *L'architettura (De re aedificatoria),* trans. Giovanni Orlandi, vol. 2, Milan: Edizioni Il Polifilo, 1966.

4   Joël Sakarovitch, *Epures d'architecture: De la coupe des pierres a la géométrie descriptive XVI—XIX siècles.*

5   Goodman, *op. cit.,* 1978; Mazzotta, *op.cit.,* 2001.

6   Leon Battista Alberti, *L'architettura di Leonbatista Alberti tradotta in lingua fiorentina da Cosimo Bartoli gentil'huomo & accademico fiorentino. Con la aggiunta de disegni.* In Firenze: *appresso Lorenzo Torrentino impressor ducale,* 1550.

7   John Dee, *The Mathematicall Praeface to the Elements of Geometrie of Euclid of Megara,* 1570, New York: Science History Publications, 1975, p. d.iiij.

8   Leon Battista Alberti, *L'Architecture et Art de bien bastir du Seigneur Leon Baptiste Albert, Gentilhomme Florentin, divisée en dix livres, Traduicts de Latin en François, par deffunct Jan Martin, Parisien, nagueres Secretaire du Reverendissime Cardinal de Lenoncourt,* Paris: [Imprimé par R. Massellin, pour] J. Kerver, 1553.

9   The Italian term *progetto* cannot be translated as "design", since it has broader and idiosyncratic phenomenological connotations. Leon Battista Alberti, *L'architettura. (De re aedificatoria)*, trans. Giovanni Orlandi, vol. 2, Milan: Edizioni Il Polifilo, 1966.

10 Susan Lang, "De lineamentis: L.B. Alberti's use of a Technical Term", *Journal of the Warburg and Courtauld Institutes*, 28, 1965, pp. 331–335.

11 Leon Battista Alberti, *On the Art of Building in Ten Books*, trans. Joseph Rykw-
ert, Neil Leach, Robert Tavernor, Cambridge, MA: MIT Press, 1988. Branko
Mitrovic, *Serene Greed of the Eye: Leon Battista Alberti and the Philosophical
Foundations of Renaissance Architectural Theory*, Berlin: Deutscher Kunst-
verlag, 2005, presents a full discussion of the different interpretations of
lineamenta but the author's conclusion is that *lineamenta* is merely a visual
shape.

12 In Ciceronian Latin, the one favored by Alberti, *natura* means also womb.

13 Leon Battista Alberti, *op. cit.*

14 Bible, New International Version, Ezekiel 40: 3, 1973.

15 Cipriano Palmira, *Templum*, Roma: University La Sapienza, 1983,
pp. 121–42.

16 *ibid.,* p. 123.

17 Leon Battista Alberti, *op. cit.*

18 Leon Battista Alberti*, op. cit.*

19 Filarete *Libro Secondo*, folio 11 recto, p. 53 … io ho già generate questa
città col mio Signore, e insieme collui l'ho esaminata più e più volte, e da
me pensata e collui diterminata. E poi io l'ho partorita, cioè glie n'ho fatto
uno disegno in liniamento secondo che vanno i fondamenti. Ègli piaciuto,
ma innanzi si cominci io gli ho detto che bisogna; sì che io, in mentre si
pena a' apparecchiare queste cose opportune per lo fundamento d'essa,
farò il sopradetto modello, o vuoi dire disegno rilevato …

20 [Marcus Pollio] Vitruvius, *On Architecture*, ed. and trans. by F. Granger,
2 vols., London: Loeb Library, 1930–1931, V, 6, vii.

21 In the Theogony, Hesiod informs us that Metis is the daughter of the Titans,
Okeanos (Oceanus) and Tethys. For the importance of *metis* in technological thought: Jean-Pierre Vernant, "Remarques sur les formes et les limites
de la pense technique chez les Grecs", *Revue d' Histoire des Sciences*, 1957,
pp. 205–225. Marcel Detienne and Jean-Pierre Vernant, *Cunning Intelligence in Greek Culture and Society*, Chicago: University of Chicago Press,
1991.

22 Italo Calvino, *Invisible Cities*, London: Picador, 1974, p. 62.

23 Carlo Ginzburg, "God is hidden in details", in G. Flaubert and A. Warburg,
Umberto Eco and Thomas Sebeonk eds., *The Sign of Three: Dupin, Holmes,
Pierce*, Bloomington, Indiana: Indiana University Press, 1988, pp. 81–118;
republished in Carlo Ginzburg, *Clues, Myths, and the Historical Method*,
Baltimore: Johns Hopkins University Press, 1989, pp. 96–125.

10 Traces and Architecture

1 Richard Krautheimer, Introduction to an "Iconography of Mediaeval Architecture", *Journal of the Warburg and Courtauld Institutes,* vol. 5, 1942,
pp. 1–33; Massimo Bulgarelli, "La Santa Casa di Loreto: L'edificio sacro e le
sue copie", *Lotus International,* vol. 65, 1990, pp. 79–88.

2 Kirsti Andersen, Brook *Taylor's work on linear perspective: a study of Taylor's
role in the history of perspective geometry, including facsimiles of Taylor's two
books on perspective*, New York: Springer-Verlag, *c.* 1992.

3 Ellis Cashmore, *Dictionary of Race and Ethnic Relations*, London: Routledge, 1996, p. 165.

4 A professor in the School of Architecture at Southern University in Baton Rouge, Louisiana, M. Saleh Uddin uses the same locution in the title a book: *Hybrid Drawing Techniques by Contemporary Architects and Designers*. However, the use of the locution indicates mere fusions of drawings with other drawings or photograph, a composite-collage-graphic-work. Furthermore, Uddins's book is an a-critical survey of contemporary architectural graphic production coupled together with ambiguously unfocused assessments of the role played by the graphic media during the processes of architectural conception producing a work that will mislead the future generation of architects.

11 Tools for Architectural Thinking

1 With technography, I am reviving in anglicized form the term *tecnografia* devised by Carlo Lodoli, an eighteenth-century Venetian architectural theoretician and master of Christian morals. Lodoli advocates a correct use of representation in the practice of architecture. He calls these drawings *tecnografie*. See Lodoli's "Outlines", in Marco Frascari, *Sortes Architecti*, PhD Dissertation, University of Pennsylvania, 1981, pp. 29 and 257.

2 William Ames was born in 1567 at Ipswich in Suffolk, that region of East Anglia where Puritanism had begun, and died in 1633. Ames is called "the father of American theology". The first books at Harvard were the ones written by Ames. He was of such profound influence upon the theology of New England that Technological Theses were routinely debated at the Harvard and Yale Commencement Exercises during the second half of the seventeenth century. Lee W. Gibbs, "Introduction" in *William Ames, Technometria*, Philadelphia: University of Pennsylvania Press, 1979. For a discussion of Ramist cultural structure and for an understanding of the complexity of encyclopedic structures and relations cf. Walter J. Ong, *Ramus: Method, and the Decay of Dialogue: From the Art of Discourse to the Art of Reason*, Harvard University Press, 1958; and Walter J. Ong, *Orality and Literacy: The Technologizing of the Word*, New York: Routledge, 2002.

3 Edward Rand, "Liberal Education in Seventeenth-Century Harvard", *The New England Quarterly*, vol. 6, 1933, pp. 525–551; and Porter G. Perrin, "Possible Sources of Technologia at Early Harvard", *The New England Quarterly*, vol. 7, 1934, pp. 718–724.

4 Lee W. Gibbs, "Introduction", in *William Ames, Technometria*, Philadelphia: University of Pennsylvania Press, 1979, p. 43.

5 *William Ames, Technometria*, Philadelphia: University of Pennsylvania Press, 1979.

6 A closer examination of Ames' conception of the arts reveals that the roots of technometry are in the exegesis of Greek and Roman Classical writings, Scholastic thought, and Renaissance humanism.

7 Lee W. Gibbs, *op. cit.*, p. 29.

8   Vincenzo Scamozzi, *L'idea dell'architettura Universale*, Venezia: Autoris expensis, 1615.
9   Lee W. Gibbs, op. cit., 1979 p.43.
10   Lettera di Mario Ridolfi in *Controspazio*, Sept. 1977, p. 3.
11   Tim Ingold, *Lines: A Brief History*, London: Routledge, p. 3.
12   R.J. Forbes, *Imhotep*, Proc Royal Society Med., October 1940; 33 (12), pp. 769–773.
13   The Cairo Museum has a fragment of a statue of King Djoser from the Third Dynasty. The base carries an inscription that cites the name of his advisor, Imhotep, and gives a list of his titles: "Chancellor to the king of Lower Egypt, a subordinate to the king of Upper Egypt, administrator of the great domain, administrator of the Pat, great visionary (high priest of Heliopolis), master craftsman of sculptors and masons." R.J. Forbes, *op. cit.*, pp. 769–773.
14   Marcel Mauss, *A General Theory of Magic*, trans. Robert Brain, 1972; reprint London: Routledge, 2002.
15   Dario Sabbatucci, *Scrivere e leggere il mondo divinazione e cosmologia*, Roma: Bulzoni, 1989.
16   Dario Sabbatucci, *op.cit.*, p. vii.
17   Plato, *Phaedrus*, 244b-c.
18   Krzysztof Pomian, *Collectionneurs, amateurs et curieux, Paris–Venise, XVIe–XVIIIe siècle,* Paris: Gallimard, 1987.

12 *Disegnare Designare*

1   Virgil C. Aldrich, "Design, Composition, and Symbol", *The Journal of Aesthetics and Art Criticism*, vol. 27, no. 4, Summer 1969, pp. 379–388.
2   "mandati i misuratori a misurare la terra di Cartagine, ficcati i pali terminali, che la disegnavano..." Bono Giamboni, *Orosio*, a. 1292 (fior.) Delle Storie contra i Pagani di Paolo Orosio libri VII, Francesco Tassi ed., Firenze: Baracchi, 1849.
3   "Cronaca senese dall'anno 1202 al 1362", *Cronache senesi*, eds. Alessandro Lisini e Fabio Iacometti, Bologna: Zanichelli, 1939, pp. 41–158, "E fecesi el disegnio di detta chiesa dove è ogi santo Pietro a Ville, e così si fece poi, quando fu chalonazzato", *c.* 1362, p. 47.25.
4   Doc. fior., 1362–75, [1367] 192, p. 207.36: "Che la detta chiesa per inanzi si deba edificare e fare sechondo ch'è edifichato il disengno o vero rilievo, il quale è murato ne la chasa de la dett'opera apresso al chanpanile." Cesare Guasti, *Santa Maria del Fiore. La costruzione della chiesa e del campanile secondo i documenti tratti dall'Archivio dell'Opera secolare e da quello di Stato,* Firenze: Ricci, 1887, pp. 144–230.
5   [Marcus Pollio] Vitruvius, *De architectura libri dece*, trans. Cesare Cesariano, commentary by Cesariano, Benedetto Giovio, and Bono Mauro. Como: Gottardo da Ponte for Agostino Gallo and Aloisio Pirovano, 15 July 1521.
6   Merlau-Ponty, *Phenomenology of Perception*, p. 23.
7   Vittorio Gallese, *Phenomenology and the Cognitive Sciences*, 2005, 4: 23–48. Vittorio Gallese, Corpo vivo, simulazione incarnata e intersoggettività:

Una prospettiva neurofenomenologica. In: *Neurofenomenologia,* M. Cappuccio ed., Milano: Bruno Mondadori, 2006, pp. 293–326.

8   Marco Frascari, "The Construction Drawings of a Blind Architect", *On Architecture, The City, and technology: Proceedings of the Eighth Annual ACSA Technology Conference*, ed. Marc M. Angilil, Stoneham, MA: Butterworth-Heinman, 1990a, pp. 52–54.

9   John M. Kennedy, *Drawing and the Blind: Pictures to Touch*, New Haven and London: Yale University Press, 1993. John M. Kennedy and Y. Eriksson, "Profiles and Orientation of Tactile Pictures", *European Psychology Society*, Tampere, July 2–5, 1993.

10   Richard Held and Alan Hein, "Movement-Produced Stimulation in the Development of Visually Guided Behavior", *Journal of Comparative and Physiological Psychology*, 1963, vol. 56, no. 5, pp. 872–876.

11   Margarita Tupitsyn, Matthew Drutt, El Lissitzky, Ulrich Pohlmann, *El Lissitzky: beyond the Abstract cabinet: photography, design, collaboration*, New Haven and London: Yale University Press, 1999.

12   Mario Bettini, *Apiaria universae philosophiae mathematicae*, Bologna: Battista Ferronij, 1642. The woodcut was probably taken from an Emblemata book and recycled by the printer as a chapter separator.

13   David Summers, "Michelangelo on Architecture", *The Art Bulletin*, vol. 54, no. 2 (June 1972), pp. 146–157.

14   Etienne de Condillac, *Condillac's treatise on the sensations*, London: Favil Press, 1930.

15   V. Gallese and M. Lakoff, "The brain's concepts: The role of the sensory-motor system in conceptual knowledge", *Cognitive Neuropsychology*, vol. 22, 2005, pp. 455–479.

16   G. Lakoff and M. Johnson, *Philosophy in the flesh: The embodied mind and its challenge to Western thought*, New York: Basic Books, 1999, pp. 124–125.

17   Elizabeth C. Evans, "Galen the Physician as Physiognomist", *Transactions and Proceedings of the American Philological Association*, vol. 76, 1945, pp. 287–298.

18   Galen, *De anatornicis administrationibus*, II 1. K II 280-f; cited by Mario Vegetti, *Il Coltello e lo Stilo*, Milano: Il Saggiatore, 1979, p. 41.

19   Galen, *De Libras*, pp. 1–2, cited by Mario Vegetti, *op.cit.*, p. 42.

20   For Manfredo Tafuri's drawings see: Anna Bedon, Guido Beltramini, Howard Burns, eds., *Questo: Disegni e studi di Manfredo Tafuri per la ricostruzione di edifice e contesti urbani rinascimentali*, Vicenza: Centro Internationale di Studi di Architettura Andrea Palladio, 1995.

21   Manfredo Taluri, "The Historncal Project," *The Sphere and The Labyrinth: Avant-Gerdes and Architecture from Piranesi to the 1970s*, Cambridge, MA: MIT Press, 1987, p. 12.

22   Michel Foucault, "Nietzsche, Genealogy, History," in *Language, Counter-4-Memory, Practice*, ed. Donald Bouchard, Ithaca: Cornell University Press, 1977, p. 140.

23   Grapaldo Francesco Maria, *De Partibus Aedium. Addita modo verborum esplicatione que in eodem libro continentur. Opus sane elegans & eruditum propter multiiugam variarum rerum lectionem cum propter M. Vitruvii & Cornelii Celsi*

emaculatas dictiones. Impressum Taurini, per Ioannem Angelum & Bernardi-num fratres de Sylva, 1517.

24 Andreas Vesalius, *De Humani Corporis Fabrica, Libri Septem,* Basileae, 1543, p. Pref. 3vr.

25 *Ibid.* p. 658, rt.

13 The Light of Drawing Imagination

1 Gregory Tullio, *Anima mundi: la filosofia de Guglielmo di Conches e la scuola di Chartres,* Florence: Sansoni, 1955.

2 David C. Lindberg, *The beginnings of western science: the European scientific tradition in Philosophical, Religious and Institutional Context, Prehistory to A.D. 1450,* Chicago: The University of Chicago Press, pp. 210–213.

3 Louis I. Khan and John Lobell, *Silence and Light: Louis Kahn's Words in Between Silence and Light,* Boulder: Shambhala Publications, Inc., 1979. Daniel Shay Friedman, "The sun on trial: Kahn's gnostic garden at Salk (California, Louis I. Kahn)", January 1, 1999, Dissertations available from ProQuest. Paper AAI9926127. http://repository.upenn.edu/dissertations/AAI9926127

4 Louis I. Kahn and Robert C. Twombly, *Louis Kahn: essential texts,* New York: W.W. Norton, 2003, pp. 222 and 236.

5 Louis I. Kahn and Robert C. Twombly, *op. cit.,* p. 229.

6 Federica Goffi-Hamilton, "Carlo Scarpa and the eternal canvas of silence", *Architectural Research Quarterly,* 2006, vol. 10, pp. 291–300.

7 Dante Alighieri, *Inferno,* XXXI, 67.

8 Francois Rabelais, *The Works of Francis Rabelais,* London: H.G. Bohn, 1854–55, vol. 2, pp. 356–357.

9 Carlo Scarpa, *Carlo Scarpa: Complete Works,* ed. F. Dal Co and G. Mazzariol, New York: Rizzoli, 1986, p. 282.

10 Carlo Scarpa quoted by Philippe Duboy, "It was long Ago", *Daidalos,* December 15, 1990, p. 8.

11 Aby Warburg, *Images from the region of the Pueblo Indians of North America,* Ithaca: Cornell University Press, 1995, pp. 277–292.

12 The template for this exercise come from Karl Wallick who learned the procedure from Daniel Freedman who learned from me.

14 Cosmopoiesis and World-Making

1 Otl Aicher, and W. Vossenkuhl, *Analogous and digital,* Toronto: John Wiley & Sons Canada, 1994, p. 64.

2 Fredrick Nietzsche, *The Gay Science,* New York: Harper & Row, 1974, p. 54.

3 *Ibid.,* p. 116

4 The book does not provide any overt details about the author. The only information given is an acrostic formed by the first letters of each chapter: POLIAM FRATEM FRANCESCVS COLVMNA PERAMAVIT, and the phrase

indicated in the first letters of the first three lines of Polia's epitaph at the end: F[rancescus] C[olumna] I[nvenit]; [Francesco Colonna] *Hypnerotomachia Poliphili ubi humana omnia nisi somnium esse docet*, Venice: Aldus 1499. Reprint 1545(Figliuoli di Aldo); [Francesco Colonna] *Hypnerotomachia Poliphili: The Strife for Love in a Dream*, New York and London: Thames & Hudson, 1999.

5 Girolamo Mancini, *Vita di Leon Battista Alberti*, second edition, 1911.

6 Jonah Lehrer, "Daydream Achiever", *Boston Globe*, August 31, 2008, p. 31. Available at http://www.boston.com/bostonglobe/ideas/articles/2008/08/31/daydream_achiever. Accessed December 30, 2008.

7 Kalina Christoff, Alan M. Gordon, Jonathan Smallwood, Rachelle Smith and Jonathan W. Schooler, "Experience sampling during MRI reveals default network and executive system contributions to mind wandering", *Proceedings of the National Academy of Sciences,* 2009, vol. 106, pp. 8719–8724.

8 David Greig, "If you want to solve a problem: forget about it", Gizmag, http://www.gizmag.com/if-you-want-to-solve-a-problem-forget-about-it/11699/, accessed March 14, 2010.

9 Matthew Battles, "In Praise of Doodling", *American Scholar*, 2004, vol. 73, pp. 105–108.

10 Anton Ehrenzweig, *The Psycho-Analysis of Artistic Vision and Hearing: An Introduction to a Theory of Unconscious Perception*, New York: G. Braziller, 1965.

11 Alfred Adler, "On Doodlings. Individual Psychology", *The Journal of Adlerian Theory, Research & Practice*, 1988, vol. 44, pp. 441–444; Guy J. Manaster, "On Doodlings and Mental Meandering: Individual Psychology", *The Journal of Adlerian Theory, Research & Practice*, 1988, vol. 44, pp. 444–447.

12 Jackie Andrade, "What Does Doodling do? Applied Cognitive Psychology", published online in Wiley InterScience, 2009 (www.interscience.wiley.com) DOI: 10.1002/acp.1561, accessed March 19, 2010.

13 To understand unconscious perception, the work of the Gestalt psychologists is consequential, because it provides descriptions of many basic perceptual phenomena that are called "Gestalt laws".

14 K. Dunlap, "The Effect of Imperceptible Shadows on the Judgment of Distance", *Psychology Review*, 1990, vol. 7, pp. 435–453.

15 *Ibid.*, p. 436.

16 Arielle Saiber, "Ornamental Flourishes in Giordano Bruno's Geometry", *Sixteenth Century Journal*, 2003, vol. XXXIV/3, pp. 729–745; Mino Gabriele, *Giordano Bruno: Corpus iconographicum*, Milan: Adelphi, 2001; Ubaldo Nicola, "Diagrammi Ermetici", in *Giordano Bruno: Sigillo dei sigilli*, Milano: Mimesis, 1995, pp. 73–112.

17 Dante Alighieri, *Purgatorio,* x, 94–96; Giovanni Pozzi, *Sull'orlo del visibile parlare*, Milano: Adelphi, 1993; Gino Casagrande, *SYNAESTHESIA AND DANTE: A Synaesthetic Approach to Purgatorio,* X, 55–63, http://www.gicas.net/purg.html#*, accessed April 16, 2010.

18 Felice Tocco, *Le opere latine di Giordano Bruno esposte e confrontate con le italiane*, Firenze: Le Monnier, 1889, available for download at http://warburg.sas.ac.uk/mnemosyne/Bruno/pdf/opTocco.pdf

19 In Greek mythology, the god Chronos, pictured as elderly, gray-haired, and bearded, was the personification of circular time. The newborn baby that ushers in the New Year is Chronos; the same personification ends the year as Father Time, a bent-over old man.

20 Callistratus, "On the Statue of Opportunity at Sicyon", http://www.theoi.com/Text/Callistratus.html#n22, accessed December 30, 2008.

21 At its completion, Town rejected the painting, and asked Cole to paint an entirely different scene.

22 Novalis (Georg Philipp Friedrich Freiherr von Hardenberg), *Philosophical Writings*, trans. Margaret Mahony Stoljar, Albany: State University of New York, 1997, vol. I, p. 82.

23 Born 1892, Pavel Florensky, theoretician of arts, theologian, engineer and mathematician taught at the Vuchtemas and was an active intellectual figure during the Russian Revolution until 1933 when he was deported in a lager. He was executed near Leningrad in 1937. Florensky's main concern was not in *philosophia* but in *philokalia*.

24 Pavel Florensky, *Iconostasis*, Redondo Beach, CA: Oakwood Publications, 1996, pp. 28–31.

25 *Ibid.*, p. 30.

26 Dimitry V. Ainalov, *Hellenistic Origins of Byzantine Art*, trans. Elizabeth Sobolevitch and Serge Sobolevitch, ed. Cyril Mango. New Brunswick, NJ: Rutgers University Press, 1961.

27 Oskar Konstantin Wulff, *Altchristliche und byzantinische Kunst*, Berlin-Neubabelsberg: Akademische Verlagsgesellschaft Athenaion m.b.H., 1914.

28 Maria Rosaria De Rosa, *Theodor Lipps: estetica e critica delle arti*, Napoli: Guida Editori, 1990.

29 VKhUTEMAS is the acronym for Higher Art and Technical Studios and was the Russian state art and technical school founded in 1920 in Moscow; in 1926 its name was modified: "Institute" instead of "Studios". It was dissolved in 1930.

30 Albrecht Dürer, *The painter's manual: a manual of measurement of lines, areas, and solids by means of compass and ruler assembled by Albrecht Dürer for the use of all lovers of art with appropriate illustrations arranged to be printed in the year MDXXV*, trans. and with a commentary by Walter L. Strauss, New York: Abaris Books, 1977.

31 Kirill Sokolov and Avril Pyman, "Father Pavel Florensky and Vladimir Favorsky: Mutual Insights into the Perception of Space", *Leonardo*, vol. 22, no. 2, 1989, pp. 237–244.

32 Raymond Queneau, *The Blue Flowers*, trans. Barbara Wright, 1967.

33 *Ibid.*

Postface

1 Alexander Gottlieb Baumgarten, *Riflessioni sul testo poetico*, Palermo: Aestetica Edizioni.

2 Filippo Tommaso Marinetti & Fillìa, *La cucina futurista*, Milano: Longanesi, 1986; Filippo Tommaso Marinetti, *The futurist cookbook*, San Francisco:

Bedford Arts, 1989; Claudia Salaris, *Cibo futurista: dalla cucina nell'arte all'arte in cucina*, Roma: Stampa Alternativa, 2000.

3   Laughter was the laxative of the Futurist body, a body trying to discover new senses. See: Lorenzo Mango, *Alla scoperta di nuovi sensi: il tattilismo futurista*, Napoli: La città del sole: Istituto italiano per gli studi filosofici, 2001.

4   Farfa, *Tuberie & sette ricette di cucina futurista*, Milano: All'Insegna del Pesce d'Oro, 1964.

Appendix

1   Egnazio Danti, *Primo volume dell'vso et fabbrica dell'astrolabio et del planisferio*, Giunti, Firenze 1578, p. 31: "Se bene questa diottra è stata modernamente da alcuni chiamata linda, che è voce spagnuola, la quale viene da 'lindero', che significa propriamente una linea tra due cose". Even if this diopter was called by some modern *linda*, which is a Spanish word, which comes from "lindero", which literally means a line between two things.

2   Aulius Gellius, *Noctes Atticae*, http://penelope.uchicago.edu/Thayer/E/Roman/Texts/Gellius/home.html, accessed November 11, 2009.

3   Pliny, *Natural History: Volume IV. Books 12–16*, Loeb Classical Library, 1952.

4   Traditional Italian naming of units of measure of length consisting of ounce (*onza*), palm (*palmo*), foot (*piede*) and arm (*braccio*), variable from city to city.

Index

Building Information Modeling (BIM)
60–64, *63, see also* digital
representation
Byzantine: art 160

Cole, T. *The Architect's Dream* 158
collage 73–75, 112, 149, 150, 201;
Blueprints Spolia 75; Vesalius' and
Rusconi's Anatomical Images 139
Collins, P.: *Changing Ideals in Modern
Architecture* 21
color 146; food 22–25; synesthesia 26–28
Computer Aided Design (CAD) 60–61,
112, *see also* digital representation
consciousness 65–86; conscious
perception 166, *see also* perception
construction: building 8–9, 49, 99–102,
99, 102, 110; built reality 49,
72–73; drawing 122–125, *see also*
facture; Roman *templum* 99; site
delineation *101;* site lines *102;*
spolia 73–75; structure 55–56, 113;
templum line tracing 99–100
contemporary architecture 23
conversion: transformation 62
cooking: metaphor *see* gastronomy
Corbusier, Le 42
cosmography 38–40; diagram *39;*
drawing *39*
cosmopoiesis 1–2, *2,* 21–28, 42, 93–108,
151–174, 180, *see also* facture;
gastronomy; world-making
Cytowic, R.E.: synesthesia 26, 28

Daedalus 112
decoupage 74–75
Delsarte, F. *77–78*
digital representation 49–50, 53, 60–62,
112; 3D/4D/5D 14, 60, 62;
Building Information Modeling
(BIM) 60–64, *63;* Computer
Aided Design (CAD) 60–61,
112; modeling *see* modeling;
photographic 14, 53, 72–73, 147;
simulation 63–64; software 112;
typographic 53, *53*
drawing: action 3–4, 132–133; anagogical
58–60; construction *see* facture;

doodle 154–155, *154,* 156–157;
equipment *see* tools; exercises
see eleven exercises; facture *see*
facture; free-hand 148, 154;
genetic 90–91; hybrid 111–115,
115; materiality 35–38; non-trivial
see representation; orthographic
160–167, *164, 165, 166,* 167,
167, 169; principle 1–7, 15–16;
reading *see* interpretation;
supports *see* supports; teaching 4,
see also architecture; education;
technique *see* technique;
transpositions 37–38
dreams 125–127, *141, 150,* 151–160,
152; Florensky 159; verso 158–160
Dunlap, K. 155–156

education 93, 105, 133; primary/
secondary 4
Egyptian architecture: Imhotep 121–122
eighteenth century architecture 121
eleven exercises 18–19; exercise #1
23–26; exercise #2 33–34; exercise
#3 60–64; exercise #4 73–75;
exercise #5 84–86; exercise #6
107–108; exercise #7 113–115;
exercise #8 133–134; exercise #9
148–150; exercise #10 164–165;
exercise #11 169–172
embodiment 5–6, *5,* 168–170, 180;
media 177, *179;* plan drawing *80*
emotion: synesthesia 26–28
equipment *see* tools
experience: synesthesia 26–28, 142–148,
178

facture 10–12, 15–16, 31–32, 45–56;
architecture 10–12, *11;* building
29–30; construction drawing
122–125; diagram *15;* drawing
3, *15,* 30–38, 40–43, 58, 70–73,
90–91, 122–125, 130; human 11,
see also cosmopoiesis
Fergusson, J. 21–22
festina lente 29–34; emblem *30;* festina
lente and slow food *16*
Florensky, P. 159, 166

food 25–26, 181; analogy 16–18, 21–22, 69–70, 178; color 22–25, *see also* gastronomy
form *see* formativity
formativity 40; Pareyson 15–16
Formenton, T. 56
Fuente, G.J. 42
futurism: cuisine 180–181

gastronomy 21–28, 31, 69–70, 178, 180–181; architectural pantry *17*, 18; Collins 21; festina lente and slow food *16*; food colors 22–25; food stuff 25–26, *25*; futurism 180–181; Glasse 22; slow food 16–18; Soyer 22; Vattimo 23; weak gastrosophy 22–23, *see also* cosmopoiesis
Gaudi, A. 113
geomancy 47–48; tablet 48; tableu *47*
geomater *see* geometry
geometry 45–46, 48–56, 50–51, *50*; affordances 54–55; analytic 54; analytic tangent *54*; angelic proportional *52*; Bruno 156–157, *156*; descriptive 48, 51–52, *51*; geomater 45–46, 48–56; geomatrician *46*; Plato 48; synthetic *47*, 51–52, *51*, 54; synthetic tangent *54*; *Thales at the foot of the Pyramids* (Serres) 53–54; vestigia 50–51
Gestalt psychology 124; Muller-Lyer arrows 155, *155*
Glasse, H.: *The Art of Cookery* 22
Greek mythology: Daedalus 112; time 157

habitus: aesthetic 40–43; Bourdieu 38–40; non-trivial drawings 38
history: architecture 172–174
human body 75–78, 80–86; anatomy 137–140; behavior 65–66, 77–78; movement 85–86; representation 78–81; scale figures 63, 81–86, *81*, *83*, *86*

ichnography 104
iconoclasm 13–20

iconophilia 13
idolatry 13
imagination 6–7, 141–142, 152–153, *179*; geomaternal articulation 46; Paracelsus 6–7
intellectual system: Ramist 117
intelligence: architectural 65–68, 76, 101, *102*
interpretation 36–38, 40–43, 124; architectural verbalization *36*; de-composition *41*; sollertia 101–102, *102*, *see also* phenomenology

Joyce, J.: geomater 45–46; graphplot 45–46; poetography 45

knowledge: cognitive awareness *176*; episodic 7; *Personal Knowledge* (Polanyi) 17; phronesis 7; tacit 17–18, 176; *The Tacit Dimension* (Polanyi) 17–18
Kundera, M.: *In Slowness* 29

Le Corbusier 42
light 141–142; indirect representation *142*
line 18, *20*, 43, 57–64, *57*, *58*, 69, 103–104, *144*, *145*, *see also* linearity
lineamenta: Alberti 96–102, *98*
linearity *20*, 94–6, 122; lineamenta 96–102, *98*, *see also* line
Lissitzky, L.M. 134, 167
Luria, A.L.: synesthesia 26

magic: three laws (Mauss) 123
making *see* facture
mano oculata: Renaissance emblem 134–137, *135*
Manuzio, A.: *Festina Lente 30*
material: spolia 73–75, *75*
materiality 32–33, 35–38, 91
materials: paper 185–186
Mauss, M.: *A General Theory of Magic* 123; three laws of magic 123
media 177; embodiment *179*
Medieval architecture 38
Medieval art 160
memory 37; speed 29

metaphor: food *see* gastronomy

modeling 187–189; Building Information Modeling (BIM) 60–64, *63*; CAD 60–61; digital 49–50, 60–64; hand-made 50, *see also* representation

modernism 21

Monge, G.: descriptive geometry 52, *see also* geometry

movement 85–86

Muller-Lyer: arrows 155, *155*

neurology 65–68, 76–78; neuro-architect *76*; phrenology head *65*; Rizzolatti *77*

nineteenth century architecture 121

occupancy: space 80–86

orthographic projection: axonometric 166–167, *166*; homo axonometrcius *169*; inverted axonometry *167*; inverted perspective 160-5, *164*, *165*; isometric *167*; oblique *160*, *166*; perspectival/oblique views *160*; recto/verso axonometry *170*; tools *168*

Palazzo della Ragione 55–56

Palazzo Steri 45

Palladio, A. 55–56; Basilica of Vicenza 56; Rotonda geometrical composition *132*; Serliana 56

Paracelsus 6–7

Pareyson, L.: formativity 15–16

perception 19, 124, 133, 136, 178; conscious *166*; synesthetic 27–28; unconscious 152–160

perspective drawing: inverted 160–165, *164*, *165*

Petrilli, A. 42

phenomenology 124; visual *124*

phrenology: head *65*

Polanyi, M.: *Personal Knowledge* 17; *The Tacit Dimension* 17–18

psychology: Gestalt 124

ramism: intellectual system 117

re-use 7, 87–91

reading *see* interpretation

Renaissance architecture 138; Alberti 96–102; Alfarano 74–75; mano oculata 134–137, *135*; Palladio 55–56; Paracelsus 6–7; Scamozzi 118, 183–189

representation: anatomical 138–140; chirographic 53; digital *see* digital representation; genetic 90–91; Gordian Knot 3–4, *3*; human body 78–81; modeling *see* modeling; non-trivial 3–4, 8–12, *9*, *10*, 30, 36–40, 112; peripheral/internal 37; photographic 14, 53, 72–73, 147; pictorial 20; re-use 87–91; rendering 14, 60, 72–73, 148; storytelling *19*, 68–75, 172–174; typographic 53, *53*

Ridolfi, M.: technography 120; technometric drawing *120*

Rizzolatti, G. 77

Rusconi, G.M. 139–140; collage *139*

St. Peter's Basilica (Alfarano, T.) 74–75

San Sebastiano (Alberti, L.B.) 55

scale 81–86, *81*, *83*, *86*

scale figures 63, 81–86, *81*, *83*, *86*

Scamozzi, V. 33, 118, 183–189; treatise frontispiece *182*

Scarpa, C. 130, 143–147; Palazzo Steri 45

senses 59, 146, 181; sensorial assimilation 1–2; sensus communis 6; sound 144–145; synesthesia 26–28, *27*, 142–148, 178; touch 130–134, 135; vision 130–131, 134–135; visual phenomenology 124, *124*

Serliana (Palladio, A.) 56

Serres, M.: *Thales at the foot of the Pyramids* 53–54

shape: grammar 48; Stiny 48

slow architecture 29–30, *see also* speed

slow food 16–18, *16*, 69

Soane, J. 74

sottolucidi 88–90, *89*

Soyer, A.B. 22

space: human behavior 65–66; occupancy 80–86, *see also* spatial representation